Educational Accountability

Educational Accountability: International perspectives on challenges and possibilities for school leadership provides an opportunity to assess, reflect on and discuss current issues surrounding accountability policies in education from around the globe and the implications they hold for school leadership. It addresses the global trend of accountability policies expanding in scope to include the education profession as well as the increasing incidence of international policy borrowing, brought on chiefly by globalisation.

Specific case studies offer a contextual examination of the theory, policy and practice of accountability and an inspection of their influence on school leadership. Cases are intentionally juxtaposed to provide a broad perspective of regional and cultural similarities and departures, and are arranged to reflect the diasporic Asian, Anglo, European and American societies.

Bringing together a number of highly regarded experts within the field, this book cultivates a global perspective on the challenges and possibilities for school leaders to foster school effectiveness and improvement. *Educational Accountability* should be key reading for researchers, policy makers and current and future school leaders.

Jacob Easley II is Dean of the School of Education and Professional Studies at Eastern Connecticut State University, USA.

Pierre Tulowitzki is a Senior Researcher at the Institute for the Management and Economics of Education at the University of Teacher Education Zug, Switzerland.

Educational Accountability

International perspectives on challenges and possibilities for school leadership

Edited by
Jacob Easley II and Pierre Tulowitzki

LONDON AND NEW YORK

First published 2016
by Routledge
2 Park Square, Milton Park, Abingdon, Oxon OX14 4RN

and by Routledge
711 Third Avenue, New York, NY 10017

Routledge is an imprint of the Taylor & Francis Group, an informa business

© 2016 selection and editorial matter, Jacob Easley II and Pierre Tulowitzki; individual chapters, the contributors

The right of the editors to be identified as the authors of the editorial material, and of the authors for their individual chapters, has been asserted in accordance with sections 77 and 78 of the Copyright, Designs and Patents Act 1988.

All rights reserved. No part of this book may be reprinted or reproduced or utilised in any form or by any electronic, mechanical, or other means, now known or hereafter invented, including photocopying and recording, or in any information storage or retrieval system, without permission in writing from the publishers.

Trademark notice: Product or corporate names may be trademarks or registered trademarks, and are used only for identification and explanation without intent to infringe.

British Library Cataloguing in Publication Data
A catalogue record for this book is available from the British Library

Library of Congress Cataloging-in-Publication Data
Names: Easley, Jacob.
Title: Educational accountability : international perspectives on challenges and possibilities for school leadership / edited by Jacob Easley II and Pierre Tulowitzki.
Description: First published 2016. | New York : Routledge, 2016. | Includes bibliographical references and index.
Identifiers: LCCN 2015042634 | ISBN 9781138777897 (hardback)
Subjects: LCSH: Educational accountability—Case studies.
Classification: LCC LB2806.22 .E37 2016 | DDC 379.1/58—dc23
LC record available at http://lccn.loc.gov/2015042634

ISBN: 978-1-138-77789-7 (hbk)
ISBN: 978-1-315-77235-6 (ebk)

Typeset in Galliard
by FiSH Books Ltd, Enfield

Contents

List of figures and tables		viii
Notes on contributors		ix
Preface		xv

1 Introduction: Conceptualizing educational accountability across global contexts 1
   JACOB EASLEY II

2 Principal leadership and accountability in Australia: A fine balance indeed 6
   SIMON CLARKE AND NEIL DEMPSTER

3 Aotearoa New Zealand: Examining the challenges of educational accountability policies and exploring possibilities for school leadership 18
   JAN ROBERTSON AND MARY F. HILL

4 From policy and practice to possibilities: The context of educational accountability in the U.S. and praxis of school leadership 34
   JACOB EASLEY II AND MOHAMMED ELMESKI

5 Chile: School leadership challenged by double accountability towards schools 54
   JOSÉ WEINSTEIN, JAVIERA MARFÁN, ANDREA HORN, AND GONZALO MUÑOZ

6 School accountability policy *in* practice: Learning by comparing Australia, New Zealand, USA, and Chile 73
   JAMES P. SPILLANE AND KATIE MERTZ

7 Teacher evaluation and educational accountability in China: Implications for school leadership 79
TING WANG

8 The School Development and Accountability Framework in Hong Kong: Possibilities of educational leadership 92
NICHOLAS SUN-KEUNG PANG

9 School education and accountability in India: Mapping current policies and practices 110
PRANATI PANDA

10 The promises and perils of school leadership for accountability: Four lessons from China, Hong Kong, and India 129
MOOSUNG LEE AND MISTY M. KIRBY

11 Accountability policies and school leadership in Austria: Increasing competition and little accountability 142
ANNA KANAPE-WILLINGSHOFER, HERBERT ALTRICHTER, AND DAVID KEMETHOFER

12 Top-down accountability and local management: Tensions and contradictions experienced by French principals as leaders 155
ROMUALD NORMAND AND JEAN-LOUIS DEROUET

13 Accountability in the German school system: More of a burden than a preference 165
STEPHAN GERHARD HUBER, BETTINA-MARIA GÖRDEL, SELIN KILIC, AND PIERRE TULOWITZKI

14 Swinging between two platforms: Accountability policy in the Netherlands and educational leadership in and around schools 184
JEROEN IMANTS, YVONNE ZWART, AND PETER BREUR

15 Emerging accountability policies and practices in education: The case of Norway 205
GURI SKEDSMO AND SØLVI MAUSETHAGEN

16 Accountability policies across Austria, Germany, France, the
   Netherlands, and Norway   224
   JORUNN MØLLER

17 Educational accountability around the globe: Challenges and
   possibilities for school leadership   233
   PIERRE TULOWITZKI

   Index   239

Figures and tables

Figures

5.1	Directive strategies	62
11.1	School leaders' (N=312) evaluation of the appropriateness of various forms of publishing inspection results	150
13.1	Strain by and preferences for the different activity fields by German, Austrian, and Swiss school leaders	175
13.2	Distribution of work time of school leaders	176
13.3	Strain and preferences on different levels of accountability for German, Austrian, and Swiss school leaders	178
14.1	Educational leadership, teacher practices, and student learning	188

Tables

5.1	Three models of accountability	56
5.2	Policies and institutional changes shaping the double accountability system in Chile	60
5.3	Strategies and practices developed by school principals to improve enrollment results	63
5.4	Strategies and practices developed by school principals to improve SIMCE outcomes	65
8.1	The pros and cons of the School Development and Accountability Framework for quality assurance	94
9.1	School accreditation models	119
9.2	School quality improvement models	120
11.1	Comparison of different dimensions of system governance	147
11.2	Evaluation of inspection goals	149
13.1	General governing levels of an education administration within a German Land	166
13.2	Models of accountability	172
13.3	Correlation between activity fields and job satisfaction and job strain for German school leaders	177
13.4	First regression model for job satisfaction and job strain	179
13.5	Second regression models for job satisfaction and job strain	179
14.1	Restricted and extended modes of result-oriented teaching	199

Notes on contributors

Editors

Jacob Easley II is Dean of the School of Education and Professional Studies/Graduate Division at Eastern Connecticut State University. His research includes a focus on contextualized leadership that attends to international perspectives of school effectiveness and improvement. He also studies educational policy and politics and the change process of organizational improvement.

Pierre Tulowitzki is a Senior Researcher at the Institute for the Management and Economics of Education at the University of Teacher Education Zug, Switzerland. He has previously worked as a researcher at Kiel University, Germany. His research interests include educational leadership, school improvement, and accountability, as well as matters of educational change.

Contributors

Herbert Altrichter is Professor of Education and Educational Psychology at Johannes Kepler University, Linz, Austria, and member of the executive committee of the European Educational Research Association. His main research interests include educational reform, governance of schooling, and educational policy as well as teacher education.

Peter Breur has received Master degrees in Special Education and Clinical Psychology. He is the Board Member for Educational Affairs of Dr. Schaepman Foundation in Hengelo, a school board with 17 schools for primary education and one special education school. Since 2014 he has served as the Chair of a regional network for primary education.

Simon Clarke is Professor in the Graduate School of Education, University of Western Australia, where he teaches, supervises and researches in the substantive area of educational leadership.

Neil Dempster is an Emeritus Professor in Educational Leadership at Griffith University and former Dean of its Faculty of Education. His research interests are in leadership for learning, school governance, school improvement, and the role that professional development plays in leadership, policy implementation, and institutional change. Neil is a Fellow of the Australian Council for Educational Leaders and a Fellow of the Australian College of Educators, where he held the post of National President in 2006–2007.

Jean-Louis Derouet is Emeritus professor at the Ecole Normale Supérieure of Lyon (Institut Français de l'Education), research unit Triangle. Since 2011, he has participated in the activities of the European Policy Network on School Leadership. He is specialized in the diversification of principles of justice in the contemporary world, the new organization of schools, the debates around the notion of leadership, and the transition of European states to a post-comprehensive school. Jean-Louis Derouet is chair of the Education, Formation, Socialisation Committee of the International Association of French Sociologists. He is the editor-in-chief *of Education et Sociétés.* He is the author of French-speaking books on leadership, including (with Romuald Normand) *La question du leadership. Perspectives Européennes*, Paris, L'Harmattan, Serie Academia, 2014.

Mohammed Elmeski is a Senior Researcher at American Institutes for Research (AIR). He has a PhD in Educational Policy and Administration with a focus on international development and evaluation. His responsibilities include conducting process and impact evaluations and technical assistance in systems change, educational leadership, and teacher training.

Bettina-Maria Gördel is Scientific Staff Member at the Institute for School Education/Didactics, University of Koblenz-Landau, Germany. Her research interests are school development, school administration and public management, and student teacher development. She has a university degree in secondary teacher-study; a Master's in Public Policy; and completed a dissertation in the field of educational governance in 2015.

Mary F. Hill is an Associate Professor in the Faculty of Education and Social Work at the University of Auckland, New Zealand. Her research interests include educational assessment, assessment education for teachers, practitioner inquiry, and the use of complexity theory and critical realism as explanatory theory for rethinking teacher education for equity.

Andrea Horn is a Doctor of Education from the Autonomous University of Madrid and Master in Educational Policies from Alberto Hurtado University (Chile). She works as an educational consultant and teaches at the Faculty of Education of the Alberto Hurtado University. Andrea has been a researcher at the Center of Innovation in Education of Fundacion Chile and at the Center for Research on Educational Policy and Practice (CEPPE). Her work has focused on educational leadership and school improvement.

Stephan Gerhard Huber is Head of the Institute for the Management and Economics of Education (IBB) at the University of Teacher Education Zug, Switzerland. His areas of interest are organization and system change, education management, school effectiveness, school improvement, professionalization of teachers, and school leaders. He conducts qualitative, quantitative, mixed-method, international comparative research.

Jeroen Imants studied organizational psychology and received a PhD degree in 1986. He is an associate professor at Graduate School of Education at Radboud University Nijmegen. His research and teaching cover the fields of school organization, educational leadership, and professional development and school improvement.

Anna Kanape-Willingshofer studied Psychology at Graz University, Austria, and currently works at the Department of Education and Educational Psychology at Linz University, Austria. Her research interests deal with the personality of leaders, especially in educational settings as well as with (educational) leadership motivation and aspirations.

David Kemethofer studied Sociology at Linz University, Austria, and currently works at the Federal Institute for Educational Research, Innovation and Development of the Austrian School Sector in Salzburg (Austria). His main research interests are educational improvement and quality assurance and evaluation with a focus on school inspections in an international perspective.

Selin Kilic is a research assistant at the Institute for the Management and Economics of Education at the University of Teacher Education Zug, Switzerland. Her research interests include educational governance and education management.

Misty M. Kirby's passion in research is grounded in the desire to improve the life chances of students through effective education leadership and high-quality, optimistic learning environments around the globe. Misty is an Assistant Professor of Education Leadership at the University of Canberra, Australia, with a PhD from the College of William and Mary in Williamsburg, Virginia, USA and a Master's degree from Teachers College, Columbia University.

Moosung Lee is the youngest Centenary Professor, one of the most prestigious professorships, at the University of Canberra. He held appointments as Associate Professor and Founding Deputy Director of Education Policy Unit at the University of Hong Kong. His current research interests are school improvement, International Baccalaureate schools, and social capital.

Javiera Marfán, a Sociologist from the Catholic University of Chile and Master in Management and Public Policy from the University of Chile, is

Coordinator of Educational Leadership at de General Education Division, Ministry of Education of Chile. She has been researcher at the Center of Innovation in Education of Fundacion Chile and research associate of the Center for Research on Educational Policy and Practice (CEPPE). Her work has been focused on educational leadership and school improvement.

Sølvi Mausethagen is Associate Professor at the Centre for the Study of Professions at Oslo and Akershus University College of Applied Sciences. Her research interests involve teacher work and professionalism, educational governance, and accountability.

Katie Mertz is the Research Project Coordinator for the Distributed Leadership Study and Dr James Spillane at Northwestern University. Her research interests include the relationship between education policy and economic development more broadly. Katie holds a Bachelor's degree in Economics and Political Science from Macalester College.

Jorunn Møller is Professor at University of Oslo at the Department of Teacher Education and School Research. Her professional interests are in the areas of educational leadership and governance, reform policies, and school accountability. She has been a manager of several research projects examining the implementation of school reform, accountability, and school leadership and identity in a Norwegian context and across countries, and she is also participating in international research networks in the field of school leadership. Recently she has participated in a project researching the spread of new public management across European education systems with a particular focus upon the implications of this development for schools serving a diverse student population. At present, she is leading a project designed to disentangle the complexity of legal standards and school leaders' professional judgment with a focus on students' right to a good psychosocial learning environment and special needs education. The project is cross-disciplinary and funded by the Research Council of Norway.

Gonzalo Muñoz, a Sociologist and Master in Sociology from the Catholic University of Chile, is Director of General Education Department at Ministry of Education in Chile. He previously worked at Diego Portales University, Fundación Chile, and Asesorías para el Desarrollo. He has published several books and articles about educational reform, school leadership, and effectiveness and improvement in disadvantaged areas. In 2012 he was appointed to the board of the Agency for Education Quality in Chile.

Romuald Normand is Professor at the University of Strasbourg (Research Unit SAGE: Societies, Actors and Government in Europe). Since 2011, he has participated in the activities of the European Policy Network on School Leadership. He has led research projects on school management, school improvement, and accountability. He is the author of French-speaking books on leadership, including (with Jean-Louis Derouet) *La question du leadership. Perspectives Européennes*, Paris, L'Harmattan. Serie Academia, 2014; (with Olivier Bachelard) *Le leadership à l'épreuve du service public*, Paris, CANOPE/ESEN, coll. Professions cadres, 2014 ; and (with François Muller), *Ecole: la grande transformation ? Les clés de la réussite*, Paris, ESF, 2013.

Pranati Panda is Professor of Education at the National University of Educational Planning and Administration (NUEPA), New Delhi, India. She is currently leading the National Programme on School Standards and Evaluation (NPSSE). She specializes in teacher education, teacher management and development, school evaluation and leadership, and internationalization of school education. She is an editorial member of various national and international journals and has presented papers at many international conferences and fora and published book chapters and articles in international journals. She is also a member of various educational committees of the federal government of India for strategic policy development in teacher and school education.

Nicholas Sun-Keung Pang is the Professor and Chair of Educational Administration and Policy at the Chinese University of Hong Kong. He specializes in educational administration, management, and leadership, as well as school effectiveness and improvement. He also serves as Director of the Hong Kong Centre for the Development of Educational Leadership (HKCDEL), Leader of the School Development and Evaluation Team (SDET), Director of the Preparation for Principalship (PFP) Course, and Director of Master of Arts Programme in School Improvement and Leadership (MASIL). Professor Pang was elected the Chairman of Hong Kong Educational Research Association and has published widely, both locally and internationally.

Jan Robertson is a Senior Researcher in the Institute of Professional Learning at the University of Waikato, New Zealand. Jan is also an Adjunct Professor at Griffith University, Australia, and the academic director of New Zealand's Aspiring Principals' programme. Her research and development work is in leadership development, education change and coaching leadership methodologies.

Guri Skedsmo is Associate Professor at the Department of Teacher Education and School Research, University of Oslo, and Senior Researcher at the Institute for the Management and Economics of Education at the University of Teacher Education Zug, Switzerland. Her research interests include educational governance, leadership, and the professionalization of school leaders.

James P. Spillane is the Spencer T. and Ann W. Olin Professor in Learning and Organizational Change at the School of Education and Social Policy at Northwestern University. Spillane has published extensively on education policy, policy implementation, school reform, and school leadership

Ting Wang is Professor in Education in the Faculty of Education, Science, Technology and Maths, University of Canberra, Australia. She specializes in educational leadership and management, cross-border educational leadership development, international education, and professional learning communities. She has presented internationally and published numerous book chapters and international peer-reviewed journal articles.

José Weinstein is a Sociologist from the University of Chile and with a PhD in Sociology from the Université Catholique de Louvain (Belgium). He was Chile's Undersecretary of Education (2000–2003) and Chile's first Minister of Culture (2003–2006). He has created and directed programs on improvement in secondary education, leadership development in vulnerable schools, and new opportunities for culture development in youth. His experience and expertise have been requested by important international organizations. He has published over 50 articles in books, reviews, and periodicals focusing on education, poverty, youth, and culture. He is currently the Director of the Center for Development of School Leadership at Diego Portales University, where he is Professor. His recent work has focused greatly on school leadership development and capacity improvement of vulnerable schools.

Yvonne Zwart has received a Master's degree in Special Education. She is a trainer and consultant at OinO-advies, an educational consultancy company in the east of the Netherlands. OinO-advies delivers services to schools and boards aimed at better learning of their students aged of 2–16.

Preface

Accountability has become the educational buzzword in the policy discourses of most countries in the globalization movement of education. It is highly influenced by waves of large-scale assessments and the introduction of new public management measures and supported by the adoption of attainment targets. Although decentralization has made schools more autonomous, the shift to local control has led increasingly to the consideration of accountability focusing on improving school quality. Very often an environment of competing policy demands asks for new leadership roles and responsibilities on all levels of school systems, with the individual schools at the heart of accountability efforts. Therefore school principals play a critical role in shaping relevant practices at the local level.

This book encompasses a collection of case studies and analyses from a multitude of countries, each providing a context-specific look at the relationship between accountability policies and practice and their influence on school leadership, reflected by theoretical implications and research data. Each case study provides deep insights into how the individual countries struggle for excellence and equity while retaining their national educational culture. This multiplicity allows different voices, points of view and complex perspectives to emerge.

The editors have intentionally juxtaposed the individual chapters to provide a broad perspective of regional and cultural similarities and departures, but have clustered them in groups, giving commentators the chance to bring in a meta-perspective. This not only draws on the essence of accountability as a ubiquitous philosophical and political concept, but also draws on highly relevant factors of professionalism in the realm of leadership and learning. The transnational dialogue ensures that the discussion about what accountability means in different countries, contexts and languages fosters debate, discussion and disagreement to promote new understanding and new knowledge on a topic that has had a controversial history.

This volume features a truly international community of authors whom the editors have brought together to share ideas, promote research and encourage practices that will enhance the quality and equity of education around the world. The authors demonstrate high standards of scholarship and intellectual wit by drawing on a wealth of research evidence over many years of debate – some of it within ICSEI (International Conference for School Effectiveness and Improvement) – about how schools and school systems become effective and can improve. The chapters provide a rich research base that can inform both policy and practice.

By sharing cutting-edge knowledge and research findings about the effects of accountability systems on school leadership, the authors touch grounds that are often neglected in the political discourse, such as the question of what accountability stressors principals perceive to be significant and how they deal with them in a productive way. They also throw light on the field of tension between political accountability and the personal and moral accountability of school principals' respectfulness for the schools and communities they serve.

Education systems are challenged to find the right balance between openness and regulation to enable each school to be responsive to the local demands of a community. The authors of the country cases critically question how professional approaches to accountability encompass both the implementation of standards and professional control of site-based management as it applies to the practices of teachers and school leaders. They aim at linking theory and practice, policy and transformation, leadership and learning through a plurality of approaches to jointly achieve in-depth understandings of what constitutes reciprocal accountability. The tensions and contradictions in balancing top-down accountability and school leadership and management at the local level seem to be similar in most cases. The question arises of whether states are becoming more alike because of the accountability movement. After having read the case studies of the authors congregated in this book, I can conclude that although local accountability demands seem to be concurrent with the development of international standards for student achievement outcomes, the policy cultures still show strong differences in the countries presented. This allows enough room to keep the pride and identity of each nation on its national education system, since the professionals of each local school are the change agents who will ultimately improve practices and their outcome.

Professor Dr Michael Schratz
University of Innsbruck
ICSEI President

1 Introduction

Conceptualizing educational accountability across global contexts

Jacob Easley II

Educational accountability and leadership are key factors commonly associated with school effectiveness and are highly inextricable from the commentary lexicon for the management of school improvement. And while globalization has had an indelible impact on accountability policy worldwide, namely due to policy borrowing from one geopolitical context to another, both educational leadership and accountability are continually defined by the historical and cultural epistemologies embedded within the core fiber of national, and in many cases, local identities of individual communities. Herein lie several tensions: one that troubles the notion of cultural sensitivity toward the conceptualization of policy and practice amid the influence of globalization on educational accountability and leadership, one that troubles the temporal-permanency continuum for sustainability as pertaining to educational effectiveness, and another that recognizes the intersections of these and others.

This edited volume brings together authors, many working in teams, who investigate these central tensions by focusing on the conditions of educational accountability, testing, inspection, and leadership within a single national context, thereby providing the readership the opportunity for broader cross-national comparisons. We have clustered national perspectives by geographical and/or cultural proximities including chapters from the following regions, in non-hierarchical order: China, Hong Kong, and India representing Asian societies; Australia, New Zealand, the United States, and Chile representing Anglo societies and the Americas; and Austria, France, Germany, the Netherlands, and Norway representing European societies. Each cluster is complemented by a synthesis and response contribution to further discussions regarding the future of school leadership within the changing context of accountability policies. Each invited contributor is noted within the profession for his or her expertise in educational policy and reform within the respective regions.

As a collective body, each chapter is largely influenced by the aims of the Educational Leadership Network (ELN) of the International Congress for School Effectiveness and Improvement (ICSEI). Undergirded by the aim to examine the intersections among accountability policy and practices from around the globe with an exploration of new possibilities for school leaders, the ELN organized a symposium occurring during the 2013 ICSEI conference in Santiago, Chile. It is from this beginning that this volume finds its roots. While many authors are members of the Network, such affiliation was not a requirement.

Offering a conceptual framework for educational accountability, we propose a multidimensional approach, one that not only describes the current contexts of educational enterprises around the globe, but also juxtaposes, questions, disrupts, and challenges them. We asked authors to investigate the philosophically, structural, and political underpinnings of educational accountability. In the advent of globalization, educational accountability has become a largely ubiquitous concept. The chapters within this volume highlight the complexity of educational accountability as enveloped by particular contexts that position accountability in unique ways. As cited by Radnor *et al.* (1996: 45), "The term accountability is used widely, vaguely, and incoherently and the issue must therefore be approached with considerable caution." Yet, it is certainly clear that the varied purposes, functions, and even the consequences of educational policies are shaped by location (Easley and Tulowitzki, 2013)—what and how education authorities and communities conceive of their role as stakeholders, resource availability, socio-cultural norms and mores (both historical and contemporary), and general intellectual capital.

As a matter of policy, educational accountability is situated in a particular vein, often beyond the reach of what some refer to as internal or self-regulatory accountability (Firestone and Shipps, 2005; Kogan, 1988; Shipps and White, 2009) that engenders an individual's moral commitment to self and others. Accountability policy conveys external obligation (see also Leithwood and Earl, 2000; Wagner, 1987) that forges a transactional relationship among individuals and groups. While less is known about the extent to which school leaders shape educational accountability, much is known about the effect of accountability on school leadership, largely informed by the obligatory and transactional function of accountability policy. For most, accountability describes a disciplinary power. Accountability describes conditionality among relations in which one body is able to exert force upon another, usually based on the actions and/or performance-based outcomes manufactured at the hands of the other. Hill and Bonan (1991: 35) further outline these conditions in four parts:

> One party expects the other to perform a service or accomplish a goal; the party performing the activity accepts the legitimacy of the other's expectation; the party performing the activity derives some benefits from the relationship; and the party for whom the activity is performed has some capacity to affect the other's benefits.

Bass (1990) describes the leader–follower transactional conditions as occurring in three prominent three ways: (1) contingent reward—whereby rewards are exchanged for effort or performance or rewards are promised to spur performance; (2) active management by exception—whereby corrective action is deliberately employed upon recognition of deviation from rules or standards of performance; and (3) passive management by exception—whereby intervention is offered only when standards or expected outcomes have not been met.

Yet, educational accountability may very well catalyze an additional dynamic beyond the noted concept of transactional leadership understood as the interactions among peoples, namely managers and employees (Bass, 1990), for an exchange of things of value (Burns, 1978), or even laissez-faire leadership (Bass, 1990; Hinkin and Schriesheim, 2008; Tejada et al., 2001) for which leaders avoid action and/or decision-making all together.

In this alternate space, the relationship between the school leader and policy itself takes center stage. This space engenders the understanding that school leaders may very well create their own accountability cultures (Shipps and White, 2009) and recognizes that the external, obligatory forces of accountability simultaneously shape leaders' self-concept. This space underscores the agentive power of school leaders as mediated by the interface among their actions and accountability policy itself—i.e., inaction, compliance, contestation, defiance, or subversive appropriation. Recognizing that school leaders do actively interpret accountability policy for use, their epistemological and ontological references for leadership inscribe new or (re)inscribe existing notions of school leader governance and performance. These notions are generative, cultural, and contextual.

Within this volume, authors explore the meaning(s) of educational accountability within their national and local contexts. They investigate the function, operations, and, more importantly, the outcomes of educational accountability, inspection, and testing within schools and on the role of school leadership. Lastly, they challenge the paradigms and practices of accountability policies and school leadership to offer new possibilities for educational effectiveness and improvement, with a particular focus on possibilities for school leadership. While in most cases, school leadership likely centers on the role of the school master or principal, we fully recognize the expanded role of educational leadership as existing both inside and outside of schools, operating across the fields of advocacy, governance, instructional practice, and policy.

In an effort to provide a structure, each national chapter addresses in some fashion, though is not limited to, the following questions to guide inquiry and collaborative analysis in a deliberate manner:

1. What is the policy that informs school accountability in your country?
    a. What philosophical underpinnings inform or define the unique perspectives of accountability within the context?
2. What happens in the practice of testing, accountability, and assessment, and how does it relate to accountability policy?

3. What does the research in your country tell us about the role of school leaders on accountability and assessment?
4. What unique research approach/design is taken to investigate questions 1–3?
5. What can we learn from an analysis of these questions to inform new possibilities for school leadership for educational effectiveness and improvement?

This design allows for a methodologically and pragmatically flexible approach (Rosenberg and Yates, 2007)—the multi-case study. The design allowed each author or teams to devise research with sensitivity to their individual research constraints as well as the context of the country, municipality, and or schools. Moreover, this design recognizes flexibility needed to allot diversity among theoretical frameworks and/or data analyses utilized by each set of authors. As a collective, the works here within seek not only to spark dialogue among those affiliated with the ELN but to provide scholars, policy-makers, and current and future school leader practitioners an opportunity to assess, to reflect on, to engage further research, and to discuss current issues surrounding accountability policies from around the globe as well as implications on school leadership. Cases are intentionally juxtaposed to provide a broad perspective of regional and cultural similarities and departures. For example, cases are arranged to reflect the diasporic Asian, Anglo and American, and European societies. In short, this work seeks to explore international perspectives on the challenges and possibilities of twenty-first-century school leadership as informed by educational accountability in an effort to advance global discussions of school effectiveness and improvement.

References

Bass, B. M. (1990). From transactional to transformational leadership: Learning to share the vision. *Organizational Dynamics*, 18(3), 19–31.
Burns, J. M. (1978). *Leadership*. New York: Harper and Row.
Easley, J. and Tulowitzki, P. (2013). Policy formation of intercultural and globally-minded educational leadership preparation. *International Journal of Educational Management*, 27(7), 744–761.
Firestone, W. A. and Shipps, D. (2005). How do leaders interpret conflicting accountabilities to improve student learning? In W. A. Firestone and C. Reihl (eds) *A New Agenda for Research in Educational Leadership* (pp. 81–100). New York: Teachers College Press.
Hill. P. T. and Bonan, J. J. (1991). *Decentralization and Accountability in Public Education*. Santa Monica, CA: RAND Corporation.
Hinkin, T. R. and Schriesheim, C. A. (2008). An examination of "nonleadership": From laissez-faire to leader reward omission and punishment omission. *Journal of Applied Psychology*, 93, 1234–1248.
Kogan, M. (1988). *Educational Accountability: An Analytical Overview* (2nd edn). London: Hodder and Stoughton.

Leithwood, K. and Earl, L. (2000). Educational accountability effects: An international perspective. *Peabody Journal of Education*, 75(4), 1–18.

Randor, H. A., Ball, S., Vincent, C., and Henshaw, L. (1996). *Local Education Authorities: Accountability and Control.* Stoke on Trent, UK: Trentham Books.

Rosenberg, J. P. and Yates, P. M. (2007). Schematic representation of case study research design. *Journal of Advanced Nursing*, 60(4), 447–452.

Shipps, D. and White, M. (2009). A new politics of the principal? Accountabilty-driven change in New York City. *Peabody Journal of Education*, 84(3), 350–373.

Tejada, M. J., Scandura, T. A., and Pillai, R. (2001). The MLQ revisited: Psychometric properties and recommendations. *The Leadership Quarterly*, 12, 31–52.

Wagner, R. (1987). *Accountability in Education: A philosophical inquiry.* New York: Routledge.

2 Principal leadership and accountability in Australia

A fine balance indeed

Simon Clarke and Neil Dempster

This chapter makes a contribution to the discussion of the effects of accountability policy on school leadership from an Australian perspective. It does so in an educational environment that is driven by policies consistent with a policy epidemic that has become known as the global educational reform movement or GERM. In Australia, these policies have been especially apparent in a move towards school markets, test-based accountability, and a focus on literacy and numeracy. GERM has affected the ideas of governments from all parts of the political spectrum, so much so that it is now difficult to find fundamental differences in the policy agendas pursued by competing parties. Indeed, it seems fair to say that the policy environment resonates with the old adage, *plus ça change, plus c'est la même chose* (the more things change, the more they stay the same). That said, it is important to understand the nature and extent of school accountability policies because of the impact they have on schools and the ways in which they are led. In undertaking a discussion of these linked issues, we structure the chapter in four parts. In the first part, we describe the background to key elements of school accountability policies and their reach into the states and territories that make up the Australian federation. Second, we dig more deeply into the testing and assessment requirements of the nation's accountability policies and the demands they place on school leaders, especially principals. Third, we outline the outcomes of Australian research into the effects of accountability policies on school leaders; and finally, we put forward some possibilities for consideration by school leaders so that they might balance the pressures of accountability while ensuring that they meet the broader aspirations of an Australian education for their students.

Policy that informs school accountability in Australia

There is an undeniable neoliberal thrust that seems to be driving contemporary Australian education policy. This can be seen in the instrumentalism of government initiatives as well as the marketised environment of schooling. The market values of competition, consumer choice, performance measurement and accountability underpin the politics of education, as does the determination to expand self-management practices in school systems. Recent moves to create 'independent public schools', especially in the states of Western Australia and Queensland, exemplify this trend. Successive governments over at least the last two decades have enthusiastically embraced neoliberal values. They were evident in the Rudd government's so-called 'education revolution' proposals (Commonwealth Government of Australia, 2008) to deliver greater accountability and better outcomes, as they were in the Gillard government's pressure to lift school performance nationally and internationally, particularly through international literacy, numeracy and science testing as a key driver. They are also evident in the Abbott government's agenda of 'accountability' and the marketisation of schooling. This is pursued mainly by means of school competition and autonomy, test-driven curriculum, school league tables and teacher performance pay, all of which leave the legacy carried over from previous political opponents largely in place. That said, there is a much broader education agenda outlined in the *Melbourne Declaration on Educational Goals for Young Australians* (MCEETYA, 2008) signed by all state and territory governments through the then Ministerial Council on Education, Employment, Training and Youth Affairs (MCEETYA).

This agenda provides an important framework within which the federal level of government, in cooperation with states and territories, has conceived school improvement initiatives. In particular, the two goals enshrined in the *Melbourne Declaration* are that (a) Australian schooling promotes equity and excellence, and (b) all young Australians become successful learners, confident and creative individuals and active and informed citizens (MCEETYA, 2008). Furthermore, the *Melbourne Declaration* was accompanied by a four year action plan for the states, territories and the federal government to work together to achieve these important national outcomes.

The practice of testing, accountability and assessment

Given the policy environment just described, it is hardly surprising that school principals are being held increasingly accountable for the educational outcomes of their students (Watterston and Caldwell, 2011). National testing, namely, the National Assessment Program – Literacy and Numeracy (NAPLAN) began in 2008 and every year, all students in Years 3, 5, 7 and 9 are assessed on the same days using national tests in reading, writing, language conventions (spelling, grammar and punctuation) and numeracy. Parents are provided with reports detailing their child's performance against national standards, national achievement levels and the national mean. Furthermore, results are reported on the MySchool website, which is a government-mandated initiative to provide online information about schools to consumers. This website makes public a synthesis of performance data and comparisons with 'like' schools from national tests, with the aim of facilitating the interpretation of results and comparisons between schools by any interested party. There are concerns held by principals, however, that MySchool, with its concentration on student achievement scores, does not accurately portray school quality (Evans, 2010). In addition, there is some consternation on the part of the education profession that the data can be used as a system of league tables based on simplistic comparisons. Cranston and his colleagues (2010: 526) have illustrated these concerns with one principal's comment found to be typical of most: 'League tables and comparisons ... that (do) not take into account the clientele of a school will create angst, division, disparity between schools […] and, ultimately destroy the morale of the teaching service'.

Beyond the generalised purposes of national testing for school and system comparisons, principals can be held accountable for an individual student's academic achievement, which can, at worst, lead to legal processes claiming negligence or educational malpractice (Teh, 2009). The political demand for high stakes national testing forces principals to make decisions, which it has been shown, at least in the English context (Cambridge Primary Review, 2010), can lead to a narrowing of the curriculum experienced by children, particularly in the period immediately preceding the tests. While there is no doubt that test results can be put to good diagnostic use to help students improve, the shortcomings associated with a one-day snapshot of academic performance attract vigorous criticism from school leaders and teachers alike.

Research on the role of school leaders on accountability and assessment

The scope of the accountabilities perceived to be the responsibility of school principals extends much further than academic outcomes for their students. Riley (2012: 8), for example, summarises some of these responsibilities in examining their impact on school principals' health:

> A significant stressor has been the increased emphasis by governments on accountability for uniform curriculum delivery along with the devolution of administrative tasks from central to local control. For example, curriculum and timetabling, once the province of the principal and fundamental to the efficient running of a school, are now more centrally controlled, while many non-educational administrative tasks such as payroll, budgeting and teacher employment have been devolved to school leaders.

Similarly, Watson (2009: 4) reports a study that again draws attention to the broader responsibilities of the school principal that go beyond educational goals: 'The Victorian study of school principals' workload identified a clear tension between a personal desire to be an "educational leader" versus the employer's imperative to be a "manager".

Accordingly, principals take a key role in staff appraisals, are held accountable for a school's finances, which are reported on MySchool, as well as for the school environment. In addition, workplace health and safety matters, including implementing policies and protocols in response to personal injuries (Teh, 2009), illicit drugs (Barnett and McNamara, 2010) and bullying (Teh, 2009) are now considered to be within the daily ambit of work for the school principal. Sport safety is also an area where school principals will need to focus their attention in the light of recent legislative changes (Poulos et al., 2010). Furthermore, child protection remains a serious realm of responsibility for which principals are required to give appropriate responses to allegations of sexual misconduct (Teh, 2009) and implement policies that effectively give due attention to legal orders placed on the family members of students in their care. These are serious matters that probably reflect the complexities of modern life. They also suggest, however, that the 'reach' of principals beyond the school yard extends further to societal priorities than might have been the case in the past, and these are now understood to be the responsibility of schools in the collective psyche of the public. To elaborate on this point, Cranston et al. (2010: 527) cite the following principal's view: 'Society keeps 'dumping' problems into schools for them to solve or teach, e.g. sex education, bike education, non-sexist education, healthy eating'. A recent addition to this inventory of measures for which principals may be held accountable is the principal's obligation to provide for healthy eating, as articulated in tuck shop or school canteen policy and practice (Andrzejewska et al., 2013).

The scope of this repertoire of responsibilities tends to be compounded because principals also encounter pressure from conflicting purposes, namely, educational and accountability responsibilities, which can result in stress when principals are held accountable for areas they cannot control. Indeed, it could be argued that principals are attempting to lead schools and improve students' education in much more challenging situations than education authorities acknowledge. Watterston and Caldwell, (2011: 649) summarise this pressure thus:

> Australia now has a national system of tests with a high level of transparency on a school-by-school basis through the MySchool web site. There is no doubt that schools and their principals are being held to account in unprecedented fashion. However, the 'missing link' in the policy-practice-accountability chain in most jurisdictions has been a lack of authority at the school level to take action in matters such as the selection of staff and the allocation of funds.

It seems clear that there has been a significant impact made by external imperatives on the role of school leaders. As a consequence, principals face enormous difficulties in achieving a balance between, on the one hand, maintaining a focus on leading learning and, on the other hand, managing the multiple accountability demands determined by the policy environment and the challenges presented for schools (McKenzie et al., 2007). From this perspective, the intriguing notion of 'bastard leadership' (Wright, 2011) is also relevant in its portrayal of the ways in which school principals are purported to be denied the full scope of authentic leadership by policy imperatives. In other words, principals may not be able to balance the impact of potentially detrimental external pressures on school improvement against what they consider to be in the best interest of the young people in their charge. Given these circumstances, the question is raised about the extent to which school leaders descend into implementing the policies and values of governments and their agencies, irrespective of the circumstances from which their students are drawn. The question is also raised about the extent to which school leaders are able to challenge or adapt government imperatives.

Lessons learned to inform new possibilities for school leadership

Taking into account the considerations that have been discussed above, we argue that it would be desirable for there to be a renewed commitment to the formation of school leaders who have the knowledge, skills and dispositions to take responsibility for their own learning as well as the learning of others. For this purpose we focus on two specific dimensions of our work designed to facilitate the agency of school leaders in taking responsibility for others' learning as well as their own. The first dimension to which we refer is the Principals as Literacy Leaders (PALL) project that has been implemented in many parts of Australia. The project assists principals to examine student achievement information, to design and implement literacy improvement in their schools and to lead a professional learning community to sustain improvement and support local and system-wide developments.

With its situated approach, PALL is enabling school leaders to adapt external system imperatives in accordance with the internal purposes of the school, highlighting that 'data literate' principals who can collect, interpret and use data effectively have a capacity to contribute to system policy and enhance the intelligence of accountability at that level. Advocated and supported by the Australian Primary Principals Association (APPA), the project has been conducted in partnership with state, Catholic and independent schools in Australia since 2010. It was originally funded as a pilot study by the Australian government under its 2012 'Closing the Gap' initiatives for schools located in low socio-economic communities. The report from that pilot study (Dempster *et al.*, 2012a) documents the impact and effect of the project on the leadership of principals and the contribution of their teachers to improving reading in their schools.

In brief, the programme employs five professional learning modules aimed at enhancing the knowledge and skills of principals to work with others on improving the teaching of reading and children's learning and achievement. Module 1 synthesises research into the actions leaders can take to connect their work better with learning; Module 2 examines the body of research, since the late nineties, to define the key elements in learning to read so that principals know about the important matters in which their teachers should be engaging; Module 3 explores the kinds of data necessary if diagnostic assessment is to be useful in finding out what children can do in order to take them further; Module 4 examines recent research literature on the planning and implementation of effective interventions in reading so that improvement planning is targeted and practice is adjusted accordingly; and Module 5 concentrates on the process of evaluation so that principals and their teachers can ascertain the impact and effect of the interventions they have been implementing. Tools and tasks, which principals use and undertake with their teachers once they are back at their schools, accompany all modules. In this way, the PALL programme acknowledges the contextual knowledge of principals and teachers, underscoring the relationship between theory and practice and the importance of learning about school improvement 'on-the-job' (Huber, 2011).

The chief impetus for PALL was the poor literacy performance of students in the schools the pilot targeted. A secondary, though clearly a strong motivation for members of the APPA, was the pressure being faced by school leaders over their students' literacy achievement. Striking a balance between the functional needs of children learning to read, the satisfaction this brings to other aspects of learning, and the political drive for increased performance accountability has weighed heavily on principals involved in the programme.

The design of the programme met this need for balance 'head on', acknowledging that principals cannot turn around student performance by hope, fiat or coercion. This requires dedicated commitment to a series of priorities derived from accumulated research into the connections between leadership and learning (Day *et al.*, 2010; Robinson, 2009; MacBeath and Dempster, 2009). These priorities are:

1. shared approaches to leadership;
2. active participation in literacy professional development;
3. attention to the physical, social and emotional conditions of learning;
4. the coordination, management and monitoring of teaching and learning;
5. partnerships with parents and others outside the school to support children learning to read;
6. a strong evidence base;
7. professional conversations about children's learning needs and what to do next based on that evidence.

Such leadership priorities, together with the 'tools' and tasks outlined during the modules referred to above, created an agenda enabling principals, in partnership with their teachers and where possible, with parents, to focus on improvements in children's reading as the foundation for literacy. That said, the PALL programme emphasised compelling research findings about learning to read, so that principals would be able to engage in discussions with their teachers about the extent of their literacy knowledge and expertise, their understanding of a range of helpful diagnostic assessment processes, the most useful evidence on reading achievement, as well as the kind of strategies most likely to take children further in their pursuit of reading improvement.

Critical amongst the priorities outlined above was the importance of professional learning (Robinson, 2009) about literacy, in which principals played an active role, not necessarily as experts, but certainly as co-learners with their teachers. As they addressed this priority, principals were encouraged to engage in ongoing dialogue with their teachers drawing on reading achievement evidence related to the reading 'Big Six' (Konza, 2011): oral language experience, phonological awareness, phonics, vocabulary, fluency and comprehension. Understanding and interpreting diagnostic assessment data related to these important building blocks for reading revealed the need for 'data literate' principals and teachers. Thus the learning of others became a significant factor in the PALL principals' school improvement journeys.

Driven by the moral purpose of improving children's lives through learning, principals and teachers were encouraged to focus on classroom activity and student progress, not on NAPLAN results. It is our view that when students and their learning needs are the perennial focus in schools, gains are achieved, teachers, children and parents alike share satisfaction, and improvements in standardised test performance follow. This claim is well supported by the findings of the PALL pilot project study (Dempster *et al.*, 2012a).

To sum up, PALL is enabling school leaders to adapt external system imperatives to mesh with the internal purposes of the school, highlighting that 'data literate' principals, with their teachers, are learning to collect, interpret and use literacy data effectively. When this is the case, they have the capacity and confidence to identify and employ teaching practices known to contribute to children's reading improvement. In so doing, they are also able to influence system policy and enhance the intelligence of accountability at that level.

The second dimension of our work to which we refer is a conceptual or analytical framework (Clarke and Wildy, 2010) with five focal points for informing principals' (and other school leaders') leadership development. Again, this framework seeks to promote a balance between, on the one hand, encouraging and supporting school leaders to take responsibility for their own learning agendas and, on the other hand, being appropriately cognizant of the normative requirements of the system.

The conceptual framework has been embedded in an interpretive approach employed over many years to investigate the principalship, an approach that has yielded a rich and realistic portrayal of Australian principals' day-to-day work from the perspectives of practitioners themselves. It is this comprehensive depiction of the problems, issues and challenges principals encounter and the ways in which these are handled, together with reflections on their experiences, that has enabled the initial focal points of the framework to be identified, namely, *place, people, system and self*.

Put simply, these focal points can be articulated as follows. Having the knowledge and understanding of *place* means that school leaders are able to read the complexities of their context, especially the people, the problems and issues, as well as the culture of the school and the community in which it is located. The necessity to be 'contextually literate' (NCSL, 2007) applies to all contexts insofar as it facilitates leaders' capacity to determine the school's priorities and interests, particularly in connection with leadership for learning. At the broader level, this 'literacy' entails familiarity with the socio-economic, demographic, cultural and historical composition of the community, which governs the intake of the school. At the school level, it means acquiring data about students' achievement and progress, turning it into useful information and ultimately into strategies for action. In other words, if student learning is to be at the focus of school leadership, principals require the ability to read the contextual circumstances so they can act in ways, which are responsive to the situation.

In its earlier iteration, having the knowledge, understanding and skill to deal with *people* meant that school leaders should be able to handle a range of complex interactions on a day-to-day basis with diverse constituent groups, such as staff, parents, state personnel and community members. These interactions highlight the importance of the interpersonal, political and ethical dimensions of the principal's role and the need to understand human nature and the motivations of individuals (Begley, 2008). More important in connection with leadership for learning, however, is the significance of *people* for its application to the development of human agency. Given the recent focus on the notion of 'distributed leadership' (Bush and Jackson, 2002) for facilitating school improvement, the ability of principals to cultivate positive and productive relationships seems to be an especially vital consideration in the formation of principals (Duignan, 2006). Similarly, Starratt (2011: xi) argues that educational leadership needs to be 'grounded in a deep appreciation of the richness, complexity and enormous potential of people'.

Having the knowledge, understanding and skill to deal with the education authority, or *system*, means that school leaders are able to navigate their way through complex and often quite baffling bureaucratic regulations, policies and protocols. Dealing with the system, therefore, takes not only functional knowledge, understanding and skill but also confidence, determination and political sophistication. In the more specific context of leadership for learning, this political sophistication may lead to an ability to adapt external system imperatives in accordance with the internal purposes of the school. The ability of school leaders to go beyond following system prescription is at the heart of achieving the balance between developing the capability to focus on leading learning and the competency to manage multiple accountability demands. To this end, the use of data and evidence is an increasingly important dimension of educational decision-making (Earl and Fullan, 2003). As with the PALL programme, outlined above, this observation is premised on the belief that 'data literate' principals who can collect, interpret and use data effectively have a capacity to contribute to system policy and enhance the intelligence of accountability at that level.

Data literacy is also critical within the school itself so that schools are able to 'know themselves, do it for themselves and give their own account of their achievement' (MacBeath, 1999: 2). In this connection, Earl's (2005: 7) distinction between what she describes as 'real' accountability and accounting is instructive, two which accounting is 'gathering, organising and reporting information that describes performance'. Accountability, however, is 'the conversation about what information means and how it fits with everything we know and about how to use it to make positive changes' Earl, 2005: 7). Earl, in fact, goes further and suggests that accountability is intertwined with 'a moral and professional responsibility to be knowledgeable and fair in teaching [and learning] and in interactions with students and their parents' (Earl, 2005: 7).

In the original version of the framework, looking after the *self* referred mainly to having the personal resilience for the job. This is because the level of personal resilience required to deal with the complexities of school leadership tends to be widely underestimated by principals, especially when they are inexperienced in the role. From this perspective, self-knowledge and the ability to contextualise, understand, accept and deal with the emotional demands of the job is a key focus of the framework for facilitating the preparation, support and development of school leaders. The significance of *self*, however, extends beyond considerations of principals' well-being and also takes into account their values and intentions. This is what Duignan (2006: 143) has referred to as personal formation and transformation, which engenders a deep understanding of personal values and a conviction that leadership is concerned fundamentally with developing the capacity of colleagues and students. This suggestion resonates with Dempster's (2009) observation that at the heart of leadership for learning is a well-defined sense of moral purpose. As he points out, 'principals are not there to make students' lives worse, they are there to see that schools concentrate on improving students' learning and ultimately their achievement' (Dempster, 2009, no page nos.).

Interestingly, although the conceptual framework was generated from principals' own perspectives of their experiences, learning *per se* did not emerge as a focal point. Perhaps, because principals are normally experienced and accomplished classroom teachers, they consider that the requisite knowledge, understanding and skills to lead learning have been acquired before entering the principal's office. It is argued, therefore, that it would be desirable for the connection between leadership and learning to be emphasised far more in the formation of school principals. Indeed, such is the significance of the principal's educative role that it would be helpful to add a further 'focal point' to the conceptual framework that may be labelled '*pedagogy*.' This addition strengthens the application of the framework because it reinforces the key purpose of school leadership – the improvement of learning and teaching. In this regard, Geoff Masters' (2008, no page nos.) observation has great poignancy: 'In a sense, [educators] can't know too much about learning'; an important reminder that a vital consideration of school leaders is to promote others' as well as their own learning.

This framework has the potential to be used as a heuristic tool by school leaders in adopting a self-study approach for enabling them to unpack the contemporary complexities of school leadership in ways that might lead to deeper understandings of their work in specific contexts. From this perspective, it may be argued that the framework has a number of key strengths. First, the framework is grounded in the realities of the school as a complex workplace. Consequently, the framework is fundamentally descriptive rather than one that is integral to a normative theory or model. Indeed, the approach that has been adopted to developing the framework may offer clearer direction for practitioners' learning because it has been based initially on a consideration of 'what is' rather than 'what ought to be'.

Second, the heuristic has the capacity to support leaders to become more autonomous in their professional learning than has tended to be the case in the past (Dempster *et al.*, 2012a). By this, it is meant that the heuristic may comprise one way in which individual school leaders can be encouraged and supported to take responsibility for their own learning agendas, rather than being overly reliant on the normative requirements of the system. Taking this into account, the framework may serve as a stark reminder that, now more than ever, school leaders need to be powerful learners themselves if they are to take responsibility for others' learning.

Conclusion

In conclusion, we suggest that the two dimensions we have outlined illustrate ways in which leadership for learning may be preserved, and even fortified, in the midst of an accountability agenda requiring a proactive response from school leaders if educational ideals are to hold sway against political ideals in the education policy environment. Such a proactive response tends to be reliant on school leaders taking responsibility for their own learning. Indeed, given the situations of complexity discussed above, which are increasingly influencing the school leader's world, it is more imperative than ever that school leaders should also be learners. If this condition can be met, both examples of professional learning reported here have the potential to enhance the ability of school leaders to go beyond following system prescription in achieving a fine balance between, on the one hand, developing the capability to focus on leading learning and, on the other hand, having the competency to manage multiple accountability demands.

References

Andrzejewska, K., Tadros, R., and Baxter, D. (2013). A descriptive study on the barriers and facilitators to implementation of the NSW (Australia) Healthy School Canteen Strategy. *Health Education Journal.* 72, 136–145. doi: 10.1177/0017896912437288.

Barnett, E. and McNamara, N. (2010). A school's duty of care and the management of illicit drug related incidents. *International Journal of Law & Education.* 15(1), 41–53.

Begley, P. (2008). The nature and specialized purposed of educational leadership. In J. Lumby, G. Crow and P. Pashiardis (eds) *International Handbook on the Preparation and Development of School Leaders* (pp. 21–24). New York: Routledge.

Bush, T. and Jackson, D. (2002). A preparation for school leadership: International perspectives. *Educational Management and Administration.* 30(4), 417–429.

Cambridge Primary Review (2010). Children, their world, their education: the final report and recommendations of the *Cambridge Primary Review.* Alexander R. J., Esmee Fairbairn Foundation. New York: Routledge.

Clarke, S. and Wildy, H. (2010). Preparing for principalship from the crucible of experience: Reflecting on theory, practice and research. *Journal of Educational Administration and History.* 41(1), 1–16.

Commonwealth Government of Australia (2008). *Quality Education: The Case for an Education Revolution in Our Schools.* Canberra: Commonwealth of Australia.

Cranston, N., Mulford, B., Keating, J., and Reid, A. (2010). Primary school principals and the purposes of education in Australia: Results of a national survey. *Journal of Educational Administration.* 48(4), 517–539.

Day, C., Sammons, P., Leithwood, K., Hopkins, D., Harris, A., Gu, Q., and Brown, E. (2010). *Ten Strong Claims about Successful School Leadership.* Nottingham: The National College for School Leadership.

Dempster, N. (2009). *Leadership for Learning: A Framework Synthesising Recent Research.* Paper 13. Deakin West, Australia: Australian College of Educators.

Dempster, N., Konza, D., Robson, G., Gaffney, M., Lock, G., and McKennariey, K. (2012a). *Principals as Literacy Leaders: Confident, Credible and Connected.* Canberra: The Australian Primary Principals Association.

Dempster, N., Fluckiger, B. and Lovett, S. (2012b). *Principals Reflecting on Their Leadership Learning with an Heuristic: A Pilot Study.* University of Sydney, Sydney, Australia: Joint Australian Association Research in Education and Asia Pacific Educational Research Association Conference (AARE & APERA), December 2–6.

Duignan, P. (2006). *Educational Leadership. Key Challenges and Ethical Tensions.* Port Melbourne: Cambridge University Press.

Earl, L. (2005). From accounting to accountability: Harnessing data for school improvement. Paper presented at Australian Council for Educational Research Conference, 'Using data to support learning', Melbourne, 7–9 August.

Earl, L. and Fullan M. (2003). Using data in leadership for learning. *Cambridge Journal of Education.* 33(3), 383–394.

Evans, S. (2010). My accountability: Do we measure up? *Accounting, Auditing & Accountability Journal.* 23(8), (no page nos).

Huber, S. (2011). Leadership for learning: Learning for leadership: The impact of professional development. In T. Townsend and J. MacBeath (eds) *International Handbook of Leadership for Learning.* (pp. 636–652). Dordrecht: Springer.

Konza, D. (2011). *Understanding the Reading Process, Department of Education and Children's Services.* Government of South Australia.

MacBeath, J. (1999). *Schools Must Speak for Themselves. The Case for School Self Evaluation.* London: Routledge.

MacBeath, J. and Dempster, N. (eds) (2009). *Connecting Leadership and Learning.* London: Routledge.

Masters, G. (2008). *Understanding and Leading Learning. Principals' Big Day Out.* Melbourne (Vic). Retrieved from: http://works.bepress.com/geoff_masters/118 Accessed 11 November 2009.

McKenzie, P., Mulford, B., and Anderson, M. (2007). *School Leadership and Learning: An Australian Overview.* Paper presented at the Australian Council for Educational Research Conference, The Leadership Challenge: Improving learning in schools, August 12–14, Melbourne.

MCEETYA (Ministerial Council on Education, Employment, Training and Youth Affairs) (2008). *The Melbourne Declaration on the Educational Goals for Young Goals for Young Australians.* Melbourne: MCEETYA. Retrieved from: www.curriculum.edu.au/mceetya/melbourne_declaration.25979.html Accessed 30 March 2009.

NCSL (National College for School Leadership) (2007). *What We Know About School Leadership.* NCSL. Retrieved from: www.ncsl.org.uk/publications Accessed 11 November 2009.

Poulos, R., Donaldson, A., and Finch, C. (2010). Towards evidence-informed sports safety policy for New South Wales, Australia: Assessing the readiness of the sector. *Injury Prevention.* 16(2), 127–131.

Riley, P. (2012). *The Australian Principal Health and Well-Being Survey.* Clayton, Victoria: Faculty of Education, Monash University.

Robinson, V. M. J. (2009). *School Leadership and Student Outcomes: Identifying what works.* Winmalee: Australian Council for Educational Leaders.

Starratt, R. J. (2011). *Refocusing School Leadership. Foregrounding Human Development Throughout the Work of the School.* New York: Routledge.

Teh, M. K. (2009). *Principals at Legal Risk: Complacency or Concern?* Paper presented at the Education: A risky business – ANZELA 2009, Australian and New Zealand Law Association.

Watson, L. (2009). Issues in reinventing school leadership: Reviewing the OECD report on improving school leadership from an Australian perspective. *Leading and Managing.* 15(1), 1–13.

Watterston, J. and Caldwell, B. (2011). System alignment as a key strategy in building capacity for school transformation. *Journal of Educational Administration.* 49(6), 637–652.

Wright, N. (2011). Between 'bastard' leadership and 'wicked' leadership? School leadership and the emerging policies of the UK Coalition Government. *Journal of Educational Administration and History.* 43(4), 345–362.

3 Aotearoa New Zealand

Examining the challenges of educational accountability policies and exploring possibilities for school leadership

Jan Robertson and Mary F. Hill

Aotearoa New Zealand (NZ) is a small country with a national school system, serving approximately 760,000 students. Performance of students in NZ sits within the top left quadrant of the OECD (Organization for Economic Co-operation and Development) results, revealing high performance but also high levels of inequity across its education population. The latest Programme for International Student Achievement (PISA) results (2012) show that although NZ is continuing to perform above average in reading, maths and science, performance in these areas has dropped against some other countries. Due to the self-managing nature of NZ's 2600 schools, school leaders have a central role to play in addressing this issue. However, as we argue below, this is neither straightforward nor static. After briefly outlining how we gathered the information for this chapter, we describe the self-managing nature of NZ schools and situate the role of school leaders within the accountability context. Next we lay out the assessment and accountability practices in primary and secondary schools. This leads to a discussion about the challenges and possibilities for school leaders within this particular context.

To gather the information needed, we initially emailed a targeted group of 12 policymakers, consultants, researchers and school leaders working in NZ and asked them to respond to four questions:

1. What is the policy that informs school accountability in NZ?
2. What happens in the practice of testing, accountability and assessment and how does it relate to accountability policy?
3. What does the research tell us about the role of school accountability and assessment?
4. What are the new possibilities for school improvement and effectiveness?

Through a process of inductive analysis, and using the four questions as a framework, we used the material to begin to develop each section of the chapter. This led to deeper consultation with members of the Ministry of Education and two additional researchers with a special interest in school leadership and assessment. This chapter draws on the multiple viewpoints of the challenges of educational accountability policies and the issues faced by school leaders and ends with a consideration of possibilities for school leadership.

Policy that informs school accountability in Aotearoa New Zealand

Over the last two decades NZ education policies have radically restructured the education system and put schools at the heart of accountability (Fiske and Ladd, 2000; OECD, 2012). Since these major reforms and the Education Act of 1989, NZ schools have been under a system of self-management. In contrast with many systems in other countries, there are no school districts or local education authorities in NZ. Each school is, in effect, its own school district operating under the control of an elected board of trustees that sets the goals and direction of the school, within government policy guidelines and in consultation with the Ministry of Education and the wider school community. The founding document for self-management of schools, the Picot Report (Ministry of Education, 1988), states that people who use public funds must be accountable for what is achieved with those funds and that to be accountable, people must know what it is they are to achieve and have control over the resources to achieve it. The Picot Report also states that it is important that the lines of accountability are clear.

The school's board of trustees appoints the school's principal and the principal is the day-to-day manager of the school, appointing the teachers. School management is guided by the regulatory and legislative requirements of the Ministry of Education as well as local policies that are developed by the school's board of trustees to meet local goals, needs and aspirations, as identified in a strategic and reporting plan. Therefore, the principal, along with other leaders in the school, implements national policies alongside local policies governed by the board of trustees.

All educators in New Zealand schools are bound by professional standards developed jointly among teachers' associations (unions) and the Ministry of Education. All schools must have performance management systems, and the principal appraises each teacher within her/his school annually. Professional development opportunities are provided for teachers by schools. Wylie (2009a: 6) describes school self-management in this way: 'The framework within which schools operated from 1990 owed much to the New Public Management reframing of public services, underpinned by separation of functions, contractual relationships, and accountability arrangements related to contracts and reporting on outputs'.

NZ, through the Ministry of Education, has a National Curriculum, National Education Guidelines and National Administration Guidelines as the main sources of accountability policy. The Ministry of Education pays teachers' salaries directly and provides all other funding for schools, directly to the individual schools. Since 2001, schools have been required to develop an annual charter, in which they set targets for achievement and report annually on progress towards these targets through the annual planning and reporting cycle. The charter is submitted annually to the Ministry of Education for approval. The planning and reporting section in the charter must report on student progress against targets agreed between the Ministry of Education and each school. However, there are many parts of this accountability framework that are not aligned. Wylie (2009b) argues that there are disconnects in the NZ education system between school planning, performance management and school review, and also between the roles of the Ministry of Education and the Education Review Office. This, she believes, means less-effective school development and inefficient use of public money for education. However, in spite of the disconnects, Wylie's research also found that the annual planning process had become a part of schools' processes and that by 2009 secondary principals were almost unanimous in stating they would use something like the current annual planning and reporting process, even if they were not required to do so.

National assessment and accountability policies

In primary (elementary) schools catering to Year 1–8 students, National Standards have been mandated since 2010. In contrast with many other jurisdictions, NZ's National Standards are not tests. The National Standards documents describe clear expectations (and provide exemplars) that students need to meet in reading, writing and mathematics in the first eight years at school. Using these descriptions and exemplars, it is the role of teachers to make overall judgements about each student's progress against the National Standards using their own professional knowledge, classroom assessment tools and other available assessment instruments (both norm and curriculum referenced within NZ) that they select to use. There has been a long-standing debate in NZ regarding the potential use of national standardized tests. Nusche (2012, blog) states:

> What struck the review team most about New Zealand's approach was the great amount of trust in the ability of students, teachers and schools to evaluate their own performance and engage in self-improvement. While accountability is not seen as a good option for New Zealand, especially in primary education, there is a general consensus against national testing and the use of test results for school rankings.

The New Zealand Ministry of Education (Sewell, 2011: 2) states in its position paper on assessment:

Unlike standards-based assessment in other countries, our standards do not rely on national testing. Instead there is an emphasis on teacher professional judgments, assessment for learning principles and practice, and the importance of information sharing to support student learning. This is a novel approach when compared with other jurisdictions.

School and student evaluation and assessment in primary schools is, therefore, very much the responsibility of the schools and their individual boards of trustees, and the main policy focus has been to build school and teacher capacity and capability in assessment and evaluation. Likewise, in NZ secondary schools (high schools) catering to Years 9–13, there has been a similar emphasis on building assessment and evaluation capability, both for formative and summative purposes. In secondary schools there are national qualifications that all students must take in the last three years of school. These are high stakes and standards-based. Known as the National Certificate of Educational Achievement (NCEA), these qualifications, in every curriculum subject, assess skills and knowledge against a number of standards. Individual students are assessed through both classroom assessment processes and external examinations. There are three levels of NCEA achievement, depending on the difficulty of the standards achieved. In general, students work through levels 1 to 3 in Years 11 to 13, gaining credits towards qualifications. Students are recognised for high achievement at each level by gaining NCEA with merit or NCEA with excellence. Appointed moderators moderate both internally within the school and externally for some of the school-based assessments, and the examinations are also marked externally. Students receive their individual results and the overall school results (percentage of students achieving at each level in each subject) are made public. Students who do not achieve the required standard at level 2 are denied access to university study. Schools' examination results are published in league tables throughout the national newspapers and media.

In addition to these assessment and evaluation practices for every student, NZ also has a system of sample-based national monitoring of student achievement at Year 4 and Year 8 in different subjects each year via the National Monitoring Study of Student Achievement (NMSSA), aiming to provide a broad picture of student achievement. These evaluations, along with the results of PISA, TIMSS (Trends in International Mathematics and Science Study) and the latest OECD study, confirm that NZ students perform very well in international comparisons. At the same time, the results show that a percentage of NZ students' achievement falls well behind the rest of students. This group (the majority of which comprises Maori (indigenous), Pacific and special needs students) is the focus of recent government policies, including the previously mentioned introduction of National Standards.

School level self-review

Schools undertake annual self-review against their strategic plan and achievement targets and are reviewed regularly by the Education Review Office (ERO), which is a government agency separate from the Ministry of Education. The ERO review occurs every five years if the ERO has been satisfied with the school's self-reviewing processes. There is a one-year cycle of review if ERO has concerns with a school. The focus of these evaluations is mainly on school self-review alongside some focus on the progress of schools in implementing priorities chosen by ERO each year in line with Ministry of Education policy implementation, for example, leadership and assessment or literacy. The ERO reports to the school's board of trustees (and thus the school community), as well as to the Ministry of Education, on its view of the school's leadership, student achievement, Maori (indigenous) student achievement and the board of trustee's governance. These reports are available for anyone to access. An auditor delegated by the Office of the Auditor General must also audit the school's annual financial accounts. The board of trustees must also ensure that the school is well maintained. There is some funding from the Ministry of Education that schools must use to maintain and upgrade their facilities.

This relatively complex policy context has arisen out of the 1988 movement to self-management and has resulted in a wide-range of accountability relationships and processes, that include: the accountability to the school, parents, students and local communities; to the Ministry of Education; to the ERO; and for secondary schools, to the New Zealand Qualifications Authority, for national qualifications and the quality of internal assessments. These accountability levers have been differently employed between compliance and improvement over the last two decades, according to political direction and individual needs of local communities. Educators and policymakers in NZ continue to discuss and debate issues related to decentralisation, accountability and support, in areas such as: whether NZ education has become increasingly more centralised in many of its accountabilities as it has become decentralised in the administrative policies; the reliability of the judgements regarding National Standards in primary schools as moderation between schools has been limited, and the effect of these standards in narrowing the primary school curriculum; whether NCEA has led to secondary teachers becoming too narrowly focused on testing rather than teaching; whether some schools conduct appraisals in a compliance mode as a perfunctory mandated process, rather than appraisal for learning; and whether communities have been as involved in education accountability as was envisaged in the formation of the policy.

Assessment practices and their relationship to accountability policy

Classroom assessment of student learning has had prominence in NZ primary schools since the 1930s with teachers responsible for regular reporting using grades until the 1960s, and since then, descriptive criteria. Rather than assigning grades, marks or assigning students to place in class or percentiles, primary teachers have described where each student is in terms of their progress towards meeting learning outcomes set out either in the scheme of work for that year level (prior to 1993) or, since 1993, in the NZ Curriculum and its associated documents such as the national literacy progressions. The purpose of descriptive assessment is to not only show where students are, but also to indicate what their next steps in learning should be. These improvement focused practices were reinforced and supported in the shift to self-managing schools through professional learning focused on assessment for learning to strengthen teachers' assessment confidence and competence. Thus, primary teachers and school leaders have responded to the new policy initiatives by continuing to focus on assessment for learning.

Studies in NZ have investigated the effects of accountability policies on assessment practices, teachers' beliefs and school systems. Since the introduction of the school self-management policies at the end of the 1980s and the introduction of a centralised, child-centred curriculum, alongside the assessment and accountability policies sketched out above, research has indicated ways in which these centralised policies have had strong influences. In primary schools, Hill (2000) investigated the effects of self-management and school evaluation by ERO and found that by making schools individually accountable, primary teachers constructed assessment and monitoring systems that tracked individual student achievements against the curriculum levels. Using both standardised assessment tools and their own professional judgement, teachers make assessment decisions informally to assist in planning for teaching. In the last decade, the curriculum has been revised, new assessment tools have been produced and disseminated, and several major professional development programmes in assessment have been 'rolled out' nationally by the Ministry of Education. These developments have occurred as a result of a major review the implementation of the 1993 curriculum, the Curriculum Stocktake (McGee *et al.*, 2003) that recommended some significant changes along with recognition by the Ministry of Education that such changes need support in order for teachers to implement new approaches. Concomitantly, a robust reserve of assessment tools has been developed both by the Ministry of Education and by specialist assessment organisations such as the New Zealand Council for Educational Research, some under contract to the Ministry of Education, to help teachers and schools. Teachers can use these to compare their students' achievements against national norms in reading, writing, mathematics, science and spelling, and schools can compare themselves against all other schools in NZ, and against schools that are similar to them in socio-economic status. One online assessment tool for teaching and learning, the e-asTTle (see http://e-asttle.tki.org.nz/), allows teachers to select items on which to assess students in reading, maths, writing, and then they receive detailed information about students' strengths and on areas of need to specifically focus their teaching. Other tools, such as reading running records and diagnostic numeracy tools are in daily use. While these many different assessment tools are available, they are not mandatory. They are used in primary schools to make decisions about where to go next for teaching and learning as well as how children are achieving against the national standards.

As explained earlier, the National Standards require primary schools to report the achievement of each student to parents and to the Ministry of Education. Rather than using national standardised tests, teachers make overall teacher judgements (OTJs) on every student against the National Standards in literacy and mathematics (Ministry of Education, 2009), which are based on the NZ Curriculum (Ministry of Education, 2007). For the first two years (2010–2011) of this policy, the results were shared with parents twice per year and in an aggregated form with the board of trustees of the school. However, to the consternation of many school leaders who felt moderation was not yet embedded sufficiently to provide rigorous and reliable data, in 2012 the Ministry of Education made the results of all schools publicly available. Many principals, school board members and communities were concerned at the haste with which these National Standards were implemented, without the necessary consultation, pilot or development of moderation processes. Wylie (2009a: 22) states:

> The sense of déjà vu is sadly also present in the way the introduction of the national standards has occurred at breakneck speed, with little inclusion of the sector in overall design. As with the development of the curriculum statements and qualifications in the 1990s, there has been some sector involvement, but often piecemeal, for particular tasks. We can feel fortunate that in the design of the national standards some of the lessons from countries that have marched down this track have been heeded; but there are some critical aspects that need collective work still.

A recent study (Thrupp and White, 2013) investigated how the national standards were being implemented and how implementation was affecting school and teacher assessment practices as well as student learning. They conclude:

> National Standards are having some favourable impacts in areas that include teacher understanding of curriculum levels, motivation of some teachers and children and some improved targeting of interventions. Nevertheless such gains are overshadowed by damage being done

through the intensification of staff workloads, curriculum narrowing and the reinforcement of a two-tier curriculum, the positioning and labelling of children and unproductive new tensions amongst school staff. These problems are often occurring despite attempts by schools and teachers to minimise any damaging impact of the National Standards.

(Thrupp and White, 2013: i)

In secondary schools, the standards-based system of national secondary school qualifications tends to drive the ways in which classroom assessment is implemented (Hill, 2011). For example, the professional development programmes in assessment for learning emphasise involving students in their own assessment, clarity of the criteria and goal setting. However, due to the high-stakes nature of the national qualifications in Years 11–13, much of the assessment in high schools is a series of summative activities, the results of which are recorded towards a summative report. In fact, the term 'formative' has been reinterpreted by some secondary schools to mean practice for the upcoming summative assessment event (Ellis, 2005; Rawlins, 2007). Where assessment for learning has been implemented successfully in secondary schools, the school principals have fully understood the changed emphasis in assessment and have developed appraisal and polices accordingly to reinforce the changed focus (Hill, 2011). A Ministry of Education (2011) policy paper on assessment for learning stated that the Ministry of Education envisages a schooling system that uses assessment effectively at every level of the system to improve both teaching and learning. The intention to have an accountable, yet self-improving, schooling system is embedded in the key principles highlighted in the position paper: namely that (1) the student is at the centre, (2) curriculum underpins assessment, (3) building assessment capability is crucial to achieving improvement, and (4) an assessment capable system is an accountable system.

The ERO also focuses on assessment as part of considering effective practice in meeting students' needs and improving learning outcomes from the schools they reviewed. In 2007, the office (ERO, 2007b: 14–21) identified the following as key features of using evidence and assessment in New Zealand schools: student involvement in assessment; students' goal setting; use of school-wide information to improve students achievement; school-wide collation, analysis and use of assessment data; use of data to evaluate teaching programmes; information used to monitor students of interest or concern; board of trustees using information to inform policy, planning and resourcing; reporting student achievement information to the community; parents' opinions and ideas valued; Maori (indigenous) community or *whanau* (family) consulted; parents informed about assessment processes; sharing achievement and progress information with parents; and parents informed about next learning steps.

NZ has had a decade-long focus on formative assessment for students, where both students and teachers receive feedback on their learning and teaching during the process, i.e., assessment for learning. However, in 2010 ERO (p. 9) found only 30 percent of schools with effective and well-established practices. In schools where assessment practices were well understood, schools used assessment data to: discuss student progress with other teachers in teams or syndicates; moderate teacher judgements; monitor students' progress; identify teaching strategies for individuals or groups of students; involve students in goal setting and deciding their next learning steps; monitor the progress of students in relation to school targets; share information with parents and *whanau*; identify professional development priorities; and critique and reflect on teaching practice.

In addition to teachers' use of assessment, the NZ Curriculum states that students should be self-regulating and involved in making their own learning decisions. ERO (2010: 12) found that:

> when schools did involve students in their learning, it was evident in: student-led conferences with teachers, parents and whanau/families; regular self-assessment and peer assessment built into learning programs; teachers sharing assessment data with students; students regularly reviewing their goals with peers, teachers and parents; student portfolios providing evidence of progress towards and achievement of learning goals; and, teachers sharing learning intentions, exemplars and success criteria with students.

From the summary above, it is clear that although the intention is to use assessment for accountability and in the service of students' learning in a balanced way, in practice this is not without its challenges. Many schools and teachers have invested time and energy on practices that do not always support students' learning or progress (ERO, 2007a). And as these ERO reports indicate, due to the self-managing nature of NZ schools, there continues to be variance in assessment and accountability practices across schools. Recent government directives that require public reporting of student performance regarding National Standards and NCEA have also reignited a historical debate regarding how schools, teachers, government and communities should address the demands for accountability while keeping the focus on student learning (see for example, Dixon *et al.*, 2011; Gilmore, 2008).

The role of school leaders in accountability and assessment

Due to NZ's self-managing school system, the tensions highlighted above regarding the use of assessment for both accountability and in the service of learning rest squarely in the domain of school leaders. The principal sits at the nexus of national regulations/policy and school policies and practices. It is the principal who has the responsibility to ensure that each student has opportunities to learn and achieve, and that teachers are using assessment practices to support learning, raise achievement and ensure accountability. And it is the principal, along with other leaders in the school, who ensure school self-review and evaluation takes place, who leads the strategic planning, target setting and professional development/support to ensure evidence-based evaluation is effective. Thus, each school leader plays a critical role in shaping accountability systems, as well as leading and improving the assessment and reporting practices in his/her school (Hill, 2000, 2011; Thrupp and Easter, 2012). Through such policies and practices, NZ school leaders develop particular school cultures and, with their boards, set the tone in the school around expectations for learning, accountability, assessment practices and teacher appraisal.

The importance of the role of the school principal in NZ has been acknowledged in a best evidence synthesis on leadership (Robinson *et al.*, 2009). A key finding of this synthesis was the potential for improving students' learning when school leaders promote and/or participate in effective teacher professional development and this finding underpins the approach to evidence-based leadership currently promoted with school principals. The NZ Ministry of Education has, more recently, acknowledged the pivotal importance of school leadership for learning and has funded leadership development accordingly with programmes for aspiring principals and first-time principals, as well as providing further support for principals in leadership and assessment.

Despite the availability of these programmes however, research and evaluations have spotlighted particular issues for school leaders (ERO, 2010; Hill, 2011; Kandasamy, 2013). These issues include principals' knowledge of assessment and the strategic use of assessment and appraisal information to make a difference, particularly for students from underachieving groups. The ERO in 2010, for example, identified that school leaders have issues in the following areas: making the best use of information to target and support (the achievement of) specific groups of students; improving their own and teachers' capabilities to analyse and interpret data; making good use of data beyond target-setting; using data to evaluate specific strategies and initiatives; and increasing the use of student achievement information as part of ongoing self-review. Furthermore, although primary school leaders have found ERO evaluations generally affirming, a New Zealand Council for Educational Research survey in 2007 found that:

> (t)hirty percent said [that school reviews helped them see] some things in a new light, and that the review did lead to some positive changes; 28 percent said it helped them get some needed changes in their school. A quarter said it gave them something they could use to promote or market their school. But around another quarter thought that they had gained nothing from the review, or felt under pressure to make changes they thought were not warranted.
>
> (Wylie, 2009b: 143)

In an analysis of the open-ended survey questions in the survey, Wylie (2009b: 143) further stated that for school principals, 'accountability is seen mainly to the school community of students, parents and the board and the role of external review is largely seen as welcome or valued if it means that external knowledge is harnessed to the school's own journey'.

A third issue for school leaders has been that even though all schools provide the Ministry of Education with their education plan each year and their annual school report, they feel that no-one beyond the school is interested in these documents. The research (Wylie, 2009b: 142) shows that these supposedly formative documents are:

> minimally used for support and challenge. Yet what is of considerable interest here is that over half of the principals would like or had such discussions, even though there remains a considerable legacy of distrust of the central government agencies from the 'hands off' stance and limited engagement on joint issues during the 1990s.

Yet, a further issue is that there is still a tendency for school leaders to see assessment as simply a data collecting, interpreting and planning tool rather than a way to access information to use with students, and their families, to take learning forward. In order to address the equity issues in achievement, school leaders in self-managing schools have an essential role in helping teachers to use 'interactive during teaching' kinds of assessment in culturally responsive ways, rather than just managing testing and the use of results for accountability purposes. Anecdotal evidence from school development consultants, as well as some of the findings from the Research, Analysis and Insights into National Standards (RAINS) project (Thrupp and White, 2013), suggests that although an evidence-based inquiry form of teaching that uses assessment to diagnose and support learning is the new rhetoric, it is rarely well finessed. One consultant to schools reported via personal communication that:

> leaders send their teachers off to inquire and write stuff up, instead of seeing these practices embedded at the department meeting level where they can usefully determine [as a collective] what is worth inquiring into [related to school goals] and how best to do this and then use that for another iteration of inquiry that supports our school development.
> (Name withheld, personal communication, 18 May 2012)

Principals in NZ schools, with their boards, have the autonomy and power, and through principal and teacher appraisal and student assessment practices, can play a pivotal part in strongly influencing teaching practices and therefore, student achievement. It is important that principals have a strong understanding of assessment, its purposes and how policies within schools can work for and against assessment that enables learning. However, the autonomy of school leaders has meant that it is difficult to ensure all those who need development are electing to have it. Since 2010, the Ministry of Education has required schools with low student achievement to be involved in leadership and assessment professional learning and development and to also receive supplementary support from their regional offices. There is still marked variation of quality of leadership in assessment and accountability practices among schools, not necessarily addressed by appraisal. Appraisal practices vary from school to school and principal appraisals are often carried out by a principal from another school or consultants, on behalf of the board of trustees. Research by Wylie (2009b: 140) found that,

> primary principals' responses to a question in NZCER's 2007 national survey indicate that these annual occasions are not working ... in many schools. In their last performance appraisal, only 65 percent said they had agreed on goals that would move the school forward, and 61 percent had goals that would move themselves as principals forward. Only 40 percent had had the opportunity in these appraisals to have frank discussion of issues or challenges at the school, and to have joint problem-solving or strategic thinking. Only 28 percent had gained new insight from their appraisal into how they could do things.

It seems that the school leaders' role at the nexus of assessment, achievement and accountability could well be enhanced by clearer communication lines between Ministry of Education, the ERO and schools related to their school plans, better alignment between aspects of the accountability system within schools and within the system, and more collaboration among schools to develop new knowledge to solve local yet complex problems.

New possibilities for school leadership

Almost 25 years after the introduction of self-managing schools, the evidence suggests that although most students are performing as well or better than those in other high-performing systems, NZ is still challenged by the under achievement of a significant proportion of students, mostly from marginalised groups. Although the underachievement of students is over-represented in schools from low socio-economic areas, all schools have students who could achieve at higher levels. In NZ's self-managing system, there is a general consensus that school leaders require further support to assist their schools to use assessment, inquiry, collaboration and accountability to address these equity issues. The ERO (2010: 13) recommended that schools through their leaders: improve formative assessment practice to increase the opportunities students have to be actively involved in assessing their learning, setting goals and identifying their next steps for learning; continue to use external support for leaders, teachers and trustees to help them understand and work constructively with the standards to raise the achievement of all students in reading, writing and mathematics; use self-review to work with the standards, specifically to review the robustness and dependability of their data in relation to the standards; and review the extent to which their curriculum is responsive to all students, including students identified as needing support to achieve success.

New Zealand's latest OECD *Improving School Leadership Country Report* (Nusche *et al.*, 2012: 138–143) highlights the following as pointers for future policy development in NZ education: (a) further strengthen consistency between different components of evaluation and assessment; (b) develop regionally based structures to support schools' evaluation and assessment practices; (c) continue to build and strengthen teacher capacity for effective student assessment; (d) enhance school capacity in the collection, analysis and interpretation of school-wide data; (e) further develop and embed the National Standards within the NZ assessment system; (f) maintain an emphasis on the improvement function of school evaluation; and (g) revisit the nature and use of annual reporting.

Government initiatives have recently been announced to cluster schools and pay some principals with proven track records of meeting achievement standards to support their colleagues to address these equity issues, along with funding for teachers to lead others in improving their use of inquiry, quality teaching and assessment for learning practices. Although it is too soon to know, the idea behind the policy is that combined with effective school self-review and robust data from assessment tools, National Standards judgements and the analysis of NCEA results, mentoring and coaching from effective principals and lead teachers will assist their colleagues in less-effective schools to boost performance.

Much of the professional learning for teachers in New Zealand takes place at the school level, sometimes within Ministry of Education projects, sometimes initiated and led by the principals and teachers within schools themselves. Coaching and learning communities, where teachers are focusing on personalising learning to address students' needs through an inquiry mindset, are positioned in the policy literature. ERO (2010: 12) found that effective schools: target groups of students needing support with their learning; set and monitor targets to improve student achievement; set increasingly challenging targets; identify school-wide patterns and trends in student achievement; identify recommendations or next steps for improvement as a result of systematic self review; identify school-wide curriculum priorities; report to boards of trustees and the wider community; and set high expectations.

School leaders of the future will therefore need to have the capability to build these capacities within their school. One initiative designed to assist with building such leadership capacity is the development of an Educational Leadership Practice Survey for the assessment of leadership and schools. Principals can elect to undertake the assessment and their teachers also fill out an online survey, anonymously. The school leader receives a comprehensive outline of the areas of strength, development and discrepancy of perception. This may well prove a valuable tool for school principals to use in the school improvement process. There is also an induction programme for first-time principals and, more recently, a national aspiring principal programme that uses blended learning with facilitator and peer coaching support and online communities to develop new generations of New Zealand school leaders who are nationally digitally connected, culturally responsive leaders, committed to equity and addressing disparities, and will lead transformation for future-focused learning environments (Robertson and Earl, 2014). Late in 2013 the government also committed over NZD$31 million (US$20 million) over the coming three years to accelerate Māori secondary student achievement in a new programme called Building on Success. Current policy documents, Ka Hikitia, Tu Rangatira, Success for All and the Pacific Education Plan, along with Kiwi Leadership, all support the leadership practice and development of New Zealand school leaders to address inequity and provide high-quality education.

In a self-managing system such as that in NZ, school leaders need to see the school system as a whole and understand their critical role in creating and developing the system. In particular, if we are to address the current inequities resulting from our social and education systems, school leaders will need to step up and ensure the very best teaching and learning exists in every school (Robertson, 2016). This will also require the Ministry of Education to undertake genuine consultation and partnership with the teaching profession, supporting educators' capability to monitor and assess progress with students and their families. Keeping student learning outcomes and equity at the centre of policy and practice, supporting self-governance of schools at the local level, while leveraging the central accountability mechanisms will be key to ensuring that all communities and learners are well served.

Acknowledgements

We would like to acknowledge, with thanks, research and policy colleagues, and school leaders, who contributed ideas and critique to the writing of this chapter.

References

Dixon, H., Hawe, E., and Parr, J. (2011). Enacting Assessment for Learning: The beliefs/practice nexus. *Assessment in Education, Principles, Policy and Practice*, 18(4), 365–379.

ERO (Education Review Office) (2007a). The Ongoing and Reviewable Resourcing Schemes: Good Practice. In *Working with National Standards within the New Zealand Curriculum* (ERO, 2010). Retrieved from: www.ero.govt.nz/National-Reports/Working-with-the-National-Standards-within-the-New-Zealand-Curriculum-August-2010.

ERO (2007b). *The Collection and Use of Assessment Information: Good Practice in Primary Schools*. Wellington: Education Review Office.

ERO (2010). *Working with the National Standards within the New Zealand Curriculum 2010.* Wellington: Education Review Office.
ERO (2011). *Evaluation at a Glance: What ERO Knows About Effective Schools.* Wellington: Education Review Office. Retrieved from: www.ero.govt.nz/National-Reports/Evaluation-at-a-Glance-What-ERO-Knows-About-Effective-Schools
Ellis, J. (2005). The Impact of the NCEA on Teaching and Learning. Thesis M.Ed. Leadership. University of Waikato, Hamilton.
Fiske, E.B. and Ladd, H.F. (2000). *When Schools Compete.* Washington, DC: The Brookings Institution Press.
Gilmore, A. (2008). *Professional Learning in Assessment: Report to the Ministry of Education for the National Assessment Strategy Review.* Christchurch: University of Canterbury
Hill, M.F. (2000). Remapping the Assessment Landscape: Primary teachers reconstructing assessment in self-managing schools. Unpublished PhD dissertation. New Zealand: University of Waikato, Hamilton.
Hill, M.F. (2011). Getting traction: enablers and barriers to implementing Assessment for learning in secondary schools. *Assessment in Education, 18*(4), 347–364. doi:10.1080/0969594X.2011.600247
Kandasamy, S. (2013). Leaders Using and Interpreting Student Assessment Data. Unpublished masters dissertation. The University of Auckland, Auckland, NZ.
McGee, C., Jones, A., Cowie, B., Hill, M.F., Miller, T., Harlow, A. and Mckenzie, K. (2003). *Curriculum Stocktake: National School Sampling Study.* Report to the Ministry of Education. Wellington, NZ.
Ministry of Education (1988). *Administering for Excellence (The Picot Report).* Wellington: Ministry of Education.
Ministry of Education (2009). *Mathematics and Literacy Standards for Years 1–8.* Learning Media. Wellington: Ministry of Education.
Ministry of Education (2007). *The New Zealand Curriculum.* Learning Media. Wellington: Ministry of Education.
Ministry of Education (2011). *Ministry of Education Position Paper: Assessment (Schooling Sector).* Learning Media. Wellington: Ministry of Education.
Nusche, D. (2012). *"We do things differently here": Evaluation and assessment in New Zealand schools.* Paris: OECD. Retrieved from http://oecdeducationtoday.blogspot.co.nz/2012/02/we-do-things-differently-here.html
Nusche, D., Laveault, D., MacBeath, J., and Santiago, P. (2012). *OECD Reviews of Evaluation and Assessment in Education: New Zealand 2011.* Paris: OECD Publishing. Retreived from http://dx.doi.org/10.1787/9789264116917-en.
Rawlins, P. (2007). Students' Perceptions of the Formative Potential of the National Certificate of Educational Achievement. Unpublished doctoral thesis. Palmerston North: Massey University.
Robertson, J. (2016). Coaching leadership: Building educational leadership capacity through coaching partnership. Wellington: New Zealand Council for Educational Research.
Robertson, J. and Earl, L. (2014). Leadership learning: Aspiring principals developing the dispositions that count. *Journal of Educational Leadership, Policy and Practice, 29*(2), 3–17.
Robinson, V., Hohepa, M., and Lloyd, C. (2009). *School Leadership and Student Outcomes: Identifying What Works and Why. Best Evidence Synthesis Iteration (BES).* Wellington: Ministry of Education.

Sewell, K. (2011). Foreword. In *Ministry of Education Ministry of Education Position paper: Assessment. (Schooling Sector)*. Wellington: Ministry of Education.

Thrupp, M. and Easter, A. (2012). *Research, Analysis and Insight into National Standards (RAINS) Project: First Report Researching Schools' Enactments of New Zealand's National Standards Policy*. Report commissioned by the New Zealand Educational Institute Te Rui Roa (NZEI). Hamilton, New Zealand: Wilf Malcom Institute of Educational Research.

Thrupp, M. and White, M. (2013). *Research, Analysis and Insight into National Standards (RAINS) Project Final Report: National Standards and the Damage Done*. Report commissioned by the New Zealand Educational Institute Te Rui Roa (NZEI). Hamilton, New Zealand: Wilf Malcom Institute of Educational Research.

Wylie, C. (2009a). What Can We Learn From the Last Twenty Years? Why Tomorrow's Schools could not achieve key purposes, and how we could do things differently with self-managing schools. Jean Herbison Lecture presented at NZARE, Rotorua, 2009.

Wylie, C. (2009b). Getting more from school self-management. In J. Langley (ed.) *Tomorrow's Schools 20 Years On …* Auckland: Cognition Institute, pp. 135–148.

4 From policy and practice to possibilities

The context of educational accountability in the U.S. and praxis of school leadership

Jacob Easley II and Mohammed Elmeski

Educational accountability has always existed within the profession, undergirded by two questions: (a) accountable for what? and (b) accountable to whom? Yet, Elmore (2005) explains the misconception that schools lacked accountability, which prevailed prior to the introduction of performance-based accountability, thereby suggesting that schools are now accountable. Kuchapski (1998) adds a third accountability question of (c) how? Taken together, these questions convey the function, structure, and strategy of accountability policy. In the case of performance-based accountability, these policies seek to improve student performance by applying a value of quality (more often than not defined by quantifiable measures of student achievement) and by leveraging rewards and punishments based on the valued outcomes.

Educational accountability has been studied and defined in different ways, resulting in analytic and descriptive typologies (e.g. Firestone and Shipps, 2005; Harris and Herrington, 2006) outlining the types, aims, mechanisms, and demands of accountability policy. While it is commonly accepted that policy-based accountability reforms typically strive to improve (and to a lesser degree sustain the improvement of) schools, these policies have dramatically altered the context of schooling. In turn, school leadership has become increasingly complex as principals are expected to navigate the internal and external accountability demands of schools in a coherent fashion.

U.S. public school districts and their schools vary due to differing state policies, economic conditions, and the socio-political milieux of the communities they serve. They share one commonality however, the expanding influence of federal authority, in particular performance-based accountability. Yet, there is a growing belief, demonstrating that school leaders "construct" their accountability environments (Firestone and Shipps, 2005; Shipps and White, 2009). Elmore (2005) distinguished these constructed environments according to the actions taken by school leaders, either by implementation/compliance—described as the aim of fidelity between policy and the actions of educators—or by response—described as the degree of agency exercised to determine collective action.

Methods

This research design utilizes a multi-case study approach. The case study approach (Yin, 2003) easily accommodates phenomenological features allowing the researcher to ascertain phenomena as well as the contextual conditions shaping these phenomena. For each case, the phenomena are bound (Miles and Huberman, 1994) by a particular performance-based policy context. And while the contexts may share certain similarities, each is unique.

As researchers, we explored each case independently. While the methods varied at a micro level, at a macro level the data collection strategy utilized the critical incident technique (Flanagan, 1954; Northouse, 2006). The technique is useful for identifying the critical perspectives or behaviors of individuals (Chell, 1998) or as explained by Shipps and White (2009: 355), "situations involving a principal['s] decision, that, in hindsight, seemed consequential." The technique relies on retrospective meaning making among participants, without the interference of any particular theoretical judgment (Northouse, 2006). Each case sought to address two global questions: what happens in the practice of testing and assessment and how does it relate to accountability policy? And, how do these conditions influence the praxis of school leadership, if at all? The data were analyzed separately for each case in order to remain sensitive to context.

Each case is described separately. A context of the accountability landscape for each is offered to contextualize the findings. The discussion seeks to draw connections across the cases. Lastly, new possibilities for school leadership are offered.

Context of school accountability in Minnesota

According to the U.S. Census Bureau (2014), Minnesota's population was estimated at 5,420,380 in 2013. Of Minnesotans aged 25 and above, 91.9 percent are high school graduates (compared to 85.7 percent nationally). According to the National Center for Education Statistics (2013), Minnesota eighth graders' average scores for mathematics and science in TIMSS 2011 (Trends in International Mathematics and Science Study) were 545 and 553 respectively, higher than both the U.S. average and TIMSS international average.

While the overall state scores are often a cause for jubilation, disaggregated scores reveal a persistent racial gap in educational achievement within the state. According to the National Assessment of Education Progress (NAEP), the "Nation's Report Card," the gaps between White and Black students have shrunk between 1971 and 2012 (National Center for Education Statistics, 2013); however, a closer look at the state data demonstrates that Minnesota's white–black gap for fourth graders remained higher than national average in both reading and mathematics between 1992 and 2007.

As early as 1997, the State of Minnesota strove to raise students' overall scores by focusing on state standards in mathematics and science, rigorous high-stakes tests, and more instructional time. While the overall scores improved, racial disparity in students' performance has persisted, even after the 2001 enactment of the No Child Left Behind Act (NCLB) that has coupled accountability based on standards test outcomes and budgetary allocations to schools, i.e., budget and performance integration. Easley (2005: 7) explains, "The idea is that in the absence of budget and performance integration," policies like NCLB "will matter little." This national mandate requires schools to demonstrate that all students, including minorities, are making adequate yearly progress (AYP), as defined by the federal government.

Minnesota's achievement gap picture is not all gloomy. North Minneapolis, with the largest concentration of African American in the state, is also home to Best Academy and Harvest Academy, two of the highest performing schools in the nation in educating students of color. Eric Mahmoud, the chief executive officer (CEO) of Harvest and Best Academies, identifies five gaps explaining the low achievement of African American students: 1) a preparation gap in adequate home and academic preparation prior to enrolling in kindergarten, 2) a belief gap consisting of low expectations among teachers, parents, and the community about the learning potential of their children, 3) a time gap in instruction that does not allow struggling students to learn at grade level, 4) a teaching gap in highly effective teachers, and 5) a leadership gap in strong and effective leadership at the district and school levels (Mahmoud and Hassan, 2013).

Case methods

One team researcher conducted phenomenologically based interviews to gain a deeper understanding of the meaning principals make of their experience (Seidman, 1991) as leaders in the context of educational accountability in Minnesota schools. Phenomenology, according to Giorgi (1986: 6), is the discipline that "studies how things appear to consciousness or are given in experience." To convey the experiences of principals with the highest integrity, direct quotes are presented to capture their perceptions of their leadership praxis as they navigate performance-based accountability.

The researcher used criterion sampling. It is a method whereby participants are selected according to specific criteria (Patton, 2002). In this study, performance on the Minnesota Comprehensive Assessments (MCAs) was the criterion for selecting three public school principals for phenomenological interviews. Each of the interviews lasted 60 minutes.

Findings

The first principal led a successful middle school (grades 7–9) in a wealthy and largely Caucasian suburb. Only 18 percent of the students received free or reduced lunch. The second principal led an urban charter school serving kindergarten to sixth grade in Minneapolis. Charter schools are public schools governed by an agreement, or "charter" with the relevant educational authority. Often students have to apply to attend. The general reform premises of charter schools follows that competition among schools will breed excellence. The school demographics were 99 percent African American, of whom 90 percent received free or reduced lunch. According to 2011 MCAs scores, this school was one of the two best schools in the state, noted for its progress toward closing the achievement gap between black and white students.

The third principal led a PreK-8 charter public urban school in Saint Paul, where 87 percent of students were English language learners (ELLs) and more than 92 percent received free or reduced lunch. Prior to 2009, this school ranked among the 5 percent consistently lowest performing schools in the state. One year into the turnaround, the primary school progressed to rank better than 25 percent of schools in Minnesota. That said, Grade 7 and 8 students were still in the lowest 5 percent when the interview was conducted.

Accountability factors impacting principals' practice

The three principals indicated that performance-based accountability raised the bar of expectations for student achievement among all learners. While the suburban school principal underscored what she referred to as "co-mutuality in accountability," she saw the policy for performance-based accountability as an opportunity to push for change by leveraging federal consequences for high-stakes testing. As she put it, "There is a co-mutuality of responsibility. The teachers need to have high standards, and the principal needs to provide adequate support to these teachers. For that, the district office needs to support me in supporting teachers."

The principal's emphasis on co-mutuality of accountability reflects her understanding of the most efficient strategies to effectuate change in a public school. She was very clear about the link between high academic standards, effective instructional practices, school leadership, and district support. With regard to the latter, the principal underscored the need to ensure that the district (superintendent and the board) provide adequate support for the school's efforts to bring all students to grade level while offering learning experiences that equitably stimulate higher-order thinking for both successful and struggling students. In this regard, her leadership challenge was to provide differentiated instruction that extends high expectations to students of color, ELLs, low-income students, and students with disabilities. Under NCLB, many suburban schools were designated as failing as their results did not demonstrate that students from racial minorities, low socio-economic status, ELL, and students with disability were learning. The principal defines her leadership practice as an advocate for minority children:

> In my old inner-city school, I had 85 percent on free or reduced lunch. Now, I have 18 percent. Here [in the suburbs], they have great family support, wonderful opportunities to learn outside the classroom, financial resources. Part of my mission is to help students understand White privilege. In this country, we have a huge problem of racism. That will not end if White people do not join, and we are perpetuating this *what is wrong with them attitude?* Another thing in this community is the bell curve mentality. "My kid is smart. My kid is in this elite program. Why is the other kid in it? They don't have the skills or the grades." I did away with barring them entry into enriched courses here.
>
> (emphasis added)

For the suburban school principal, the NCLB requirement to achieve AYP across disaggregated groups of students shone the light on the historically obfuscated low performance of minority, underperforming students due to aggregated reporting. Meeting the aim to shine a light on failure (U.S. Department of Education, 2002), NCLB forced schools to look at their results differently.

Under NCLB, successful suburban schools faced the threat of being labeled as failing to make AYP because many of their minority students did not perform at grade level. This diversity penalty, according to Darling-Hammond (2007), constituted a major bone of contention against NCLB. The introduction of the Minnesota Multiple Measurement Ratings (MMRs) has helped principals, especially in suburban schools by focusing on closing the achievement gaps while buffering struggling students and their parents from being blamed for the school failure to make AYP. Reflecting on the MMRs waiver to the NCLB threat of disbanding schools failing to make AYP, the following principal highlights the role of wealthy suburban communities in advocating against performance accountability when judged as unfair to their schools:

> I always thought that this whole accountability thing will be looked at differently once it hits the suburbs. The reason they got the waiver (MMRs) is all those suburbs having been declared as having failing schools. So now this suburban school which has a great reputation could be classified as a failing school.

Negotiating the balance between the needs of high achievers for intellectually stimulating learning opportunities and advocating for social justice for underperforming and usually invisible students is a painstaking process. The suburban principal's response to performance accountability demands is a multipronged strategy that is premised on close collaboration with teachers, constant coordination with the district, and a disposition to communicate and educate the community about the importance of balancing the drive for competitiveness alongside commitment to equitable learning opportunities for all students.

For the two charter schools, NCLB was viewed as the ultimate motivator. According to the high-performing charter school principal, high-stakes testing acted as a constant reminder to schools of the achievement gap they need to close. The principal of the charter school going through a turnaround process shared the same position. Their views on NCLB are respectively summarized as follows:

> I didn't mind NCLB the way it was. I liked it. I felt those were my goals. Some people think of it as an imposition, I think of it as goals. Just like any business, if you don't have goals, you don't have a business. Students need to read at their grade level. If you are not doing that, then there is something wrong.

> NCLB nudges people to open their eyes and see the problem within the school and start addressing them. The effort of NCLB allows those who are serious to be very specific about what to do and how to do it. Having some pressure to be able to drive learning and instruction forward from a federal level does make you think about what you do every day.

The performances of the two charter schools are almost at opposite ends of the spectrum for MCA scores. However, they are characterized by similar challenges. Most of the students are racial minorities. More than 90 percent of them receive free or reduced lunch, and parents' involvement in education is very low. The two principals' reflections indicate a *no excuses* mindset that is rooted in a strong belief that quality education represents their students' only hope for closing the persisting achievement gap in reading and mathematics with white and non-low-income peers.

The principal of the suburban school, by contrast, recognized that her students can succeed, in spite of school. This is consistent with the literature of the role of the non-low-income home advantage (Lareau, 2000) in providing children with early education programs, literacy-rich home environments, and active parental involvement in their children's well-being at school. The principal's cognizance of the academic advantages accruing to non-low income students by virtue of their socio-economic head start suggests two important realizations: 1) achieving equity in quality, while noble, may be fraught with tension. Influential parents see struggling children and families as a drag on their children's progress and may fight the principal's efforts to provide equitable learning opportunities perceived to lower the bar for their children's achievement in school; and, 2) in traditional public schools, where principals are required to work closely with their multiple stakeholders at the political and social support levels, accountability for quality and equity, and accountability to distinct entities with agendas that are not always compatible make for a messy exercise in educational accountability.

Principals' response to the challenges of performance accountability

Principals responded to the challenges posed by performance accountability in ways that are reflective of their leadership mission and their perceptions of their margins for maneuver as change agents. Robert Marzano's (2009) analogy of silver BBs (ball bearings) vs. silver bullet arose as a reference. The suburban principal highlighted the need for multiple interventions, instead of one magic solution, to solve complex issues. By contrast, charter school principals highlighted a direct chain of command that ends with them as ultimately responsible for school improvement. These perspectives are as much philosophical as they are influenced by principals' interpretations of their contexts.

The suburban principal described her synergistic approach to performance accountability in the following words:

> The state asks for your structures, your strategies, and your professional development plan. For me, professional development is key and it has to be articulated so that for each time we meet, we are building on it. And it builds in my mind year to year. I had a four-year plan coming to this school. We have a team focused on problem solving. We have an academic focus team and a student socio-emotional assistance (SA) team. Teachers meet. They have a students' protocol to discuss kids. They provide interventions in the classroom. If students are not making progress, then they can refer them to the RTI team [Response to Interventions] or the SA team. At that point, we have counselors, social workers, and psychologists working with teachers on what other additional support we could offer. You can do many small things that work. However, there is no big thing that works because if it were, we would be all doing it.

The principal of the high-performing charter school depicted her direct responsibility amid the charter context as follows:

> The charter is like my own business. I sit down with my staff and we take the budget, and I say a year from now, I will not have a job and half of you won't either. In the [traditional] public school, I don't remember having that freedom ... I have the power and the freedom to change, and we turned it around and we achieved the top reading scores in the state two years ago ... We knew what had to change. Students had to be at school for longer hours. They were behind. If I had a union to fight with, I could never extend those days. I paid them for Saturdays. The union would not let me do that at all. That freedom allowed me to allow more instructional time and keep the teachers who were willing to do it.

She continued:

> My students have to be at fourth grade level by the end of the year. What does that mean I have to do? That means I am on the phone at night talking to them. That means I pay home visits. I send the van to their homes when they are not in school. Those things do not cost any [extra] money. It is a philosophy that I have versus I cannot control whether they are not coming to school.

The principal of the school undergoing a turnaround process emphasized his direct responsibility for the school's improvement strategy. He initiated intensive classroom observation protocols to ensure that instruction is delivered following specific criteria of best practices in instructional delivery. He explained:

> I am the instruction leader. As a framework of practice, I need this to be my emphasis. In the past, observations were done once a year. In my school, the teachers are observed more than 20 times and given support. This is my approach to leadership that I proposed, and my admin staff supported, and my teaching staff is subject to. One thing that became clear to me was that inspecting what we expect, will give us a good idea of what is happening in the classroom. I, the assistant principal, the curriculum coordinator, and ELL coordinator act as coaches. The teachers know we have their best interest in mind. We will come to their classroom and we will give them feedback. We want them here at the end of the year, so we are coming to provide support. We identify all the areas that we need to focus on in order to inspect what to expect.

The suburban principal and the two principals of the two charter schools are at opposite ends of the silver bullet vs. silver BBs analogy. The suburban principal's strategy leverages the effect of multiple actions to effect change. Her multifaceted approach incorporating support from the district and community levels, her silver BBs leadership philosophy recognizes the multiple fronts and the complex issues that can only be addressed with a package of complementary solutions.

By contrast, the charter schools' principals' response to the challenges and constraints associated with performance accountability is more aligned with the silver bullet approach. They sought to ensure instructional fidelity through intensive testing and monitoring. In the high-performing charter school, the principal was clear about who will be fired when things go wrong. The fact that the consequences of performance accountability are stark in terms of loss of jobs for the principal and the teachers resulted in a form of budget and performance integration whereby the performance level of teachers is coupled with the price of employment.

The Minnesota case study demonstrates that the governance structure of schools (traditional public vs. public charter), the socio-economic characteristics of their local environments, and the accountability structure determine the opportunities and boundaries of leadership practice. In the suburban school, the flexibility waiver provided relief from the drastic implications of NCLB and allowed the school principal to align multiple stakeholders around long-term strategies for enabling minority children to benefit from the same learning opportunities available to their non-minority peers. By contrast, public charter school principals described their charter governance structure as characterized by higher decision-making discretion. They praised NCLB as a catalyst of their school turnaround. NCLB legitimated their fortitude to enforce what they expect as the intensity and quality of performance necessary for administrators and teachers to keep their employment.

New York State and New York City

The state of New York recently undertook an unprecedented reform of public education, largely in response to its 2010 receipt of federal Race To the Top (RTTT) funds. Unlike the NCLB, which was a reauthorization of the Elementary and Secondary Education Act, RTTT is a contest designed to catalyze educational innovation and funded as part of the American Recovery and Reinvestment Act of 2009. States seeking funds are scored on several criteria for educational policy and practice reform, to include performance-based standards, or evaluation systems for teachers and principles. In step with the criteria of RTTT, the state Regent's reform agenda is outlined by four interlocking goals:

1. to adopt internationally benchmarked standards and assessments that prepare K-12 students for success in college and the workplace,
2. to build an instructional data system to measure student success and inform teachers and principals on how to improve their practice,
3. to recruit, develop, retain, and reward effective teachers and principals,
4. to turn around the lowest-achieving schools.

The accountability lynchpin of reform is Education Law §3012-c and the Commissioner's Regulations for the annual professional performance review (APPR) of teachers and principals. Beginning in the academic year of 2011–2012, 40 percent of principal and teacher's annual evaluation is based on student achievement. The remaining 60 percent of the evaluation, rating, and scoring is developed locally, consistent with the commissioner's regulations. The evaluations are used as a significant employment factor to include, but not limited to: promotion, retention, tenure decisions, termination, and supplemental compensation.

New York City, however, began to employ similar performance evaluation mechanisms nearly a decade prior. Given its status as the nation's largest public school district with nearly 1 million students (Sable *et al.*, 2010), its governance structure of mayoral control and its unique policy relations with the New York State Board of Regents (i.e., the governing body that supervises all educational activities within the state, presiding over the university system and the New York State Education Department), the district serves as a case study not only for the state of New York but also for the nation.

In 2001 Michael Bloomberg became the mayor of New York City. A keystone of his campaign was his promise to overhaul the school system. According to Viteritti (2009: 217), Bloomberg, accustomed to working in the private sector, "lacked patience with the bureaucratic ways of city government and seemed to resent the limited checks on his power that remained in the city charter." In an effort to leverage educational reform, he instituted the annual progress report, grading New York City schools A, B, C, D, or F based on multiple measures and renegotiated contracts to reward teachers and principals based on the graded performance. A school's yearly grade is weighted 60 percent on student progress, 25 percent on student performance, and 15 percent on school environment in comparison to the results for peer group schools serving similar student populations (New York City Department of Education, n.d.a). Principals of persistently low performing schools can be removed in as little as two years (New York City Department of Education, 2008b).

Prior to the administration's changes, school performance was measured primarily on the State Report Card—based on test scores from the Regent's Exam that all New York State high school students must pass in order to graduate. According to Shipps and White (2009), there were no special consequences for performance unless schools were judged so poor as to be taken over by the state. Historically, those held most accountable were the students (Klein, 2003) by way of promotion and graduation exams (PGEs). PGE accountability measures require that students either pass a grade level for promotion or the Regent's Exam requirements for a high school diploma. It should be noted, however, that since the time of the study and with the election of the subsequent mayor, Bill de Blasio, New York City schools are no longer scored by letter grades.

In addition, all schools undergo a Quality Review (QR). The frequency is determined by several factors such as prior performance on annual progress reports or QRs as well as new school status. QRs measure school performance by assigning an overall score based on four ranges: well developed (WD), proficient (P), developing (D), and underdeveloped (UD).

To better understand the context of policy reform within the city, it is important to point out that according to public memory, the co-opting of corporate tactics for school accountability by both the mayor and the chancellor, Joel Klein, and the responsibility they shouldered for the control of schools, was unprecedented. Equally unheard of, the New York City Department of Education (NYCDOE) removed 45 principals for not meeting performance standards in 2004 (Morello, 2004). According to the chancellor, the challenge was "to change a culture built on avoidance of accountability." (Hunt, 2003: A15)

Keeping in line with the Chancellor's belief that "every great school has a great principal," (Hunt, 2003: A15) the new, accountability policies of New York City schools are designed to spur greater entrepreneurialism among principals (Shipps, 2012), placing them directly in charge for the instructional effectiveness of programming. Choice and competition underscore the levers for school effectiveness and improvement, with principals having greater control over the selection and budgeting of support services for their schools, increased opportunity for performance pay based on outcomes compared with those of peer schools (in upwards of US$25,000 if their scores fall in the top 20 percent), as well as pressures for the recruitment and retention of students under the district-wide school choice option for students attending school in "Need Improvement" status for two or more years or Persistently Low Achieving (PLA) schools.

Case methods

Twenty-two (n=22) New York City school principals were interviewed by a group of research assistants between the years of 2009 and 2011, supervised by one of the team researchers. Following a uniform interview guide, only a subset of questions focused on performance accountability and these principals' critical incidents related to the construction of the accountability contexts for their schools. Ninety-five percent of the schools were in the Bronx and 5 percent in Manhattan. Fifteen were elementary schools, five high schools and two middle schools. Of these, three were charter schools. Each principal, with the exception of one, had more than five years of school leadership experience with the district. The outlier participant was a first year employee of the district with only three months experience as the school's executive administrator and a graduate of the district's Leadership Academy. Each of the principals identified their student populations as "at-risk" or traditionally underperforming based on standardized tests.

Each school leader participated in a single interview. Their participation was voluntary; yet the sampling was convenient, given that each research assistant was an educational leadership graduate student who either had or currently worked in the schools of the participants. The relationships between the participants and research assistants served dual purposes: (1) to facilitate access to schools, and (2) to maximize candor among participants' responses. Each research assistant possessed a grounded knowledge of research methods and interviewing strategies and utilized a structured protocol based on Flanagan's (1954) framework of critical incident technique for fidelity. The technique focuses on principals' reflections on accountability conditions and experiences that they judge to have had a critical impact on their leadership behaviors or perspectives—i.e., the construction of their accountability context. The team researcher, serving as the primary investigator, conducted member checking by stratified random selection to ensure the trustworthiness of the data.

Each transcript underwent three independent reads by a different research assistant. Each critical incident was coded for accountability and coded incidents were the unit of analysis (Shipps and White, 2009). The codes were categorized according to their efficacy (Merriam, 1998) in order to establish themes. Two themes emerged related: (1) accountability stressors and (2) accountability implementation. For the latter, sub-themes were identified.

Findings

Accountability stressors principals perceive to be significant

The principals identified client-based factors as key attributes influencing their accountability contexts, chief among them, student demographics and parental behaviors. When indicated as critical incidents shaping their accountability context, principals consistently identified either a history of chronic low performance among students (23 percent) or a lack of parental/home support for their children's academic success (18 percent). Each of the principals described their schools as serving predominately African American and Hispanic populations of low economic status. One school leader further explained the pressure to graduate eighth grade students in order that they not be retained in the school for an additional school year. In fact, the elimination of social promotion for grades 3–8 was a key agenda item during Bloomberg's bid for a third term re-election.

New York City school system, as a district, represents a demographic outlier in comparison to districts across the rest of the state. The percentage of racial minority students attending the district's schools nearly, if not more than, doubles that for the entire state, with 15 percent Asian, 31 percent African American, and 40 percent Hispanic populations in comparison to the state's totals of 8 percent, 19 percent, and 21 percent, respectively. Conversely, the percentage of white school goers within the state nearly triples that of NYCDOE at 51 percent compared to 14 percent (Council of Great City Schools, 2011).

Household demographics for those living below the poverty level between 2008 and 2012 within the represented boroughs of the Bronx and Manhattan, in comparison to the state, shine a light on the conditions referred to by the principals. The aggregate levels, regardless of race, were 29.3 percent for the Bronx, 17.5 percent for Manhattan and 14.9 percent for the state (U.S. Census Bureau, 2013).

Performance-based accountability's impact NYC school leaders

Each principal interviewed reported on actions that may be associated with Elmore's (2005) notion of policy implementation/compliance. None of the principals shared critical incidents that may be defined as response actions, in particular, collective agency that influences policy. Yet, their critical incidents directly emanated as implementation strategies aimed to address the stressors mentioned above. At every turn, the unforgiving pressure to pass the QRs filtered these stressors. The implementation strategies were grouped into three sub-categories: (1) curriculum and assessment, (2) intervention supports, and (3) instructional oversight.

Curriculum and assessments. Principals (36 percent) identified curricular and assessment responses as a means to improve student achievement. Their strategies varied to include instituting collaborative curriculum planning among teachers, project-based learning, differentiating instruction, curriculum placing, rewriting curriculum in alignment with college readiness standards, and using assessment data to inform instruction. Particular attention was given to the use of periodic assessments, a requirement for every New York City school.

Intervention supports. Several principals (41 percent) noted the use of intervention programs. While some saw these as a means to support character development and students' overall interest in school by bolstering culturally relevant pedagogy for the largely racial minority student populations, others focused primarily on academic supplements. Principals availed themselves of the resources offered by the district's Academic Intervention Services (AIS), allowing them to hire additional support personnel to provide one-on-one and small group instruction to struggling students. These services were predominantly for mathematics and literacy lessons. In addition, principals reported on the implementation of after school programs.

Instructional oversight. In addition, school leaders (18 percent) explained that they focused on instructional leadership to encourage quality teaching. Most noted was the use of walkthroughs, in which principals and other instructional specialists and district officials briefly visit classrooms during instruction to observe teaching and learning. These occurrences are shorter than a structured observation and often focus on general practices across classrooms. Feedback is often shared with groups of teachers for school improvement. Another strategy discussed was the use of data walls and rooms in which the administrative team and grade-level teachers report on, track and use student assessment data to inform the instructional program for groups of students, grade levels, and the whole school.

The strategies that define these themes do not represent exclusionary attempts implemented in isolation. Often a single principal identified strategies across the sub-themes. In order to better understand their intersections, a closer look at the Department's infrastructure for school improvement is needed. By and large, the above strategies follow the logic of a larger district-wide design for reform accented by performance-based accountability.

The political and structural design of New York City school accountability policy leverages both centralization and decentralization simultaneously.

Educational accountability in the U.S. 47

While principals are individually held responsible for school level outcomes on the QR, the Department rolled out a comprehensive reform agenda that directly shapes teaching and learning across schools. In 2006, the Department piloted a project in 332 Empowerment Zone schools, a model in which schools assume greater autonomy in exchange for increased responsibility for producing student academic achievement. Empowerment Schools differ with regard to accountability, goal setting, autonomy, and support structures. A common practice within Empowerment Schools, teams of teachers diagnosed the needs of select groups of struggling students in their respective schools and developed strategies to improve their learning (New York City Department of Education, 2008a; Robinson, 2010). This inquiry model was adapted from the Scaffold Apprenticeship Model of School Improvement through Leadership Development (SAM)—developed through collaboration among the School of Public Affairs at Baruch College (City University of New York), New Visions for Public Schools, and the New York City Leadership Academy. In 2007, the Department supported the proliferation of the Inquiry Team approach in every school as part of its Children First reform. The aim of the reform is to grow the number of educators participating in Inquiry Teams, year-over-year, with the desired goal of 90 percent teacher participation (Robinson, 2010). Each of the above sub-themes for accountability implementation is, in one way or another, interfaced with the collaborative inquiry process.

The Department provides support and guidance to schools for teachers' engagement in collaborative inquiry and for school leaders to launch the process. School leaders are expected to avail themselves of the assistance of one of nearly sixty network teams (New York City Department of Education, n.d.b). Principals are instructed to selectively choose a network based on the specific needs of the school community. In turn, each network is organized around specific instructional designs and philosophies. All networks, working closely with the Department's central leadership, are overseen by the Office of School Support, and are evaluated annually.

As is the nature of large-scale reform implementation, particularly in large districts such as New York City (NYC), the decentralized roll out of a centralized agenda yielded uneven results. Robinson (2010) conducted research on the outcomes of collaborative inquiry in NYC schools at different stages of the Department's described process, some beginning and others well defined. Of the participating schools, "variation across teacher inquiry teams was moderate to high, largely due to the newness of the process and a history of weak teacher relations." (Robinson, 2010: 10). Likewise, principals demonstrated varied leadership "styles" and approaches in accordance with the context of their school cultures and their respective, professional leadership acumen. The researcher reported on three distinct leadership styles for accountability-driven school improvement—participatory, delegative, and authoritative.

Participatory leadership style. Robinson (2010) defines the first style as participatory leadership, similar to shared leadership in which "principals collaboratively change classroom practices to support and improve student learning." (Wahlstrom *et al.*, cited in Easley, 2016). Wahlstrom *et al.* (2010: 10) further classify shared leadership as "teachers' influence over, and participation in, school-wide decisions with principals." Vis-à-vis the participatory leadership, teachers expressed an increased sense of ownership for student learning and professional growth for data-based decision-making. Principals and teachers alike described inquiry teams as the vehicle for driving forward a culture of fluid leadership shared among all members.

Delegative leadership style. Principals employing this style took a hands-off role for inquiry. They delegated the facilitation of inquiry teams to teachers. Robinson (2010: 18) explains one principal's justification as, "'We, administrators, try to stay away from teacher inquiry meetings so teachers can have an honest conversation about what is working or not.'" School leaders often provided support when requested in the form of literature, and coaching from data specialists. While this approach seemed to foster support for individual teacher teams, inquiry informed decision-making did little to benefit the school as whole.

Authoritative leadership style. Occurring in only two of the participating schools, school administrators took full control for facilitating inquiry teams. Robinson (2010: 20) describes the core inquiry team as "dominated by the input and presence of administration, with teachers in a listening role and simply expected to 'report back' conversation topics and new directions." Teachers on these teams expressed a lack of trust between administration and themselves and little benefit worth sharing beyond the team.

As previously mentioned, the NYCDOE principals did not directly cite broader district accountability policies as primary levers informing their practice; rather, they noted local conditions as critical incidents. These findings corroborate the work of others (Firestone and Shipps, 2005; Shipps and White, 2009) upholding the axiom that school leaders indeed construct their accountability context. It is clear that their work largely focused on the conditions of teaching and learning germane to their unique student populations and communities.

The result is a double-barreled or dual bureaucracy that administers centralization and decentralization concomitantly. In this case, centralization is played out at the system level, holding schools accountable by way of QRs, the incentivized threats of competition and job loss, and by shaping leadership practice through its Children's First reform. Decentralization is played out at the school level, in which leaders are responsible for finding unique and novel ways to improve the conditions of their individual communities. In essence, school leaders craft their own accountability context by mediating not only the political and bureaucratic accountabilities but also by their professional, moral, and personal accountabilities (see Firestone and Shipps, 2005; Møller, 2009) that are informed chiefly by the aims they hold for educational quality and their altruistic spirit to improve the lives of others.

Summary

Minnesota and New York are representative specimens of the U.S. context of school accountability and praxis of school leadership. Minnesota is a local-control state that values community and government partnership to support school improvement. New York City is one of only a few U.S. school districts with a history of mayoral control. Interviews with school principals across St. Paul, Minneapolis, and NYC, though not unique only to their educational contexts, suggest that many struggling schools are located in neighborhoods with high incidence of poverty among racial minority communities, particular those of African American and Hispanic heritage. While principals in each locale expressed an internalized and largely personal accountability for school improvement, it is clear that their decision-making discretion for improving the outcomes of their most struggling students is varied. Yet, for each, discretionary power is mediated along the double-barreled accountability continuum between degrees of centralization and decentralization. Easley and Tulowitzki (2013: 750) explain that, "Decentralisation is not equivalent to deregulation and does not necessarily lead to greater autonomy. When the regulating power changes from the state to the municipality, for example, it is even possible that schools lose part of their autonomy." Such is the case for New York City principals who are required to implement inquiry teams within their schools and participate in a district network while being held individually accountable for school improvement.

Implications: From policy and practice to possibilities

In full recognition of the steady vicissitudes of policy as new federal, mayoral, school board, and other administrations of public authorities are named, school leaders' potential to establish sustainable improvement for underperforming schools is greatly challenged. With each new top-down policy brought on within these vicissitudes, school leaders are continually redefining their accountability contexts for school improvement and effectiveness. Elmore (2000: 12) posits, "Improvement implies not just that any given unit in a system is improving (classroom, grade level, school, etc.) but that all units are improving at some rate." This perspective guides our implications for school leadership possibilities. While our recommendations are not exhaustive, they are presented in response to the findings from this study, and likewise, reflect interconnectivity.

Personal and moral accountability

We understand personal and moral accountability as school principals' genuine respect for the schools and communities they serve. As such, morally accountable leaders are stewards of social change. They recognize that their actions directly shape the lives and wellbeing of others. They are guided by moral ideals that aim to improve the human condition (Dewey, 1909). For schools defined as underperforming, serving communities placed at risk by historical and structural conditions of economic disenfranchisement, categorical discrimination, dominant language barriers, and limited access to the social capital and material resources associated with academic success, their moral accountability is imperative.

Morally accountable leaders serving schools like those in this study are public advocates. They seek to foster transformative and empowering conditions both within and outside of the school, reaching deep into the communities they serve.

Instructional accountability

Instructional leaders advance educational improvement for students by continuously focusing on the core, interdependent functions of schools—teaching and learning. In this regard, both their moral accountability and instructional governance are quickened as they grapple with important questions such as, what is student success? And how do I define educational equity for the community I serve?

Elmore (2000) explains that policy (e.g., accountability policy) can set the initial expectations and conditions for school improvement, performance indicators and targets, performance-based incentives, as well as the tone for public discussion of school improvement. From our understanding, policy is continually created, interpreted, and mediated across the educational enterprise, at the system and unit levels, and varies in degrees of coupling. Yet, policy alone will not ensure an efficacious educational core for teaching and learning. Strong leadership that is morally steeped and adept at mitigating the aforementioned barriers to teaching and learning is vital. It has become common practice for schools to use test data to monitor student learning and to inform instruction. Furthermore, instructional leaders help others understand educational equity and the pluralistic knowledge, skills, and dispositions that students will need for their personal and civic wellbeing within and beyond their immediate communities. Lastly, highly effective instructional leaders seek to create systems for sustainable learning across classrooms that transverse the borders of an individual school.

Reciprocal accountability

Reciprocal accountability shoulders the notion of dual bureaucracy such that accountability is simultaneously top-down and bottom-up. While personal and moral accountability are likely to expand the hierarchical structure to whom schools are accountable, reciprocal accountability is more likely to disrupt this linear structure. Mutuality is espoused. A synergy among the enterprise's parts is necessary for functional coherence and cohesiveness. This does not mean that both top-down and bottom-up levers are applied evenly and with the same intensity.

Reciprocal accountability is responsive to the performance-based accountability demands faced by teachers to the extent that instructional leaders assure the necessary resources needed at the educational core. Reciprocal accountability implicates school, district, and other educational leaders along with teachers in a mutually respectful way for school improvement. In this regard, both the means and ends of school improvement are valued and attended to.

Balanced accountability

Lastly, Elmore's (2005) distinctions between accountability implementation/compliance—described as the aim of fidelity between policy and the actions of educators—and response accountability—described as the degree of agency exercised to determine collective action, merit a particular discussion for leadership possibilities. Holding to the premise that school leaders construct their accountability contexts and that interconnectivity exists among personal/moral accountability, instructional accountability, and reciprocal accountability, we posit that school leadership is dynamic. In order to foster the conditions for equitable and sustainable school improvement, a single accountability paradigm is highly insufficient. This is particularly true if school effectiveness and accountability is to be scaled upward beyond a single school or school district. We call for calibrated and amalgamated levers of educational accountability to meet these aims. We call this approach balanced accountability. We do not suggest that perfect equilibrium among levers of educational accountability is a prerequisite for action, particularly as a constant. It aims to leverage equitable practices both inside and outside of schools for high levels of educational improvement. The various accountability types are mediated in such a way by school leaders who are advocates for educational equity, focus on instructional leadership, and hold themselves accountable for the function of education, while simultaneously seeking to scale up best practices in policy and school improvement that advance students' learning and wellbeing.

References

Chell. E. (1998). Critical incident technique. In G. Symon and C. Cassell (eds), *Qualitative Methods and Analysis in Organizational Research* (pp. 51–72). Thousand Oaks, CA: Sage.

Council of Great City Schools (2011). *Beating the Odds: Analysis of Student Performance on State Assessment and NAEP.* Washington, DC: Author.

Darling Hammond, L. (2007). Race, inequality and educational accountability: The irony of 'No Child Left Behind'. *Race, Ethnicity and Education*, 10(3), 245–260.

Dewey, J. (1909). *Moral Principles in Education.* London: Feffer & Simons.

Easley, J. (2005). A struggle to leave no child behind: The dichotomies of reform, urban school teachers, and their moral leadership. *Improving Schools*, 8(2), 161–177.

Easley, J. (2016). The audacity to teach: An examination of reform policy, school leadership, and their relationships mediated by instructional capacity. *Urban Education*, 51(1), 108–137.

Easley, J. and Tulowitzki, P. (2013). Policy formation of intercultural and globally minded education leadership preparation. *International Journal of Educational Management*, 27(7), 744–461.

Elmore, R. F. (2000). *Building a New Structure for School Leadership*. Washington, DC: The Albert Shanker Institute.

Elmore, R. F. (2005). Accountable leadership. *The Educational Forum*, 69(2), 134–142.

Firestone, W. A. and Shipps, D. (2005). How do leaders interpret conflicting accountability to improve student learning? In W. A. Firestone and C. Reihl (eds) *A New Agenda for Research in Educational Leadership* (pp. 81–100). New York: Teachers College Press.

Flanagan, J. C. (1954). The critical incident technique. *Psychological Bulletin*, 51(4), 327–358.

Giorgi, A. (1986). Theoretical justification for the use of descriptions in psychological research. In Ashworth, P. D., Giorgi, A. and De Koning, A. J. J. (eds) *Qualitative research in psychology: Proceedings of the International Association for Qualitative Research* (pp. 3–22). Pittsburg, PA: Duquesne University Press.

Harris, D. N. and Herington, C. D. (2006). Accountability, standards, and the growing achievement gap: Lessons from the past half-century. *American Journal of Education*, 112(2), 209–238.

Hunt, A. R. (2003). Bringing accountability to New York City Schools. *The Wall Street Journal*, January 2, p. A15.

Klein, J. (2003). Accountability for all. *The New York Post*, December 7, p. 26.

Kuchapski, R. (1998). Accountability and the social good: Utilizing Manzer's liberal framework in Canada. *Education and Urban Society*, 30, 531–545.

Lareau, A. (2000). *Home Advantage*. Oxford, England: Rowman & Littlefield Publishers, Inc.

Mahmoud, E. and Hassan, J. (2013). *Best in Class: How We Closed the Five Gaps of Academic Achievement*. Brooklyn Park, MN: Papyrus Publishing, Inc.

Marzano, R. (2009). What do we know about the effect of technology on student achievement? Palm Springs Convention Center, Computer Using Education Conference keynote Speech. Palm Springs, CA, March, 6.

Merriam, S. B. (1998). *Qualitative Research and Case Study Applications in Education: Revised and Expanded from Case Study Research*. San Francisco: Jossey Bass.

Miles, M. B. and Huberman, A. M. (1994). *Qualitative Data Analysis: An Expanded Source Book* (2nd edn). Thousand Oaks, CA: Sage.

Minneapolis Foundation (2012). Education. Retrieved from www.minneapolisfoundation.org/CommunityIssues/Education.aspx

Minnesota Department of Education. (n.d.). 7-point plan. Retrieved from http://education.state.mn.us/MDE/Welcome/OfficeCom/BetterSchBetterMN/

Møller, J. (2009). School leadership in an age of accountability: Tensions between managerial and professional accountability. *Journal of Educational Change*, 10(1), 37–46.

Morello, S. J. (2004). Solving the principal problem. *The New York Post*, July 10, p. 18.
National Center for Education Statistics (2013). *The Nations Report Card: Trends in Academic Progress 2012* (NCES 2013 456). Institute for Education Sciences, U.S. Department of Education. Washington, DC: National Center for Education Statistics.
New York City Department of Education (2008a). *Children First Intensive: Inquiry Team Handbook*. New York: New York City Department of Education.
New York City Department of Education (2008b). *School-wide Performance Bonus Plan* (C43 Program Area: Teacher and Principal Quality Initiatives, ed.) New York: New York City Department of Education.
New York City Department of Education (n.d.a). Progress Report. Retrieved from http://schools.nyc.gov/Accountability/tools/report/default.htm
New York City Department of Education (n.d.b). School Support. Retrieved from http://schools.nyc.gov/AboutUs/schools/support/default.htm
Northouse, P. G. (2006). *Leadership: Theory and Practice* (4th edn). Thousand Oaks, CA: Sage.
Patton, M. Q. (2002). *Qualitative Research & Evaluation Methods* (3rd edn). Thousand Oaks, CA: Sage.
Robinson, M. A. (2010). *School Perspectives on Collaborative Inquiry: Lessons Learned from New York City, 2009–2010*. New York: Consortium for Policy Research in Education.
Sable, J., Plotts, C., and Mitchell, L. (2010). *Characteristics of the 100 largest Public Elementary and Secondary School Districts in the United States: 2008–09* (NCES 2011-301). U.S. Department of Education, National Center for Education Statistics. Washington, DC: U.S. Government Printing Office.
Seidman, I. E. (1991). *Interviewing as Qualitative Research: A Guide for Researchers in Education and Social Sciences*. New York: Teachers College Press.
Shipps, D. (2012). Empowered or beleaguered? Principals' accountability under New York City's diverse provider regime. Education Policy Analysis Archives, North America, January, 20. Retrieved from http://epaa.asu.edu/ojs/article/view/892.
Shipps, D. and White, M. (2009). A new politics of the principalship? Accountability-driven change in New York City. *Peabody Journal of Education*, 84(3), 350–373.
U.S. Census Bureau (2013). *State and County Quick Facts*. Washington, DC: U.S. Census Bureau.
U.S. Census Bureau (2014). *State and County Quick Facts*. Retrieved from http://quickfacts.census.gov/qfd/states/27000.html
U.S. Department of Education (2002). *What to know and where to go: Parents' guide to No Child Left Behind*. Washington, DC: U.S. Department of Education
Viteritti, J. P. (2009). New York: Past, present, future. In Viteritti, Joseph P. (Ed) *When Mayors Take Charge: School Governance in the City* (pp. 206–234). Washington, DC: Brookings Institution.
Wahlstrom, K. L., Seashore Louis, K., Leithwood, K., and Anderson, S. E. (2010). *Investigating the Links to Improved Student Learning: Executive Summary of Research Findings*. New York, NY: The Wallace Foundation.
Yin, R. K. (2003). *Case Study Research: Design and Methods* (3rd edn). Thousand Oaks, CA: Sage.

5 Chile

School leadership challenged by double accountability towards schools

José Weinstein, Javiera Marfán, Andrea Horn, and Gonzalo Muñoz

Literature distinguishes between different forms of accountability that respond to different purposes. Leithwood (2001) shows how pro-accountability policies have existed in pursuit of different objectives, such as making the decision-making process more accessible to schools, favoring the performance of the education market, promoting professionalism amongst the leading players of the schooling process (teachers and administrators), or improving the educational and institutional management of schools. Similarly, differentiating accountability types according to their main aims, the Organization for Economic Co-operation and Development (OECD) (OECD, 2009) has distinguished between accountability focused on the requirements of the school system (contractual accountability), accountability focused on responding to the needs of students and parents (moral accountability), and accountability designed to meet the expectations of teachers and administrators (professional accountability), creating the concept of multi-accountability in order to describe the way in which these simultaneous processes operate. Meanwhile, Darling-Hammond (2004) identifies (though not exclusively) similar types of accountability: legal and bureaucratic accountability, in which schools operate according to legislation or to regulations set by the state that are intended to ensure that schools follow certain procedures; market accountability, which allows parents to choose courses or schools; and professional accountability, in which the school staff are expected to acquire specialized knowledge in order to meet professional standards of practice in their work. The later can be understood in terms of internal accountability, a concept introduced by Elmore (2010) alluding to the link between the results and the development capacities of the school, showing the need to prioritize it over external accountability.

The presence of accountability conceptualization in educational research is related to a pro-accountability trend in school systems, which has been described, among others, by OECD (2009) and specifically for the United States by Darling-Hammond (2004). This trend has gone hand in hand with an increasing decentralization of educational decision-making, as well as with a greater observance of countries that comply with the quality of learning achieved at different levels of the system as a whole, requiring improvement on the effectiveness of school systems in the context of a more demanding and globalized economy and society (OECD, 2009). This process would not have been possible if the techniques of measurement of the quality of education had not had a dramatic change from their focus on the integration and preservation of community values and knowledge to individual results of performance based on quantitative goals (Mauroy and Voisin, 2013). These different forms of accountability implicate schools and their administrators to take responsibility for the quality of the education they provide, having to respond to the consequences derived from their results. Market accountability considers that families have the possibility to choose their school, and by choosing it over others, reward it for its performance, a material reward that implies payment to the school. For example, one may assume that a family's preference could express particular satisfaction with the education provided by, and would contribute to, greater quality levels from education service across providers, thus having a positive systemic effect. This subject has been put at issue by different studies (Carrasco and Flores, 2013; Corvalán and Román, 2012) in particular due to its impact on greater social segmentation (OECD, 2004). Therefore, schools would have incentives to improve their results in order to attract families. However, state accountability's rationale is to set incentives for schools in order to foster the achievement of certain standards that have been set by educational authorities, expecting by this to enhance school improvement efforts. If the expected outcomes are not achieved, consequences could imply even the closure of the school as an educational organization. This chapter addresses only those types of accountability that could be considered as external, examining their consequences over schools and specifically their influence over principals' professional behavior.

In school systems, some types of accountability tend to predominate among the others, and it is not unusual that they coexist. The features of a certain combination of accountability types will depend on the history and reality of each school system. There are socio-political and institutional dynamics that may push a certain system in one direction or another. There are school systems, such as those in the English or the U.S. contexts, which have evolved from forms of accountability structured around the state, to other forms that are open to the market (Ravitch, 2013), while other systems, such as the Chilean one, have gone in the opposite direction, adding state regulations for schools to a system that historically has been mostly market based (Cox, 2012). Either way, the resulting system of school accountability may end up being a combination of elements from different origins, as shown in Table 5.1.

When both types of external accountability, market and state, are present in a certain school system, a model of double accountability emerges. Inasmuch, competition between schools to obtain the approval of families coexists with the requirement to comply with performance standards set and monitored by authorities. Hence, the resulting pressure on schools is

Table 5.1 Three models of accountability

Measure	Market	State	Market plus state
Who is accountable?	The school and its administrator	The school and its administrator	The school and its administrator
Accountable to whom?	To the families (within the existing legal and administrative frame)	To the Ministry of Education	To the families and the Ministry of Education
How does one yield accountability?	Through the satisfaction of the families for the educational services offered	Through meeting the required standards	Through the satisfaction of families and meeting the required standards
What are the consequences in cases of success in meeting accountability expectations?	Preference showed by families (viability) leads to success of the school unit and its administrator	More incentive for good performance and greater autonomy in management	Preference showed by families, more incentive and greater autonomy in management
What are the consequences in cases of non-success in meeting accountability expectations?	Exit by families (or not showing up) and failure of the school unit and its administrator	Progressive sanctions (could even close down) and greater external control in educational management	No preference showed by families, sanctions and greater external control in educational management
What basic systemic prerequisites must be met?	Existence of diverse educational offers available to families and the freedom for them to choose	Existence of quality standards and the capacity from the Ministry of Education to monitor and sanction (if needed)	Existence of diverse educational offers available to families together with standards that are monitored with consequences

amplified, as discussed later in the description of how this impacts on the work of school principals in Chile.

However, these models of accountability do not necessarily follow the conceptual itinerary as planned because sometimes certain assumptions or conditions of viability are not met. The last line of Table 5.1 exposes this shortcoming: unsatisfied families are not always able to exert options for changing schools within the market model. In fact in Chile, schools can select their students. For example, the lack of nearby alternative high-quality schools available to families, in case their own low-quality schools close down, has been documented (Elacqua *et al.*, 2011). Furthermore, public bureaucracies do not always have the skills to effectively develop appropriate standards, nor to monitor and enforce them. However, it is clear that the organization of the system based on these two main orientations leads schools and responsible authorities to try to respond to a number of significant results in terms of standards achievement and enrollment.

An education system built on competition with increasing public regulation

Under the dictatorship of General Pinochet (1973–1989), Chile experienced a sort of "capitalist revolution," becoming a country where the neoliberal ideas of Milton Friedman were put into full swing, elevating the market as playing a significant role in national development. In the educational field, market-based influence was observed via the establishment of a system governed by competition between public and private service providers throughout the school system, requiring schools to try to attract students and their families. In theory, families would "vote with their feet" for the best possible deal available. In fact, state financing consisted of the payment of a subsidy to the service provider named the "*sostenedor*" for each student attending classes. The *sostenedor* is responsible for defining the educational project, for staffing school and managing the financial and other resources. While the municipality administrates public schools, *sostenedors* of private schools typically own the school itself. The amount of the subsidy does not depend on whether the *sostenedor* is public or private. The system also promotes the installation of new private providers by means of low entrance barriers to access this market and by making low-quality compliance requirements for the school service itself. In addition, public education is *deeply decentralized*, as the management of school services was transferred from the Ministry of National Education to over 300 municipalities, due in part to a lack of experience in school administration and insufficient institutional capability (Marcel and Raczynski, 2010). Meanwhile, subsidized private education greatly expanded, accounting for nearly 60 percent of national enrollment.

The main achievement attained by this market system was the growth in numbers of students inside the school systeme. This achievement has also been made possible by non-education-related factors, such as the sustained increase in living standards (Gutierrez and Paredes, 2011), significant poverty reduction, down from over 38.3 percent to 14.4 percent between 1990 and 2011 (Ministerio de Desarrollo Social de Chile, 2012), and the general increase in educational expectations. In fact, the percentage of the Chilean population under 25 years old that is expected to complete upper secondary is higher than the average for OECD countries (OECD, 2013).

We cannot say the same in terms of the learning quality of students and even less in terms of learning equity,, areas where this model failed to achieve significant progress and even increased preexisting levels of class-based segregation. When compared with other OECD countries, taking into account the variance of the Programme for International Student Assessment (PISA) 2009 results that are explained by socio-economical factors, Chile ranks above the OECD average (Ministerio de Educación de Chile, 2013).

Once Pinochet's dictatorship concluded, democratic governments (post-1990) introduced improvements to the original model by placing greater demands on the quality of school service, empowering the state as the central governing agent of the education system, systematically multiplying sector financing and encouraging a set of compensatory measures to the most socioeconomically disadvantaged schools and students (Weinstein and Muñoz, 2009). Additionally, with the Statute of Professionals in Education (1991), teachers' working conditions improved (e.g., increased salaries, job security, diverse benefits, etc.), especially for those teachers working in the public sector (Weinstein and Muñoz, 2009). The improvements were implemented in phases. In the first phase (1990–2007), reforms were focused on building educational infrastructure, improving school staff working conditions, investing in educational resources, introducing changes to curricula, extending the school day and implementing centrally defined programs for learning improvement (Raczynski and Muñoz, 2007). Finally, the co-finance law strengthened the conditions of private, subsidized schools. This allowed these schools to charge students' families whilst continuing to receive funds from the state.

After the emergence of a student movement in 2006 called the "Penguins' Revolution," where the claim for higher quality and educational equity enjoyed massive public support, a new phase of educational reforms began, with especial focus on educational quality and equity improvement. Hence, in 2008 the Preferential School Subvention Law (SEP) was announced: a vast initiative for schools serving disadvantaged students to receive significant additional funding to be used in improvement plans they themselves developed and in which certain academic goals were to be met within four years. The SEP law revolutionized the top-down support forms, based on centralized programs, which in the 1990s the Ministry of Education set in motion in order to boost the educational quality of the most vulnerable facilities (Núñez and Weinstein, 2008; Weinstein et al., 2010). In 2009, the General Education Law (LGE) deepened the definition of roles for each school player, including a greater participation of the state as guarantor of education quality (Weinstein and Muñoz, 2009). The LGE refashioned institutions' responsibility for guaranteeing educational quality by setting learning standards, measuring student learning, and defining consequences for those schools that failed to meet the standards set. In this respect, LGE emphasized the state's leading role (Banco Mundial, 2010) and even questioned some pillars of the market model (Cox, 2012).

For these recent policies to be implemented, the national system for measuring student learning played a major role. Having a national, standardized test to measure student learning has been a prerequisite to rank schools while establishing the conditions to set incentives and to deliver state support. This system, called Sistema de Medición de la Calidad de la Educación (SIMCE), has been in operation for more than 25 years. As a result, information on curricular coverage and different subjects is periodically collected at the student, school, municipality, and national levels. Every year, language, math, and science census tests are carried out with 4th grade students, and every other year with students from the 8th and 10th grades. These tests have recently been enhanced by the introduction of new levels (6th and 2nd grades) and disciplines (English, technology, and physical education). This system is considered a big jump forward compared to the information provided previously regarding the educational system (Meckes and Carrasco, 2010).

SIMCE results were not initially made public. This changed in 1995, leading to an annual ranking of the schools published in the press, thus becoming a tool for families' school choice. Although it should be noted that even though Chilean families can choose among schools, the criteria they use to make school choice decisions are not always reliant on the SIMCE scores. Studies have shown that their decision is likely to be based more on school proximity, the social status of the family, the school's infrastructure and other factors (Elacqua and Fabrega, 2004; MacLeod and Urquiola, 2009). Nevertheless, SIMCE has increasingly been used as a key tool for building and regulating actions that the state has been assuming regarding the school system, by promoting a standards-based reform that takes SIMCE scores as its main source of information (Espinola and Claro, 2010). For example, SIMCE has been a key factor for the implementation of the law of preferential school subvention (SEP). In effect, schools that do not meet the SIMCE goals they have committed to may be sanctioned for closure (Elacqua *et al.*, 2013), thereby introducing key principles of high-stakes school accountability. Therefore, SIMCE has put learning information at the center of the two forms of accountability that the Chilean school system has been settling into throughout the last decade. The main milestones of the Chilean double accountability system are synthesized in Table 5.2.

The role of the school principal and the results promised by double accountability

In line with international trends (Leithwood, 2001; West *et al.*, 2010) over the past decades, and particularly in the past five year period, there has been an important transformation of the role of the school principal: primarily from implementing and administrating centrally defined educational policies in the school to rapidly becoming the person in charge of certain key results that the school must reach (Montt *et al.*, 2006; Núñez *et al.*, 2012). This includes a shift towards a stronger emphasis on managerial aspects. School leaders are responsible for leading the educational and institutional projects

Table 5.2 Policies and institutional changes shaping the double accountability system in Chile

Era	Year	Milestones
Pinochet dictatorship	1980	The establishment of financial system based on student attendance. The amount of financing is the same for municipal and private subsidize schools. This marked the beginning of "competition for students."
	1981–1986	The development of a decentralization process. Schools stopped being managed by central government, as management was transferred to the local level (municipalities).
	1988	The creation of SIMCE, which realized national examinations for the students of certain grades and certain subjects to determine quality of learning.
Democratic governments	1991	The introduction of Statute of Education Professionals regulated the working conditions of teachers, in particular for those in the public sector.
	1993	The approval of co-finance law allowed private schools to charge students' families whilst still receiving funding from the state. This created an imbalance in the funding between the public and the private subsidized sectors.
	1995	The SIMCE results were made public and the press began to construct league tables among schools.
	2008	The New Preferential Subvention Law (SEP) was established, where schools accepting underprivileged students received extra funds, in return for committing to achieve certain established learning goals.
	2009	New General Education Law established education quality objectives to be accomplished by schools and *sostenedores*. Quality standards were put in place.
	2012	The New Quality Assurance Law created institutions such as the Quality Agency to monitor the schools achievement of the national standards.

of the school in their charge, making sure they meet the goals and processes necessary to achieve the agreed targets in the context of SEP and the Educational Quality Guarantor System. Weinstein *et al.* (2012b) explain that this task implies that they must not only transform their relationship with respect to the upper levels of the school system, but they must also change their inward work towards the school—acquiring authority and decision-making as expressed clearly in the new legal requirement for which principals should observe classes and discharge teachers. This new legal scope of the principal's role focuses on the capacity for leading the school's educational project and also includes new administrative powers that, in general, provide greater autonomy.

In this context, school leaders are compelled to try to achieve two kinds of results, directly related to each type of accountability present in the Chilean educational system. First, a direct *derivative* of the competitive financing system, in which schools receive their funding according to student attendance, indicates that school principals must deal with matters of enrollment. Not having a suitable number of enrolled students leaves the school not only with an "idle capacity," but also generates a financial deficit for the *sostenedor*. However, ensuring the necessary annual enrollment is not a simple task as the number of educational service providers is growing, particularly in light of the expanding private subsidized sector. Paradoxically, there are fewer students, due to changing youth demographics (Marcel and Raczynski, 2010). Hence, the *sostenedor* puts pressure on principals to assure "proper" enrollment numbers by increasing the existing enrollment rate, if found insufficient, or by maintaining it, if found satisfactory. This goal is part of the usual discussion between *sostenedores* and principals. Yet, an analysis of enrollment (MacLeod and Urquiola, 2009) reveals that despite these demands, municipal schools have shown a trend of declining enrollment whereas private, subsidized school enrollment is growing.

The second result expected of principals follows from the growing weight of quality measurements of student learning, which is expressed by individual schools' ranking in the SIMCE annual standardized tests. Even though this information originally was supposed to only have a referential value for the school and its *sostenedor* (who could learn of the school's health and take remedial measures), for the families (who could use the information for school choice) and for the Ministry of Education (which could identify problems and establish ad hoc improvement programs), SIMCE test scores have had increasingly direct consequences on schools (Meckes and Carrasco, 2010). At first, these consequences were only positive. For example, in schools reaching a certain SIMCE score, teachers were awarded additional economic incentives through the National System of Performance Evaluation (SNED). More recently though, with the implementation of the SEP and its resulting SIMCE goals to be reached in four years, these consequences could also be negative, including the possibility of school closure. The *sostenedor*, therefore, puts pressure on principals to assure a certain SIMCE score or student outcome level.

The main results that principals are supposed to achieve are in line with the two forms of accountability that have become prevalent in the Chilean school system. So while achieving and maintaining adequate student enrollment meets the requirements of a market-based system for the attraction and retention of families, getting and maintaining adequate SIMCE results is in line with the requirement to comply with the academic standards fixed and operationalized in the SEP act. While these matters do not necessarily correspond to the discourse on the alleged role principals should fulfill (Pont *et* al., 2008), these two requirements determine the work of the principals, setting the priorities by which they will be evaluated by their employers, whether public or private.

School principals response to double accountability

In this context of double accountability, school principals have developed specific strategies to mobilize their schools towards meeting the enrollment targets and developing SIMCE score strategies. These strategies were identified in the qualitative phase of a research project entitled School Leadership and Educational Quality in Chile, directed by José Weinstein and Gonzalo Muñoz between 2009 and 2011. The research is based on an in-depth study of 12 urban elementary school principals in disadvantaged social educative situations and aims to identify the strategies they implemented in compliance with the two accountability demands. Figure 5.1 presents the conceptual device underlying the identified strategies.

The strategies are a set of initiatives that are strongly aligned to goals for increasing student enrollment and learning agreed upon by principals and their school boards. The principals operate different strategies to achieve those results, and so they must get families to choose their school and their pupils must reach a certain level of academic performance.

Two caveats are needed. Considered in isolation, the strategies have a rather tactical purpose and do not necessarily point towards further development of school capacity. As other authors have claimed about the American school

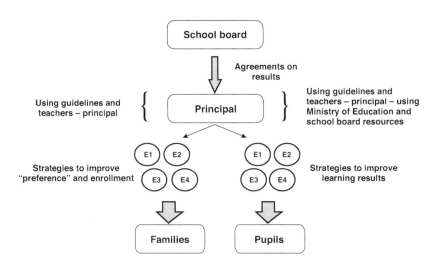

Figure 5.1 Directive strategies
Source: Weinstein *et al.* (2012b)

system, some policies of accountability can reach academic goals at the expense of other long-term educational aims (Jacob, 2005; Ravitch, 2010). Additionally, the possibility of implementing some of these strategies, as well as their chances of success, depends heavily on factors outside the principal's control, such as the administrative unit of the school, the school's previous results and the socio-economic profile of the families it serves. Research in primary schools (Weinstein *et al.*, 2012a) identified 12 strategies carried out by the directors, five of which are focused on improving the results of enrollment (see Table 5.3), while the other seven are designed to increase scores on SIMCE (see Table 5.4).

Table 5.3 Strategies and practices developed by school principals to improve enrollment results

Strategy	Examples of practices related to the strategy
1. Starting pupils earlier at school	– Offering lower levels (such as pre-kindergarten) which enables children to start school earlier – Setting up a special needs language school in the institution, for preschool children with (suspected) language difficulties
2. Gaining loyalty, developing a local identity for the families living in the area near the school	– Facilitating the use of the sports facilities, the stage, computer rooms, and the library by neighbors in the area and their organizations – Developing courses and training for adults aimed at the parents, but open to other neighbors
3. Promoting differentiated characteristics of the families accepted by the school (by selecting students and attracting the target group)	– Economic filter: the family accepted must have some ability to make co-payments for the child's schooling – Values ideological filter: the family accepted must share certain principles or specific beliefs promoted by the institution – Academic merit filter: the applicant accepted must have certain academic qualifications that differentiate him/her from other pupils
4. Improving school's supply by complements and features that distinguish them among others	– Offering infrastructure (such as buildings, land, or equipment) that make the school different from others – Offering full-time schooling – Offering additional learning opportunities (school activities and extracurricular activities)
5. Informing families of the good academic results	– Having their results in official standardized tests and university selection examination known to the families, by comparing them with those of other institutions in the areaMaking parents and pupils aware that the school provides good opportunities to continue their secondary education

In terms of improving school enrollment, the first strategy, *starting pupils earlier at school*, consists of schools offering an educational service at lower levels (such as pre-kindergarten). Another alternative is to set up a special needs language school in the institution, for preschool children with (suspected) language difficulties that welcomes and provides treatment for them, acting as a *bridge* to later attend normal school, where they can continue their schooling by being integrated gradually into different courses while having the possibility of continuing their remedial classes at the same time.

The second of these strategies, *gaining loyalty, developing a local identity among the families living in the area near the school*, has to do with the schools offering an education service that is renowned for its identity within the proximity of the local community, maintaining a close link with families in the area and social organizations (neighborhood associations, sports clubs, etc.), which other schools find difficult to do.

A third strategy for enrollment results is *promoting differentiated characteristics of the families accepted by the school*, which implies the integration of pupils and families that share the same social and cultural characteristics distinctive to them. This strategy was also validated by other studies demonstrating that many subsidized private schools selected those students with more resources and academic skills (Elacqua and Fabrega, 2004). In many cases, these resources are not available to public schools. There seems to be three filters that principals must use during selection: (1) an economic filter, which incorporates families as long as they can make a prepayment in addition to the scholar grant, (2) a values ideological filter, which only incorporates those families who share certain principles or specific beliefs promoted by the institution and, (3) a filter related to the pupil's academic merit, which favors the incorporation of those pupils that are able to comply with schools' predetermined academic requirements.

The fourth strategy is *improving the school's supply by complements and features that distinguish them among others*. This means that the school provides an education and non-academic services that make it different from other schools. Families will associate it with achieving better welfare and the comprehensive development of their children. Therefore, this prestige is not based on the type of education provided or the academic performance of the pupils. For this reason Chilean parents have been labeled as uninformed consumers when it comes to choosing a school for their children. Other researchers (Waslander and van der Weide, 2010) in other contexts have distinguished between internal and external answers to market pressures, demonstrating that the latter (which does not touch upon the hardcore of education) were prevalent.

Finally, the fifth strategy is *informing families of the good academic results*. The school actively presents the results achieved every academic year, which are officially recognized by education authorities and the media, in order to convince new families to choose that school and for their children to remain in the schools they already attend.

Leadership and accountability in Chile 65

With regard to compliance with standards of academic performance, research has identified seven alternatives commonly developed by principals in schools to improve scores on standardized tests (see Table 5.4).

Table 5.4 Strategies and practices developed by school principals to improve SIMCE outcomes

Strategy	Examples of practices related to the strategy
6. Selecting pupils in a way that excludes problem students	– Selecting applicants to the school in the admission process (pre-kindergarten, kindergarten or first grade at primary level) – Dismissing '*problem*' students in third or fourth grade so that they are no longer in the school to take the national standardized examination
7. Organizing pupils' support according to academic ability	– Offering remedial classes for pupils experiencing the most difficulties in school, who are also responsible for *lowering* the SIMCE results – Provide specific support to students with the greatest difficulty, either individually or collectively, by psychologists or other special needs education specialists – Sorting pupils into groups of the same academic level (or tracking them down)
8. Giving priority during school time to SIMCE assessed subjects	– Dedicating time that could be used for different types of workshops and activities of interest to the pupils (such as sports, art, or culture) to assessed subjects – Complementing language and math classes (usually identified as core subjects) with some of the activities carried out in non-core subjects to practice them as well
9. Enhancing or maximizing teaching skills in accordance with SIMCE	– Designating teachers with the right skills for grades that must take the SIMCE examination, in particular fourth grade – Seeking secondary school teachers, particularly language specialists and math teachers to support those grades
10. Adopting a specific teaching method for the assessed subject	– Training teachers to use a specific technology for teaching pupils and monitoring them when using it – Adopting specialized support from private technical assistance institutions or the Ministry of Education
11. Training the pupil with SIMCE practice assessments	– Conducting trial SIMCE tests throughout the course of the school year – Incorporating the SIMCE format of evaluation into regular learning assessments that teachers use from first grade level
12. Awarding special incentives for achieving good SIMCE results	– Rewarding teachers with either symbolic (a tribute of some form or a small gift) or material incentives (computers, training courses, trips) – Rewarding classes that achieve good SIMCE results

The sixth strategy consists of s*electing pupils in a way that excludes 'problem' students*. This means that the school examines the applicants' academic ability and discards those who are *problematic* in terms of SIMCE results. This can be done by way of selection in the process of student admission, or subsequently, by expelling those who may underperform in SIMCE. These strategies are similar to those found by Figlio and Getzler (2002) and by Cullen and Reback (2006) in the U.S.

Strategy number seven, *organizing pupils according to academic ability*, makes the school institute teaching methods used with pupils according to their academic ability and difficulties. This strategy recognizes that each pupil, regardless of his/her background or competencies, is different, and that the implementation of the teaching support system for pupils accommodates their differences. This approach has been a great change for many schools.

The eighth strategy developed to improve scores is *giving priority during school time to SIMCE assessed subjects* by focusing on subjects relevant to the SIMCE examination, under the assumption that more class time focused in this regard will mean that pupils perform better. The first decision made in this respect is to use the "free time available" on the current course program and dedicate it to assessed subjects so that the number of hours for languages and mathematics would be more than is required. Hannaway and Hamilton (2008) and Ravitch (2010) warn about this curriculum distortion in the U.S.

The ninth strategy identified by the research has to do with *enhancing or maximizing teaching skills in accordance with SIMCE*. This means that the school allocates its teachers in a certain way in order to achieve the best SIMCE results possible. Nevertheless, it should be pointed out that there is a sharp contrast between principals' *room for manoeuvre* in private subsidized schools and municipal schools. Principals in municipal schools contend with several constraints, for example, they cannot dismiss teachers who they believe are incompetent; they cannot hire new teachers; and they usually have to deal with greater levels of teacher absenteeism (Weinstein and Muñoz, 2013). For this reason, they must resort to ingenious and intricate ways to encourage their teaching staff.

In tenth place, schools seek to raise SIMCE results by *adopting a specific teaching method for the assessed subject*. School incorporate a particular method of teaching for one or several of the SIMCE subjects, believing that this *teaching strategy* will enable them to improve teaching and results. For the adopted method, teachers must be involved; they must be trained on how to use this technology and they must be monitored when using it. Regardless of their technical qualities, the key to lasting success is the principal and teachers' commitment, deciding how to adopt and implement the adoptions.

An eleventh strategy is *training the pupil with SIMCE practice assessments* by developing assessment procedures similar to those used in the national tests. This not only prepares the pupils by familiarizing them with the tests, but it also gives the school an idea of its *current situation* so that it can implement corrective measures in time. This means that the principal can use the information to intervene, as Jacob (2005) noticed on the impact of the accountability system in the schools of Chicago and Koretz *et al.* (1993) in Vermont.

The last strategy identified to foment the improvement of results of standardized tests, is *awarding special incentives for achieving good SIMCE results*. Whether the incentives are symbolic or material, the objective is to motivate the different players involved with SIMCE, in particular the teachers, to work hard to achieve the best possible result.

In general, the first group of strategies linked to market accountability is less described by the literature than the second. Indeed, the principals' strategies focused on raised test scores have some similarities to other school systems that have implemented these types of accountability policies. Spillane *et al.* (2002) also reported finding strategies 8 to 12 in Chicago. In the case of strategies 7, 8, and 10, Rouse *et al.* (2007) reported similar results for accountability pressure in the state of Florida.

Conclusion

It is commonplace in the global characterization of education today to say that in seeking to improve educational quality, school systems are involved in significant change processes. These processes often include increased accountability of the various units, beginning with the school, for the desired results to be achieved (Pont *et al.*, 2008). But the institutional improvement sought, as well as specifically who needs to achieve the results, varies according to the history and characteristics of each educational system and its country. These idiosyncratic elements are also reflected in the combinations of different ways of accountability that eventually amalgamate and form the particular system of educational accountability.

In Chile, the accountability system is based on the combination of two different models. The first, foundational and instituted under a dictatorial political order, was based on the creation of an educational market, where competition amongst public providers (municipalities) and private ones is encouraged by state funding for recruiting families. The underlying assumption is that this competition between different schools leads to the development of a quality school system. It is important to note that this hypothesis has not been verified in the case of Chile, which, although it has achieved historical rates of access and student retention, has not achieved any significant progress in terms of quality of learning and it has had to pay a high price in terms of segregation, being actually the most segregated system amongst those who participate in PISA testing (Valenzuela *et al.*, 2013). Later, under pressure from citizens and a democratic political order, a public System of Quality Assurance has been gradually installed, which is based on the requirement that schools meet certain basic standards of academic performance. This second model of accountability has been introduced with the implementation of a comprehensive remedial action, the SEP law, in which schools that serve the more disadvantaged students receive substantial financial support from the state, but in exchange, should follow actions for improvement and achieve certain scores on standardized tests of learning (SIMCE). These two accountability systems coexist and have effects upon each other, forming what we call "double accountability."

This system strongly influences the principal's work in the school. It is no coincidence that in parallel to the progress of these new demands, there has been a redefinition of the school principal's role. So if, in the past, they were responsible for the proper implementation of policies and programs that came from other forums and educational levels, particularly the central Ministry of Education, principals are increasingly viewed as the ones who should lead the educational/institutional school project, taking responsibility for the results that are achieved. New laws have sought to enhance the management status and deliver greater power to principals that affect them in their relationships with superiors (Ministry of Education and *sostenedores*) and with their learning communities. So, while greater local leadership is expected from them, it is also demanded that they clearly differentiate themselves professionally from classroom teachers, acquiring greater decision-making powers and pedagogical supervising obligations.

Beyond the rules, this redefinition of the role of the principal can also be analyzed from the main results they are required to achieve by their *sostenedores* and also by the educational authorities themselves. Therefore, two priority results are clearly shown: (a) achieve or maintain certain student enrollment (which determines the financing of the facility), and (b) achieve or maintain certain results on standardized learning SIMCE tests (fulfilling of the commitments made by the SEP law and others). As we have seen, these two results are closely related to the model of double accountability, each corresponding to one of the types of accountability that constitute it.

Attaining these two results is not easy to achieve and principals are under intense pressure to try to reach them. Many times the resources and supports come from their *sostenedor*, and as well, the socio-cultural characteristics of students and the community context affect their action frame.

The importance of achieving both results is so relevant to the "success" of the principal and school in the Chilean context that to some extent it comes into conflict with what the recent literature (Leithwood and Seashore Louis, 2012) has identified as effective and sustainable leadership. In Chile, other strategic areas of management practice have notably decreased (e.g., the development of teacher collective effectiveness or confidence within the educational community) because of this concentrated pressure on short-term results in restricted areas. At the same time, the current legal regulations framing principals' actions make invisible the functions related to "marketing" and seeking to strengthen the fidelity of families. These are quite often found outside the pedagogical functions of schools, yet are highly relevant in the actual exercise of principals in school contexts that encourage competition, like the Chilean one does. The conditions are not optimal to develop a leadership focused on building capacities inside the school community.

This makes it difficult, but not impossible, for principals to lead the school improvement process, particularly for disadvantaged schools. Indeed, a recent study (Bellei et al., 2014) followed the results of Chilean primary schools over a period of a decade. It concluded that 10 percent had managed to achieve consistent improvement, while 40 percent made partial academic improvements. When the researchers looked closer at the successful schools, they confirmed that principals play a crucial, irreplaceable function in the improvement process. These leaders were capable of managing short-term accountability pressures, while at the same time building capacities of the school community and effectively using the resources available to them. More generally, the principals have the strategic role of mediating national policies regarding their own schools (Fullan and Hargreaves, 2012). Some leaders are capable of managing accountability pressures and go beyond short-term goals that the system pushes for (Moos, 2005). Others, possibly the majority, only transfer the pressure to their communities or turn to frenetic activism. Only the first ones are able to successfully navigate the tumultuous waters of double accountability.

In sum, the Chilean experience shows that the predominant accountability in a school system is far from irrelevant for the leadership role. It has significant effects on the practices and priorities established by principals. Therefore, if the Chilean school system seeks to advance towards a genuine improvement of its schools, especially those most disadvantaged, it will require principals being able to exercise powerful pedagogical leadership within a new intelligent and authentic accountability framework (Fullan and Hargreaves, 2012). Building a system of accountability, less stressed by the market and state regulations, which guides a more comprehensive view of the quality of education, looking beyond the results on standardized tests, and promoting a better balance between internal and external accountability, seems to be a decisive road for a better future of school leadership.

References

Banco Mundial (2010). *Diseño de una nueva organización institucional para el aseguramiento de la calidad de la educación: Lecciones para la República de Chile de experiencias internacionales y locales.* Washington, DC: Banco Mundial.

Bellei, C., Valenzuela, J.P., Vanni, X., Contreras, D. (coord.) (2014). *Lo aprendí en la escuela ¿cómo se logran procesos de mejoramiento escolar?* CIAE-UNICEF, Santiago.

Carrasco, A. and Flores, C. (2013). *(Des)igualdad de oportunidades para elegir escuela: Preferencias, libertad de elección y segregación escolar.* Documento de Referencia Nº2. Espacio Público. Santiago de Chile.

Corvalán, J. and Román, M. (2012). La permanencia de escuelas de bajo rendimiento crónico en el cuasi Mercado educativo chileno. *Revista Uruguaya de Ciencia*

Política, Vol. 21, Nº1. ICP, Montevideo.
Cox, C. (2012). Política y Políticas Educacionales en Chile 1990–2010. *Revista Uruguaya de Ciencia Política*, 21(1), 13–42.
Cullen, J.B. and Reback, R. (2006). Tinkering toward accolades: School gaming under a performance accountability system. *NBER Working Paper No. 12286*. Retrieved from www.nber.org/papers/w12286
Darling-Hammond, L. (2004). Standards, Accountability, and School Reform. *Educational Leadership*, 55(5), 6–11.
Elacqua, G. and Fabrega, R. (2004). *El consumidor de la educación: El actor olvidado de la libre elección de escuelas en Chile*. Universidad Adolfo Ibáñez, Santiago.
Elacqua, G., Santos, H., Urbina, D., and Martínez, M. (2011). *¿Estamos preparados para cerrar las malas escuelas en Chile? Impacto sobre equidad en el acceso a educación de calidad*. Reporte Final Proyecto FONIDE. Ministerio de Educación, Chile.
Elacqua, G., Martínez, M., Santos, H., and Urbina, D. (2013). Escuelas bajo amenaza: Efectos de corto plazo de las presiones de accountability de la ley SEP en las políticas y prácticas docentes. *Documentos de Trabajo, 16*. Retrieved from http://politicaspublicas.udp.cl
Elmore, R. (2010). *Mejorando la escuela desde la Sala de Clases*. Fundación Chile. Santiago, Chile.
Espínola, V. and Claro, J. (2010). El sistema nacional de aseguramiento de la calidad: una reforma basada en estándares, in Bellei, Contreras and Valenzuela (eds 2010) *Ecos de la revolución pingüina. Avances, debates y silencios en la reforma educacional*. Santiago, Chile: Universidad de Chile – UNICEF.
Figlio, D. and Getzler, L. (2002). Accountability, ability and disability: Gaming the System? *NBER Working Paper No. 9307*. Retrieved from www.nber.org/papers/w9307
Fullan, M. and Hargreaves, A. (2012). *Professional Capital: Transforming Teaching in Every School*. Teachers College Press. USA.
Gutierrez, A. and Paredes, R. (2011) Desempeño y Brecha Educativa en Chile: ¿Existe un Sesgo por Cobertura?, *Economía Chilena*, 14 (1), 39–51.
Hannaway, J. and Hamilton, L. (2008). *Performance-Based Accountability Policies: Implications for School and Classroom Practices*. Retrieved from www.urban.org/UploadedPDF/411779_accountability_policies.pdf
Jacob, B.A. (2005). Accountability, incentives and behavior: The impact of high-stakes testing in the Chicago public schools. *Journal of Public Economics*, 89, 761–796.
Koretz, D., Klein, S., McCaffrey, D., and Stecher, B. (1993). *The Reliability of Vermont Portfolio Scores in the 1992–93 School Year*, CSE Technical Report 370. Retrieved from www.cse.ucla.edu/products/reports/TECH370.pdf
Leithwood, K. (2001). School Leadership in the Context of Accountabilities Policies. *International Journal of Leadership in Education: Theory and Practice*, 4(3), 217–235.
Leithwood, K. and Seashore Louis, K. (2012). *Linking Leadership to Student Learning*, San Francisco: Jossey-Bass.
MacLeod, B. and Urquiola, M. (2009) *Anti-lemons: School Reputation and Education Quality*. NBER Working Paper No. 15112. USA.
Marcel, M. and Raczynski, D. (2010). *La Asignatura Pendiente. Claves para la revalidación de la educación pública de gestión local en Chile*. Santiago: Uqbar Editores.

Mauroy, C. and Voisin, A. (2013). As Transformacoes Recentes das Politicas de Accountability na Educacao: Desafios e incidencias das ferramentas de acao publica. *Educacao e Sociedade*, 34(124), 881–901.
Meckes, L. and Carrasco, R. (2010). Two decades of SIMCE: An overview of the National Assessment System in Chile. *Assessment in Education: Principles, Policy and Practice*, 17(2), 233–248.
Ministerio de Desarrollo Social de Chile (2012). *Informe de Política Social 2012*. Ministerio de Desarrollo Social, Gobierno de Chile.
Ministerio de Educación de Chile (2005). *Marco para la Buena Dirección: Criterios para el Desarrollo Profesional y la Evaluación de Desempeño*. Santiago de Chile: MINEDUC.
Ministerio de Educación de Chile (2013). *Equidad en los Aprendizajes Escolares en Chile en la última Década*. Serie Evidencias. Centro de Estudios Ministerio de Educación de Chile. Mayo.
Montt, P., Elacqua, G., González, P., Raczynski, D., and Pacheco, P. (2006). *Hacia un Sistema Escolar Descentralizado, Sólido y Fuerte. El diseño y las capacidades hacen la diferencia*. Serie Bicentenario, Ministerio de Educación. Santiago, Chile.
Moos, L. (2005). How Do Schools Bridge the Gap between External Demands for Accountability and the Need for Internal Trust? *Journal of Educational Change*, 6, 307–328. DOI 10.1007/s10833-005-2749-7
Núñez, I. and Weinstein, J. (2008). *El Caso de Chile: Una reforma educacional ¿sin reforma del ministerio? (1990–2007)*. Serie Rethinking Capacity Development, UNESCO-IIPE, Paris, April.
Núñez, I., Weinstein, J., and Muñoz, G. (2012). ¿Posición Olvidada? Una mirada desde la normativa a la historia de la dirección escolar en Chile. In Weinstein, J., and Muñoz, G. (eds) *¿Qué sabemos de los directores de escuela en Chile?* Santiago: Centro de Estudios de Políticas y Prácticas en Educación.
OECD (2004). *Revisión de Políticas Nacionales de Educación: Chile*. Paris: OECD.
OECD (2009). *School Evaluation: Current Practices in OECD Countries and a Literature Review*. Paris: OECD.
OECD (2013). *Education at a Glance*. OECD Indicators. Paris: OECD.
Pont, B., Nusche, D., and Moorman, H. (2008). *Improving School Leadership, Volume 1. Policy and Practice*. Paris: OECD.
Raczynski, D. and Muñoz, C. (2007). *Reforma Educacional Chilena. El Difícil Equilibrio entre la Micro y la Macro Política*. Serie Estudios Socio-Económicos n° 31. Santiago: CIEPLAN.
Ravitch, D. (2010). *The Death and Life of the Great American School System: How Testing and Choice are UnderminingEeducation*. New York: Basic Books.
Ravitch, D. (2013). *Reign of Error: The Hoax of the Privatization Movement and the Danger to America's Public Schools*. USA: Knopf.
Rouse, C.E., Hannaway, J., Goldhaber, D., and Figlio, D. (2007). Feeling the Florida Heat? How low-performing schools respond to voucher and accountability pressure. *NBER Working Paper 13681*. Retrieved from www.nber.org/papers/w13681
Spillane, J.P., Diamond, J.B., Burch, P., Hallet, T., Jita, L., and Zoltners, J. (2002). Managing in the Middle: School leaders and the enactment of accountability policy. *Educational Policy*, 16, 731–762.
Valenzuela, J.P., Bellei, C., and de los Ríos, D. (2013). Socioeconomic School Segregation in a Market-oriented Educational System. The Case of Chile, *Journal of Education Policy*, DOI:10.1080/02680939.2013.806995.

Waslander, S., Pater, C., and van der Weide, M. (2010). *Markets in Education: An analytical review of empirical research on markets mechanisms in education.* OECD, Education Working Paper 52, Paris: OECD.

Weinstein, J. and Muñoz, G. (2009). Calidad para Todos. La Reforma Educacional en el punto de quiebre, in Bascuñán, G., Correa, G., and Maldonado, J. (eds) *Más acá de los sueños, más allá de lo posible: la Concertación en Chile.* LOM, Santiago.

Weinstein, J. and Muñoz, G. (2013). When Duties Are Not Enough: Principal leadership and public or prívate school management in Chile. *School Effectiveness and School Management*, DOI 10.1080/09243453.2013.792850.

Weinstein, J., Fuenzalida, A., and Muñoz, G. (2010). La Subvención Preferencial. Desde una Difícil Instalación Hacia su Institucionalización. In Matinic, S., and Elacqua, E. (eds) *¿Fin de ciclo? Cambios en la gobernanza del sistema educativo.* UNESCO – Pontificia Universidad Católica de Chile.

Weinstein, J., Marfán, J., and Muñoz, G. (2012a). ¿Colegas y jefes? La visión de los docentes sobre el liderazgo directivo en Chile. In Weinstein, J., and Muñoz, G. (eds) *¿Qué sabemos sobre los directores de escuela en Chile?* Santiago : Centro de Innovación en Educación de Fundación Chile y Centro de Estudios de Políticas y Prácticas en Educación.

Weinstein, J., Muñoz, G., and Marfán, J. (2012b). Liderar bajo presión: Las estrategias gestionadas por los directores de escuelas para alcanzar los resultados comprometidos. In Weinstein, J., and Muñoz, G. (eds) *¿Qué sabemos sobre los directores de escuela en Chile?* Santiago : Centro de Innovación en Educación de Fundación Chile y Centro de Estudios de Políticas y Prácticas en Educación.

West, D., Peck, C., and Reitzug, U. (2010). Limited Control and Relentless Accountability: Examining historical change in urban school principal pressure. *Journal of School Leadership*, 20(2), 238–266.

6 School accountability policy *in* practice

Learning by comparing Australia, New Zealand, USA, and Chile

James P. Spillane and Katie Mertz

The four preceding chapters center on a policy instrument that has become commonplace in education policymaking in many countries over the past few decades, that is, holding schools accountable for their performance. While the authors capture the particulars of accountability in *place* (Australia, Chile, United States, and New Zealand) and *time*, together their accounts document the spread of this policy instrument in four very different geopolitical territories. The rich descriptive accounts document the emergence of accountability as a favored government policy instrument, capturing the particulars in four different school systems nested in distinct systems of government from parliamentary democracies such as Chile and New Zealand to federalist systems such as Australia and the US. Moving beyond describing the accountability policy environment of the four countries the authors examine how accountability works in practice inside the schoolhouse. In particular, the chapters examine how school principals apprehend and grapple with accountability policy in their work as school leaders and managers. This commentary identifies three themes and two puzzles prompted by a reading of the chapters in an effort to engage the reader in learning by comparing these four cases of accountability policy and practice.

The potency of government accountability in school principal practice

In all four cases, the reach of standards and accountability into schools is striking, occupying a very prominent, if sometimes problematic, position in school principals' day-to-day work. Even in New Zealand where schools are 'self-managing,' national accountability mechanisms figure prominently inside schools. Specifically, in all four systems we observe school principals heeding government accountability efforts, actively trying to make sense of what accountability initiatives mean for their schools, and struggling to figure out the entailments of these demands for everyday school and classroom practice. Although the accountability mechanisms vary by country and by the stakes attached, principals in all four countries still reported that accountability featured prominently in their work.

These accounts contrast sharply with a half-century of implementation scholarship, albeit much of it done on US school systems, that mostly laments the failure of government policy, especially policy related to classroom instruction, to make much of a difference in schools and classrooms. These chapters tell a very different story, one where government efforts to hold schools accountable for instruction through various mechanisms get taken up by school leaders, influencing both their practice and priorities. In these chapters we see accountability mechanisms, and by extension government policy on instruction, figuring prominently in work on instruction and instructional improvement in schools. These accounts of policy getting beyond the schoolhouse door are consistent with research over the past couple of decades that shows how standards and accompanying accountability mechanisms do influence what goes on in schools.

Of course, acknowledging the reach of accountability is not to evaluate its efficacy in transforming the quality of teaching and learning in schools. As Robertson and Hill state, "many schools and teachers have invested time and energy on practices that do not always support students' learning or progress." (ERO, 2007: 41) The four chapters capture the good, the bad, and the ugly of accountability mechanisms as they are taken up in local schools and classrooms. They document the upsides and downsides of accountability mechanisms in school efforts to manage instructional quality and lead instructional improvement. They also capture tremendous variability within school systems in how schools respond to accountability initiatives, suggesting that while government policy may be exercising influence inside schools, policy remains a blunt instrument when it comes to the work of leading and managing instruction (Green, 1983). The variability in local response to accountability policy in part reflects the tremendous variation among schools in terms of student learning needs and the capability of school staff.

Accountability mechanisms and educational infrastructure

The four chapters also underscore the critical role of the educational infrastructure in the way accountability policy is taken up on the ground, inside schools. It is noteworthy that each of these chapters, in describing accountability mechanisms and exploring school principals' responses, pay attention to a variety of other aspects of the educational infrastructure including professional learning opportunities, student assessment instruments, and so on.

This is to be expected because standards and accountability do not operate in a vacuum, and on their own they do not constitute an educational infrastructure for supporting instruction and its improvement. Rather, these are but two components of the educational infrastructure (e.g., curricular materials, organizational routines, and so on) that enable and constrain practice related to instruction inside school. These chapters capture how understanding relations between accountability mechanisms and the work of school principals must take into account several other components of the educational infrastructure. Further, what is key here is understanding how these various components, including standards and accountability, interact with one another to more or less structure school principals' and teachers' practice related to instruction. As a result, how accountability policy gets played out in everyday practice inside schools depends in great measure on other core components of the educational infrastructure that supports teachers' and school leaders' work. These chapters then point to the importance of designing and redesigning educational infrastructures as a whole (rather than just the accountability component) in efforts to improve and maintain the quality of instruction (Spillane *et al.*, 2011).

The chapters also capture the importance of time and taking a historical approach to policy analysis. The accounts suggest that change is a constant in the practice of education policymaking. New policies and new policy instruments (or sometimes just relabeled or renamed instruments) are the norm rather than the exception. While it is the case that standards and accountability have been popular instruments with policymakers for a quarter-century or more (and they were mobilized in much earlier school reform efforts), there has still been tremendous policy churn in the education sector. Take the US where standards and accountability have been commonplace in local, state, and national education policy since the 1990s. Still, standards and accountability have had several incarnations over this relatively short time period. At the national level alone there have been several different incarnations of accountability and standards, the most prominent being No Child Left Behind (NCLB) and more recently the Common Core State Standards initiatives.

This policy churn is consequential for local schools and their efforts to support classroom instruction and improve its quality. When new policies are introduced, they are often layered on top of existing ones. As a result, education policy often sends mixed signals to schools about instruction and instructional improvement. Moreover, the constant policy churn, and at different levels of the school system as Easley and Elmeski document in their chapter, creates a lack of stability for local school staff who have to manage a constantly changing and unstable policy environment. Each new incarnation of accountability and standards creates new demands on school principals – demands that at times have to be met while still attending to extant policies. We find evidence of this in all four chapters but especially in José Weinstein and his colleagues' chapter on Chile and the challenge of what they call 'double accountability,' where school principals have to contend with both market and state models of accountability together.

Leading and managing in a pluralistic institutional environment: Accountable to many stakeholders and for different things

While the deployment of standards and accountability in the education sector differs in terms of form, focus, and function between countries (and indeed over time), these four chapters document several similarities across countries. A key and striking similarity captured in all four chapters are the challenges faced by school principals regardless of country. School principals have to contend with multiple stakeholders – parents, students, teachers, local community members, board of trustees, government policymakers, and so on – who place different and sometimes conflicting demands on them and their schools. This is the reality of leading and managing organizations situated in "pluralistic" institutional environments where "persistent internal tensions" arise in response to sometimes "contending logics." (Kraatz, 2009) School principals have to address the dual imperatives of organizational legitimacy and integrity but they have to do so for diverse stakeholders who can have different and sometimes conflicting ideas about what makes a 'real' or legitimate school. Organizational legitimacy involves gaining the support of diverse stakeholders by demonstrating to those stakeholders a school's 'cultural fitness.' 'Organizational integrity' refers to the need to knit together the expectations of diverse stakeholders in order to create an 'organizational self' that is minimally coherent, integrated, and self-consistent (Kraatz, 2009; Mead, 1934; Selznick, 1992). Setting direction for the school and developing short- and long-term goals to realize this direction are critical for organizational integrity. In these four chapters, we see school principals who work in four very different school systems grappling with organizational legitimacy and organizational integrity.

Efforts to address the demands of external stakeholders so as to preserve the legitimacy of the school organization can come into conflict with efforts to address organizational integrity and the demands of internal stakeholders such as teachers. Moreover, accountability and standards do not appear to have eased the challenges of organizational legitimacy and integrity that school principals must address. Indeed, as evidenced in the case of Chile, accountability mechanisms may have served to exacerbate the challenges of addressing organizational legitimacy and integrity. Accountability mechanisms can serve to privilege one group of stakeholders (e.g., parents) over another (e.g., government policymakers) at different times and can also created mixed signals about to whom schools should be accountable. Regardless, as the four chapters document, school principals are left to figure out how to manage these challenges on the ground as they contend with diverse stakeholders who place different, and sometimes conflicting, demands on them. Managing in the middle between these multiple stakeholders is the lot of the school principal, something that these chapters suggest holds across countries (Spillane and Kenney, 2012).

A puzzle: Where is professional accountability?

In reading these chapters, the limited attention given to professional models of accountability is striking. José Weinstein and his colleagues discuss professional accountability, but it does not appear from their account to be a prominent model in the Chilean school system. Robertson and Hill refer to how New Zealand schools are held to professional standards that are jointly developed by teacher unions and the New Zealand Ministry of Education, but here too there is limited evidence that a professional model of accountability is thriving in any of these systems. Juxtapose this limited attention to professional accountability against references throughout these chapters to 'teachers' professional judgment,' 'professional development,' 'professional leadership,' and 'leading a professional learning community.'

This is not to say the authors omitted something, but rather that it is remarkable and rather puzzling, especially considering the references to professional judgment and professional learning communities, that professional accountability models are not prominent in these school systems. In some respects, it may reflect the weak status of teaching as a profession, what scholars of professions often refer to as a semi-profession (Etzioni, 1969; Ingersoll and Perda, 2008). It likely also reflects the privileging of market and state or bureaucratic models of accountability in policy discourses and texts in these four countries and many others over the past several decades. By professional accountability I do not mean accountability models that are focused on the individual school but rather models of accountability that go beyond the particular school in which the profession itself takes responsibility for monitoring professional practice and holding members accountable for certain standards of practice.

Another puzzle: Moving beyond an exclusive focus on the school principal

All four chapters focused on the school principal with some attention to school leaders more broadly, especially in the chapter on New Zealand. There is good reason to do so: the school principal is the denotative leader, the one charged with managing the demands of diverse stakeholders in all four school systems. Still, the focus on the school principal suggests a second puzzle concerning how these accounts might change (if at all) should the authors, moving forward, focus their analyses on school leadership and management practice (for shorthand we might say school administrative practice) as distinct from focusing more narrowly on the school principal. Again, this is not a critique of the chapters, but instead an attempt to puzzle over whether and how the reach and influence of accountability policies would look any different if we conceptualize school leadership and management differently rather than equating it with the work of the school principal.

Such an approach would entail at least two things. First, it would involve attending to whether and how accountability mechanisms matter in the work of other formally designated school leaders involved in leading and managing the quality of instruction in their schools such as assistant or deputy principals, mentor teachers, and so on. As research increasingly documents the critical and unique role of these other school actors in leading and managing instruction and its quality, it seems imperative that future work on the influence of accountability mechanisms attends to these other school leaders. Second, it would require attention to the actual practice of leading and managing instruction, as distinct from focusing only on what school leaders tell us about what they do and how accountability mechanisms matter to this. Specifically, if we studied the day-to-day practice of leading and managing instruction inside schools, we would be better able to understand how standards and accountability policies get taken up in practice and how their meanings for extant practice are negotiated among school staff.

Individually and collectively these four chapters offer rich descriptive accounts of the particulars of accountability mechanisms in four countries as well as how these mechanisms are being negotiated inside schools by school principals. There is much to be learned about standards and accountability from engaging the chapters in a conversation with one another. We can learn by comparing how roughly similar policy instruments (e.g., standards and accountability) played out in distinctly different education systems, related with school and classroom practice.

References

Education Review Office (2007). *The Collection and Use of Assessment Information: Good Practice in Primary Schools*. Wellington: Education Review Office.

Etzioni, A. (1969). *The Semi-professions and their Organization: Teachers, Nurses, Social Workers*. New York: Free Press.

Green, T. F. (1983). Excellence, equity, and equality. In L. S. Shulman and G. Sykes (eds) *Handbook of Teaching and Policy* (pp. 318–341). New York: Longman, Inc.

Ingersoll, R. M. and Perda, D. (2008). The status of teaching as a profession. In J. H. Ballantine and J. Z. Spade (eds) *Schools and Society: A sociological Approach to Education* (pp. 106–118). Thousand Oaks, CA: Sage Publications Inc.

Kraatz, M. S. (2009). Leadership as institutional work: A bridge to the other side. In T. B. Lawrence, R. Suddaby and B. Leca (eds), *Institutional Work: Actors and Agency in Institutional Studies of Organizations* (pp. 59–91). Cambridge, UK: Cambridge University Press.

Mead, G. H. (1934). *Mind, Self, and Society: From the Standpoint of a Social Behaviorist*. Chicago: The University of Chicago Press.

Selznick, P. (1992). *The Moral Commonwealth: Social Theory and the Promise of Community*. Berkeley, CA: University of California Press.

Spillane, J. P. and Kenney, A. (2012). School administration in a changing education sector: The U.S. experience. *Journal of Educational Administration*, 50(5), 541–561.

Spillane, J. P., Parise, L. M., and Sherer, J. Z. (2011). Organizational routines as coupling mechanisms: Policy, school administration, and the technical core. *American Educational Research Journal*, 48(3), 586–620.

7 Teacher evaluation and educational accountability in China

Implications for school leadership

Ting Wang

Over recent decades, the quality of school education has become a high-priority policy issue in many education systems where attention has focused on ways of identifying factors associated with effective schooling and thus to achieve further improvements in quality (e.g. Darling-Hammond and Bransford, 2005; McKinsey and Company, 2007; OECD, 2001, 2005; Rowe, 2007). If teacher performance and practice are the most important factors in achieving improved learning for all students, then teacher evaluation may be considered as a quality assurance mechanism (Danielson and McGreal, 2000; Kleinhenz and Ingvarson, 2004). To improve teaching effectiveness, many countries have developed teacher evaluation systems in response to the demands for high educational quality (Teddlie *et al.*, 2003). Teacher evaluation has two major purposes: (1) to ensure that teachers perform at their best to enhance student learning, and (2) to improve the teachers' own practice by identifying strengths and weaknesses for further professional development. An evaluation process should ideally be directed towards both educational efficiency and educational equity (Isoré, 2009).

The prevailing performance discourse in education claims school improvement can be achieved through transparent accountability procedures. The purpose is to make teachers' work transparent through inspections, observations, appraisals, and public reporting of test scores. Accountability has become a core concept under educational reforms in the age of neoliberal governance, which emphasizes devolution, performativity, productivity, efficiency, and effectiveness (Ball, 2003; Ranson, 2003; Webb, 2006). Anderson (2005) proposes three main types of accountability systems in education, namely compliance with regulations, adherence to professional norms, and results-driven accountability. The accountability system should be built upon aligned components: objectives, assessments, instruction, resources, and rewards or sanctions. The three types coexist in different combinations and a range of instruments to evaluate and improve performance may be used in different contexts.

Educational accountability in China

China has a strong tradition of centralization policy, but there is a trend toward reducing the centralized control over education in the reforms implemented after 1985. Decentralization was considered a key element in educational policies and larger systematic reform movements to implement economic reforms and marketization. This process of decentralization revealed the political paradox of the coexistence of decentralization and centralization in educational transformation in China. Qi (2011) argues that in the decentralization process, the central state concentrates on regulating Chinese education through building a rigorous legal and policy framework.

The Ministry of Education (MOE) is responsible for formulating laws, regulations, and policies and providing guidance for the work of provincial, municipal, and local education authorities (MOE, 1993; People's Congress of China, 1986). Since 1986, a centralized education inspection system has been strengthened to monitor school reforms with corresponding regulations and procedures in both local and central administrations. Municipal and district educational inspection agencies conduct the actual inspection and evaluation of local schools. School administrators are responsible for evaluating teachers (Liu and Teddlie, 2003; MOE, 2010). The new National Regulations on Educational Inspection highlight two elements: higher level government's inspection on lower-level administration's implementation of educational law, regulations, and policies; and local government's inspection of schools in their educational activities (MOE, 2012). The inspection focuses on the evaluation of school activities and site visits by specialized experts reviewing the comprehensiveness of internal documents, efficiency in resource utility, enhancement of teaching quality, and holistic development of students.

Improving teacher quality and student learning has become a major theme in the educational reform agenda over the past two decades. The establishment of teacher evaluation and designation systems evidences result-based accountability in China. Since 1986, an integrated national, provincial, municipal, and school-level teacher evaluation and designation/ranking system has been implemented nationwide. A new teacher evaluation and designation policy was piloted in China in 2009–2010, and then to be implemented across the nation in 2014 (MOE, 2011). Through linking the evaluation results with teachers' pay and professional progression, teacher performance-based pay reform, which has been implemented nationwide since 2009, strengthens teacher evaluation and accountability procedures (MOE, 2010). National professional standards for kindergarten, primary, and secondary teachers were issued in 2012.

An important aim of recent education reforms in China is to establish transparent, reliable, and comprehensive educational evaluation systems and accountability mechanisms. Chu (2012) argues that both accountability mechanisms and evaluation systems are intertwined. The educational evaluation and accountability policies in China highlight the principles of effectiveness, efficiency, transparency, and performance. Education authorities endeavor to establish a transparent and effective evaluation system to assess and monitor teacher performance. This is linked to an evidence-based accountability system with explicit reward and sanction measures. High-performing teachers are rewarded through promotions, salary increments, and awards. However, in some regions and schools, the evaluations of schools and teachers are primarily based on student academic performance and high-stakes test results. The accountability policy has a narrow focus on obligatory and transactional functions.

Teacher evaluation and designation policies in China

The Teacher Evaluation and Designation policy (1986–2009) emphasizes teachers' professional status and collective responsibilities for improving teaching performance and student learning. The aim is to enhance teacher quality and establish strong school communities through evaluation, promotion, and professional development and training (MOE, 1993, 1995). Teachers are evaluated and designated to different levels. Primary and secondary schools adopt different designation/ranking systems. Each system has three designations/levels: junior-, senior-, and master-level teachers. The highest rank for primary school teachers is equivalent to that of a university lecturer, and the highest rank for secondary teachers is equivalent to that of an associate professor. Typically all three levels with different pay rates and prestige are employed in a single school. Only few exemplary teachers are promoted to master teachers due to a restricted quota. Teachers are evaluated according to the following criteria: morality, diligence, teaching abilities, and student performance. Evaluation materials are submitted to the provincial or municipal educational authorities. Evaluations are primarily conducted by external experts and are differentiated across these levels of expertise.

The recent Teacher Evaluation and Designation policy aims to improve teaching quality, encourage healthy competition, and enhance teachers' holistic development by prioritizing professional growth (MHRSS and MOE, 2009; MOE, 2010, 2011). Some specific measures include the integration of two previously separated primary and secondary evaluation systems into one system with five designations/levels: junior 3rd, 2nd, 1st, senior, and master levels (junior 3rd is the lowest). Explicit evaluation standards are set for each level, emphasizing student-oriented education and teachers' work ethic, competence, achievements, and contribution. Improved evaluation mechanisms include peer reviews, teacher interviews, and class observations. The highest rank for primary and secondary teachers is now equivalent to that of a professor.

External teacher evaluations and designation are conducted to differentiate performances and provide incentives for teachers to achieve high teaching performance and career progression. Teachers are initially evaluated internally in the school. External evaluators at municipal/provincial levels assess their applications and supporting materials. Each level has different requirements on the balance of teaching and development responsibilities. The outcomes of promotion applications are mainly based on the evaluation of submitted materials and internal evaluation recommendations from school leaders.

Numerous researchers argue that the implementation of the teacher evaluation policies has promoted school improvement by inspiring teachers and acknowledging their contributions to student learning through professional titles and high social status (Yao, 2006; Zhang, 2010). Evaluating teachers in relation to specific criteria makes comparisons possible, which are used for promotion opportunities. This system provides an opportunity for high-performing teachers to achieve fast-track promotion. Teachers engage in professional learning activities to enhance professional growth and improve teaching practices, leading to the improvement of the school's and students' learning. The systematic approach is essential to retain excellent teachers in schools and make teaching an attractive career choice in China.

However, other researchers argue that this system is problematic and in the need of reform (Chen, 2006; Yao, 2006; Ying and Fan, 2001). The evaluations rely heavily on teaching performance and students' test scores. The mechanism is primarily used to reward excellent teachers and punish low-performing ones, which may not foster all teachers' passion for teaching. Xia (2004) contends that this evaluation mechanism does not allow for a dialogue between teachers and administrators. Teachers are excluded from participating in reviewing the evidence and decision-making regarding the evaluation. External evaluators have limited chances of observing classes or interviewing teachers and students. Moreover, schools receive quotas for promotion from the government annually, and unhealthy competition may arise among teachers competing for limited positions (Zhang, 2009). Increased competition also puts more pressure and accountability demands on teachers, which may lead to loss of enthusiasm and burnout of teachers (Xu and Shen, 2008; Zhao, 2006).

Despite a growing research interest in educational reforms in China, there is limited empirical research on teacher evaluation and educational accountability. Drawing on data from a larger study on professional learning communities and school leadership in China, this chapter investigates the experiences of principals and teachers in two case-study schools and seeks to answer the following research questions: what internal and external evaluation procedures are implemented in schools? And what are the impacts of evaluation systems upon teachers and school leaders?

Methodology

The study was primarily qualitative and interpretative. The purpose of interpretive research is of paramount importance for envisaging the social reality of the case setting, which is initially unknown until the investigator understands the way participants interact in their world (Radnor, 2001). A case-study approach was utilized because case studies investigate the complex dynamic and unfolding interactions of events and human relationships in a unique instance, and penetrate situations in ways that are not always susceptible to numerical analysis (Cohen et al., 2000). The decision to focus on two schools was on the grounds that each case would generate considerable and manageable data from which initial conclusions could be drawn.

This study involved the collection of data derived from semi-structured interviews of 20 participants, a review of relevant documents, and observations in two senior high schools in Harbin, North China in 2012. Two schools were identified based on an enviable reputation for excellent teaching quality and a willingness to participate in the study. These two schools enroll Years 10–12 students. School A has 2700 students and 220 teachers, and School B has 3000 students and 200 teachers.

Participants were selected through purposeful sampling, ranged from varied disciplines, ages, teaching experience, and designations of levels. The 20 participants included 2 principals, 4 deputy principals, and 14 teachers at different levels with teaching experiences ranging from 2 to 35 years. Participants included 9 master teachers, 3 senior teachers, 2 level 1 teachers, and 6 level 2 teachers. Their disciplines covered Chinese language, mathematics, biology, geography, physics, chemistry, and history.

An in-depth and semi-structured interview technique was used to explore participants' experiences. The average time for each interview was approximately one hour. The interview questions were related to internal and external evaluation measures implemented in the school and the impacts of teacher evaluation systems. Each interview was digitally recorded and transcribed verbatim, with relevant sections of the transcripts fully translated from Chinese into English by the researcher, an accredited translator.

The transcripts were coded, based on emergent themes and categories, and summarized into a report on each case-study school. Data analysis took the form of constant comparative analysis whereby themes were identified and coded as they surfaced (Miles and Huberman, 1994). As new themes emerged from patterns and units of relevant meaning, these were compared with the previous ones and regrouped with similar themes. The responses were sorted into categories on the basis of similarities and differences. The researcher looked for the themes common to most or all of the interviews as well as individual variations.

Findings

The findings were categorized into three major themes to address the two research questions regarding internal evaluation, external evaluation, and the impacts of evaluation systems. Challenges for school leaders in the accountability environment are also discussed.

Internal evaluation focuses on inspection and monitoring

Most interviewees commented on teachers' professional responsibilities to meet the requirements of internal and external teacher evaluations. Both schools implement formative and summative evaluation procedures to assess and monitor teachers' performances through regular observations, inspections, and annual performance reviews using explicit evaluation criteria. Teachers indicated that internal evaluations were used to "keep teachers on constant alert," "ensure quality teaching and learning," and "maintain discipline and effective management." A junior level 2 teacher commented on the regular inspections and "rigorous school management" in School B:

> The school leaders review lesson plans monthly, observe classes from time to time, monitor, and supervise teaching periodically. Therefore, we are under constant surveillance and need to take each class seriously. I cannot slack off. I feel this is like an invisible, ongoing evaluation and monitoring.

Internal evaluation primarily focused on monitoring and assessing teaching practice and student learning. Principals in both schools commented that internal evaluations were not utilized to differentiate or punish teachers because "all teachers are committed and work hard." In School B, teachers receive a comprehensive internal evaluation of performance annually. School leaders fill in the forms provided by the municipal education authorities and assess teachers' performance using the criteria provided. A deputy principal explained:

> The student university entrance exam results and research outputs account for about 50 percent of the evaluations. Other evaluation criteria include teaching attitude, professionalism, student feedback, parent feedback, and peer review. All teachers were rated as excellent because we believe they all work hard and there is no need to rank them in the order of A, B, C, D.

External evaluation focuses on differentiation and promotion

The findings reveal that external evaluations are conducted to differentiate performances. Outstanding teachers are rewarded and promoted but rarely are teachers punished. Teachers who are underperforming or deemed unsuitable for teaching may be transferred to general administrative positions. According to the principal, only one underperforming teacher was transferred to the library over the past 30 years in School A.

This evaluation system aims to hold teachers accountable for their continuous professional development and teaching performance. In order to meet the criteria for promotion, teachers must demonstrate that they have provided "hard evidence" and met "non-negotiable requirements." These include completing prescribed training courses, participating in professional development activities within and across schools, such as class observations and open lessons, publishing a required number of articles related to teaching practices and action research, and achieving sustained quality teaching and student learning outcomes, as evidenced by high-stakes test results, internal and external recognitions and awards. As commented by a deputy principal in School B:

> We must follow the criteria and standards stipulated by the national and provincial governments and give specific scores. Teachers should participate in mandated training programs and achieve certain credit points. These hard evidence or hard standards are non-negotiable.

A junior level 2 biology teacher in School A commented on his pressure to "work hard and accumulate sufficient evidence to justify the promotion." He explained:

> To be honest, I need to make a lot of effort to prepare for the open lessons. At the beginning, I feel nervous and frustrated. Without the pressure of evaluation and promotion, I may not sign up to participate in the open lesson competitions.

Teaching effectiveness is a key criterion for promotion. Teaching is recognized as a research-oriented profession and research achievements are part of the requirements for evaluation and promotion. Conducting demonstration lessons at the district, city, provincial levels, mentoring junior teachers, and leading curriculum development are also part of requirements for promotion to senior and master teacher levels. A master-level mathematics teacher in School A confirmed that teachers received rigorous evaluations before being promoted:

> Firstly, teaching ability must be excellent. This teacher must earn the acknowledgment from students and parents. His students' university entrance exams performance is an important indicator. Secondly, he must demonstrate strong research ability and achieve publications and research outputs. Moreover, he should make significant contributions to the school.

Impacts of the evaluation systems

Most interviewees reported positive impacts of teacher evaluations on their professional growth, such as providing clear expectations, guidance, and structural support to meet the evaluation requirements. The findings indicate that external evaluations and promotion criteria place a strong focus on differentiation and evidence. The internal evaluations appear to be more lenient and less strict than the external evaluations.

Teachers are paid according to their rankings and performance-based bonuses do not reveal much difference among them. Respondents generally reported a high level of job satisfaction. Most teachers commented that intrinsic motivations such as passion, professionalism, and dedication to education primarily sustained their efforts, not just external recognition and promotion. Some teachers commented that they strived for promotion to a higher level, mainly aiming to "seek reputation" and not to "lose face." A senior-level geography teacher in School B believed this system was "transparent and fair," explaining:

> Had it not been for this system, I would feel content and over confident. It may be hard for me to see other teachers' strengths or have a strong motivation to improve. It seems that Chinese people like pressures and they are motivated to work best under some pressure. Moreover, Chinese people attach much importance to reputation and face. Qualities of teacher forces are also improved incrementally through this system.

Assigned evaluators and expert panels carried out the evaluation process for designation/promotion. Principals and teachers commented on a positive shift in recent years from a focus on the judgment of external expert panels to the school-based evaluation and peer reviews regarding individual teacher's performance. They also acknowledged increased social status and benefits of teachers, particularly the master-level teachers, who are now officially equivalent to professors.

It should be noted that interviewees had mixed feelings towards the evaluation and designation system. School leaders and master-level teachers generally believed this evidence-based system played an important role in enhancing overall teacher quality. It facilitated a competition mechanism and supported the mission of striving for excellence. A deputy principal commented, "This system is transparent and objective. The designation can reflect a teacher's professional standard. The system has provided an effective platform and pathway for teacher professional development."

A master teacher shared similar views, "Promotion requires meeting the standards and criteria. If a teacher wants to have career progression, he must work hard to enhance teaching and research capabilities, which in turn facilitates his professional development." As for young teachers who have just started their career, they were optimistic about their career development and held a proactive attitude towards the system.

However, the teachers at the senior level and junior level 1 tended to express dissenting views on the designation system. They were disappointed at limited promotion opportunities. There are restricted percentages for master- and senior-level teachers in a school, according to government policies. It may take up to ten years for an eligible level 1 teacher to be promoted to senior teacher. In 2012, no quota was allocated for master-level teachers in both schools; 44 eligible level 1 teachers competed for 3 positions of senior teachers in School A, and 39 eligible level 1 teachers competed for 6 positions of senior teachers in School B. Competition for promotion has become increasingly fierce and the limited annual quota creates disincentives and tensions among some teachers. Two level 1 teachers commented that the system dampened their enthusiasm for professional progression.

In order to address the dilemma and provide incentives for teachers, School A has implemented an experimental internal designation system, acknowledging the contribution of teachers using school recognized professional titles. Because the provincial department of education does not recognize these, the issue is yet to be resolved.

Challenges for school leaders

The findings show that the evaluations of schools, principals, and teachers are explicitly linked to students' academic performances. Most interviewees commented that the Chinese education system is still examination oriented. Principals and teachers are under tremendous pressure from various stakeholders. They are held accountable for students' academic performance, particularly in high-stakes exams, like the university entrance examinations (*Gaokao*). Making all students learn and achieve high academic performance is considered a top priority for schools. Teaching activities primarily focus on the development of students' fundamental knowledge and basic skills. Students in both schools are required to complete daily homework and various exams, such as monthly exams, mid-term, and end of term exams. Senior high schools in the region continue to be ranked according to *Gaokao* results and the rates of student admission to universities, particularly to top universities.

In this study, the evaluation of principals was mainly based on overall teaching quality, student academic performance and school improvement. Students' *Gaokao* results are still considered an important indicator in assessing teachers' teaching ability and performance. *Gaokao* results usually account for 30 percent of teacher evaluation in School A and up to 50 percent in School B. As indicated by a deputy principal in School B, school leaders are facing a dilemma of "how to cope with a test driven, performance-based education and survive in a constrained space to allow teachers and students to enjoy autonomy and happy lives."

Many interviewees indicated that teachers were under tremendous pressure to meet the performance expectations. Heavy workload and long working hours are common. They teach classes of 40–60 students for 10–12 hours per week. Besides lesson preparation, they spend 2–3 hours on marking and student consultation each day. A typical working day for a teacher is from 7 am to 4:30 pm with take-home work thereafter. School leaders commented that teachers were under heavy pressure and it would be sensible to release some stress and reduce teacher burnout.

The findings show that school leaders demonstrate strong instructional leadership and play an important role in creating the conditions for school improvement. Two principals and four deputy principals in this study were master-level teachers with strong expertise in leading curriculum development and supervising teaching and learning. Interviewees commented on their critical role and engagement in "supervising teaching and curriculum," "promoting teacher professional learning," and a consistent focus on "improving teaching quality" and "enhancing student learning and holistic development."

Leaders in both schools engaged in fostering an inclusive school culture and committing teachers to a shared vision of learning for all. Collective efforts were made to foster a culture of trust and collaboration. Professionalism and dedication were considered essential to achieve continuous improvement. A deputy principal in School A commented:

> Our school culture has a feature of trust. The school is running smoothly thanks to each teacher's work ethics. Each member endeavors to teach every class well and accomplish every task satisfactorily. This kind of *ocean culture* seems to look loose but never affects our performance. So long as teachers fulfill their obligations, there is no need to implement numerous inspections.

Conclusion

This chapter has presented the findings of a qualitative study utilizing data collected from 20 interviews with principals and teachers in two senior high schools in North China. There is a limitation imposed by the sample size. The generalizability of findings to other parts of China and different types of schools would require caution. Further research with a larger sample of schools in other regions could be conducted.

In this study, both schools implemented internal and external evaluation procedures to monitor teachers' professional learning and ensured this was supported in an aligned manner to meet the national/provincial requirements and individual teacher's needs. This was a dynamic process focusing on assessing and monitoring as well as providing strong support for continuous improvement. In the two schools, internal evaluation focused on inspection and monitoring while external evaluation focused on differentiation and promotion. Evaluations generally had a positive impact on the improvement of overall teacher quality, but there was a tension between accountability demands for school leadership and the need for enhancing teacher well-being and reducing burnout.

The study suggests that the three types of accountability coexist in China to balance the requirements of adherence to laws, regulations, and professional standards, as well as results-driven accountability. The Chinese government mandates policies on teacher evaluation, designation, and professional standards. The alignment of the national, provincial, and municipal/local policies using a coordinated approach enables policy implementation at different levels with less ambiguity. School leaders play a critical role in creating the conditions for school improvement. They continuously negotiate their practice in a mandatory accountability policy context, and take into account local and institutional contexts to address specific issues. They are faced with challenges of balancing the demands from stakeholders to be accountable for teaching quality and student learning, and the demands from the governments to reduce students' workload and enhance their holistic development. These mediating forces shape their leadership practices and demand creative school leadership for the future.

References

Anderson, J. A. (2005). *Accountability in Education*. Paris: International Institute for Educational Planning and The International Academy of Education.

Ball, S. J. (2003). The teacher's soul and the terrors of performativity. *Journal of Education Policy*, 18(2), 215–228.

Chen, W. (2006). Constructing new discipline for school teachers' appraisal and designation system. *Sichuan Education*, 10(5), 1–13.

Chu, H. (2012). *Transforming the Chinese Educational Development Mode*. Keynote address at the 2020 Education Vision International Conference, 9–10 November, Taipei.

Cohen, L., Manion, L., and Morrison, K. (2000). *Research Methods in Education* (5th edn). London and New York: RoutledgeFalmer.

Danielson, C. and McGreal, L. T. (2000). *Teacher Evaluation to Enhance Professional Practice*. Princeton, NJ: Educational Testing Service.

Darling-Hammond, L. and Bransford, J. (eds) (2005). *Preparing Teachers For a Changing World: What Teachers Should Learn and be Able to Do*. San Francisco, CA: Jossey-Bass.

Isoré, M. (2009). Teacher evaluation: Current practices in OECD countries and a literature review. *OECD Education Working Papers*. No. 23, OECD Publishing.

Kleinhenz, E. and Ingvarson, L. (2004). Teacher evaluation uncoupled: A discussion of teacher evaluation policies and practices in Australian states and their relation to quality teaching and learning. *Research Papers in Education*, 19(1), 31–49.

Liu, S. J. and Teddlie, C. (2003). The ongoing development of teacher evaluation and curriculum reform in the People's Republic of China. *Journal of Personnel Evaluation in Education*, 17(3), 243–261.

McKinsey and Company. (2007). How the world's best-performing school systems come out on top. Retrieved 16 November 2012 from http://mckinseyonsociety.com/how-the-worlds-best-performing-schools-come-out-on-top/.

MHRSS and MOE (Ministry of Human Resources and Social Security and Ministry of Education) (2009). *Guidelines on Deepening the Reform of School Teacher Evaluation and Designation System*. Beijing: Ministry of Human Resources and Social Security and Ministry of Education.

Miles, M. B. and Huberman, A. M. (1994). *Qualitative Data Analysis: An Expanded Sourcebook of New Methods* (2nd edn). Thousand Oaks, CA: Sage.

MOE (Ministry of Education) (1993). People's Republic of China Teachers Law. Retrieved 16 November 2012 from www.moe.edu.cn/publicfiles/business/htmlfiles/moe/moe_619/200407/1314.html

MOE (1995). People Republic of China Education Law. Retrieved 26 November 2012 from www.moe.gov.cn/publicfiles/business/htmlfiles/moe/moe_619/200407/1316.html

MOE (2010). Ministry of Education work priorities in 2010. Retrieved 25 November 2012 from www.moe.gov.cn/publicfiles/business/htmlfiles/moe/A02_zcwj/201005/xxgk_87820.html

MOE (2011). Ministry of Education: Promoting the expedition of pilot experiment of China's school teacher appraisal and designation system reform. Retrieved 20 October, 2012 from http://edu.people.com.cn/GB/8216/36635/17011713.html

MOE (2012). Press release on 'Ministerial Opinions on Further Enhancing the Inspection of Primary and Secondary Schools'. Retrieved 20 November 2013 from www.moe.edu.cn/publicfiles/business/htmlfiles/moe/s271/201209/142328.html

OECD (2001). *Teachers for Tomorrow's Schools: Analysis of the World Education Indicators*, 2001 edition. Paris: OECD and UNESCO Institute for Statistics.

OECD (2005). *Teachers Matter: Attracting, Developing and Retaining Effective Teachers*. Paris: Organization for Economic Cooperation and Development.

People's Congress of China (1986). Compulsory Education Law. Retrieved 7 September 2012 from www.moe.edu.cn/jyfg/laws/jyfgywjy.htm

Qi, T. (2011). Moving toward decentralisation? Changing education governance in China after 1985. In T. Huang and A. W. Wiseman (eds) *The Impact and Transformation of Education Policy in China*. Bingley, UK: Emerald.

Radnor, A. H. (2001). *Researching Your Professional Practice: Doing Interpretive Research*. Buckingham: Oxford University Press.

Ranson, S. (2003). Public acccountablity in the age of neo-liberal governance. *Journal of Education Policy*, 18(5), 459–480.

Rowe, K. J. (2007). School and teacher effectiveness: implications of findings from evidence-based research on teaching and teacher quality. *Springer International Handbooks of Education*, 17(6), 767–786.

Teddlie, C., Stringfield, S., and Burdett, J. (2003). International comparisons of the relationships among educational effectiveness, evaluation and improvement variables: an overview. *Journal of Personnel Evaluation in Education*, 17(1), 5–20.

Webb, P. T. (2006). The choreography of accountability. *Journal of Education Policy*, 21(2), 201–214.

Xia, X. (2004). Teacher evaluation: Professionals' perspective. *Studies of Educational Development*, 10, 19–22.

Xu, F. and Shen, J. (2007). Research on job satisfaction of elementary and high school teachers and strategies to increase job satisfaction. *Chinese Education & Society*, 40(5), 86–96.

Yao, W. Z. (2006). *Understanding the Life and Career Meaning of Professional Titles*. (Vol. 16). Chengdu, Sichuan: Sichuan Education Press.

Ying, P. C. and Fan, G. R. (2001). Research on traditional cases of teachers' evaluating patterns-on the disadvantage of traditional pattern of teachers' evaluation and study of a new pattern. *Theory and Practice of Education*, 2(3), 22–25.

Zhang, X. M. (2009). Vanity Fair of professional titles. *Journal of Sunset, 24*(22), 4–9.

Zhao, M. Y. (2006). General analysis on the reasons for school teachers' psychological pressure. *Journal of Huaibei Professional and Technical College, 5*(3), 58.

8 The School Development and Accountability Framework in Hong Kong
Possibilities of educational leadership

Nicholas Sun-Keung Pang

Globalization and changes in information processing during the last two decades have had a great impact on education systems and organizations. The modern values of sub-contracting, market, competition, efficiency, accountability, planning, continuous evaluation, quality assurance, and so forth, have been emphasized, one might even say exaggerated, in the education system under the impact of globalization. There have certainly been some noticeable changes in schools and numerous scholars have warned educators that public (state) schools must keep pace with societal changes and expectations, in order to survive in such a changing environment (Gamage and Pang, 2003). Now, almost daily, educators are confronted with demands, ostensibly from society, to reform the organizational structures and educational processes.

According to Beer and Nohria (2000), two dramatically different approaches to organizational change are being employed in the world today, namely: Theory E and Theory O of change. Different assumptions by corporate leaders about the purpose and means for change inform the two theories. Theory E changes aim at the creation of economic value and maximizing shareholder values. It emphasizes the changes in structures and systems, motivates through financial incentives, and involves the processes of planning and establishing programs. Thus, Theory E changes are managed from the top down, planned, and programmatic. Theory O changes, by contrast, are emergent, and less planned and programmatic. It aims to develop organizations' human capability to implement strategy and to learn from actions taken about the effectiveness of changes made. It encourages participation from the bottom up, focuses on the building up of a corporate culture, motivates through commitment, and makes use of the processes of experimentation and involvement. Both Beer and Nohria (2000) regarded these theories as archetypes. An examination of many organizations will show that a mixture of these strategies often coexists, and it is suggested that a hybrid of these theories is likely to produce better results in organizations.

Hong Kong schools are confronted with more or less the same challenges as those in other countries, brought by the huge information flow and vigorous innovation due to globalization. Hong Kong policy necessitates that schools transform into learning communities so as to meet the expectations of their stakeholders (Pang and Cheung, 2004). If a school has to become a learning community, it needs to enhance its own learning capacity in such a way that the whole school seeks organizational improvement in a continuous process. School leaders have to submit to a paradigm shift from hierarchical, supervisory, and controlling roles to facilitative and supportive roles with careful planning.

The quality assurance movement in Hong Kong

There have been rapid changes in both the education system and schools themselves in Hong Kong due to the recommendations of the Education Commission Report No. 7 (ECR7) issued in 1997. The ECR7 recommended a two-pronged approach to ensure the quality of education in Hong Kong: an external quality assurance mechanism and an internal quality assurance framework. While the external quality assurance mechanism has been achieved through the establishment of the Quality Assurance Inspectorate (QAI) in 1997, to which schools are accountable, the internal quality assurance framework relies on schools' own capability at self-evaluation as the process of school improvement. The external quality assurance mechanism is done through adopting a whole-school approach to inspection by the QAI, which assesses schools' effectiveness, identifies their strengths and weaknesses, makes suggestions for improvement and development in the schools, and releases inspection reports for public reference. In order to improve the quality of school education continuously, all schools are also expected to engage in cyclical processes. Every school must work towards meeting the educational needs of its students as effectively as it can and self-evaluation provides information on which to base plans for improvement. All schools should produce documents that outline the long-term goals, prioritize development areas, set out specific targets for implementation, evaluate progress of work during the school year, and set improvement or development targets for the coming year (Ministry of Education, 1984; Scottish Office, 2002).

In the year of 2003, the Education Bureau revised the two-pronged approach to quality assurance of education in Hong Kong and introduced the School Development and Accountability (SDA) Framework (Education and Manpower Bureau, 2003). Since then, the external quality assurance mechanism is achieved through the conduction of external school review (ESR) by the Quality Assurance Division (QAD) for accountability purposes, whereas the internal quality assurance mechanism relies on schools' capability of school self-evaluation (SSE) within the process of continuous improvement. Evidence-based organizational change has become a major trend in the school reform in Hong Kong. It is important that organizational change be based on objective and reliable evidence of school performance.

Schools can only improve continuously when they have institutionalized a self-evaluation framework in daily practice and when there is a set of valid, reliable, and school-based performance indicators available for use in self-evaluation (Pang *et al.*, 2004). Practicing self-evaluation enables schools (1) to develop formal procedures for setting school goals; (2) to promote participation of teachers in school management, development, planning, evaluation, and decision-making; (3) to assess their progress towards goals, as well as their performance over time; and (4) to take appropriate steps for improvement (Pang, 2006a). When school-based indicators are translated from the aims of the schools, they are useful tools for measuring and monitoring school performance in areas of interest. Self-evaluation with appropriate school-based indicators provides information to schools, teachers, parents, students, and the community with the general profiles of schools for reference and for comparison among schools of similar background. School self-evaluation and school-based performance indicators are the crucial elements for continuous improvement in schools (Cuttance, 1994; Scottish Office, 2002). A summary of the pros and cons of the SDA Framework for quality assurance in education is given in Table 8.1. It shows that the external mechanism of quality assurance through the practice of external school review is usually a top-down approach. This innovative, crash-through approach will bring radical changes in school organization and management. Its effects are fast and on schedule, but intermittent. On the contrary, the internal mechanism of quality assurance, through the practice of self-evaluation, is usually a bottom-up approach from within. This incremental approach is likely to bring about evolutionary changes to the school culture, with slow, but continuous and long-lasting effects. Both the internal and external mechanisms of quality assurance have their respective advantages and disadvantages in the school development process. So, a flexible and good blending of both mechanisms should be needed for invasive significant changes in school management and development, while maintaining continuous and long lasting effects (Pang, 1998).

Table 8.1 The pros and cons of the School Development and Accountability Framework for quality assurance

Quality assurance	External mechanism	Internal mechanism
1. Approach	An innovative approach	An incremental approach
2. Changing agent	External school review	School self-evaluation
3. Changes	A "crash-through" approach with radical surgery	An evolutionary development
4. Drives	Top-down and external	Bottom-up and internal
5. Pace of change	Fast, on schedule, and intermittent	Slow, continuous, and long lasting

Leading and managing change through the School Development and Accountability Framework

The SDA Framework introduced in the 2003/04 school year emphasizes SSE in recognition of the school's central role in its improvement. SSE, complemented by ESR, helps promote continuous self-improvement in schools through the planning-implementation-evaluation (PIE) cycle. With concerted effort over the past years, schools are making better use of data and evidence to evaluate work effectiveness, resulting in more open classrooms and increased transparency in school management. In the coming years, the Education Bureau (EDB) will help schools embed SSE and formulate their school development plans more systematically, and promote schools' reflection on their developmental needs and areas for improvement (Education Bureau, 2012a).

Evidence-based organizational change has been a very recent trend in the school reform and improvement movement. It is important that organizational change should be based on objective and reliable evidence of school performance. Schools should have a self-renewal mechanism (with the implementation of school self-evaluation) to manage change, which can be built upon (1) clear and appropriate diagnosis of the school as an organization and (2) the role of administration in the organization (Pang, 2006a). Experience in both research and practice has shown that if school reforms are to succeed, organizational changes need the active support of the principal (Gamage and Pang, 2006; Pang, 2010). The principal needs to be an advocate of self-evaluation and be prepared to articulate a vision of self-renewal for the school. School development cannot be copied and imposed from outside. The leader needs to understand the current situation, including strengths and weaknesses, opportunities, and threats (SWOT) to the organization, determine the goals to be attained within the next one to three years, and develop the strategies to be pursued in order to achieve them. Institutionalization of self-evaluation in the organizational framework and daily managerial practices allows the principal to lead and manage the school towards effective educational change (Macbeath *et al.*, 2000).

Although schools conduct self-evaluation according to the SDA Framework prescribed by the EDB, an expert team conducts external school reviews to validate the exercise of school self-evaluation. SSE is important in school improvement and development, and ESR will play a complementary role to SSE and to facilitate SSE in a more focused manner and alleviate teachers' workload. In line with the spirit of embedding SSE in ongoing school practice and encouraging schools to take greater responsibility for continuous development, the EDB will conduct ESR in a school-specific and focused mode, putting emphasis on how schools apply the PIE exercise in SSE to identify and meet their specific needs.

To successfully institutionalize a self-renewal framework in daily managerial practices as well as to lead and manage change effectively, the leader needs to: (1) acquire appropriate knowledge and understanding of the theoretical framework and concept of SSE, (2) develop and acquire the necessary skills and attitudes for self-evaluation and manipulation of performance indicators, (3) think through the leadership role as a guide to action; and (4) clarify for themselves the strategic elements that are essential for an effective implementation of the school development plan (Gamage and Pang, 2003). Then, the principal should examine the types of knowledge, kinds of skills, and the attitudes needed for successful implementation of organizational change.

Research into the effectiveness of the SDA Framework

After implementing the SDA Framework in Hong Kong schools for nearly ten years, the author conducted qualitative research, soliciting the school leaders' views of the effectiveness of the SDA Framework and exploring possibilities of professional development for school leaders in Hong Kong schools. A sample of 10 schools was randomly selected for this qualitative research project, along with 18 school leaders, including school managers, principals, vice-principals, and senior teachers. They were invited to a focus group discussion and to respond to a protocol linked to the research questions (see Box 8.1). The respondents' views and opinions, were collected, summarized, transcribed, and subsequently analyzed. The following sections summarize findings, which are categorized into themes, such as (1) the factors that hindered the effective implementation of the SDA Framework in Hong Kong both at the education system level and the school organizational level, as well as (2) the factors that facilitated the effective implementation of the SDA Framework, respectively at the system level and the school level.

Findings show that most school leaders had positive views of the SDA Framework and got used to the cyclical practice of SSE and ESR. In terms of effectiveness, most school leaders agreed that the SDA Framework and the developed tools for evaluation have helped schools to build a culture of questing for quality, to find out their strengths and weaknesses, and to redefine schools' aims and visions, as well as the directions and action plans in school development. Though many school leaders agreed that the SDA does have an accountability function, the accountability system was not well and clearly defined within the school level or at the system level.

Factors that hindered the implementation of the SDA Framework

Generally, most principals opined that the SDA Framework had initially not been the normal practice in schools and it was, to them, a new and innovative concept when introduced. They thought that since the implementation of the SDA Framework involved a paradigm shift in school management and

> **Box 8.1** The protocol for interviewing the school leaders
>
> **What have been the impacts of the SDA Framework on your school?**
>
> On June 12, 2003, the permanent secretary for the Education and Manpower Bureau stipulated a circular (No. 23/2003), entitled *Enhancing School Development and Accountability (SDA) through School Self-evaluation and External School Review*, and sent to all schools to mandate that they carry out SSE to assess their own performance, with the aid of some measurement tools such as the framework of performance indicators (PIs) for Hong Kong schools, stakeholders' questionnaires to teachers, students, and parents, key performance measures (KPMs), and the Assessment Program for Affective and Social Outcomes (APASO), and to prepare for ESR.
>
> Q1. Has your school undergone the second cycle of the SDA Framework? If no, when will your school be under the next ESR? What are your feelings and views now, being a staff member of your school?
> Q2. Has your school undergone the process of ESR in the first cycle? If yes! What were your feelings and views before and during the review process?
> Q3. What are/have been the positive and negative effects of the SSE process on your school?
> Q4. What are/have been the positive and negative effects of the ESR process on your school?
> Q5. What are your views of the development of the SDA Framework in Hong Kong in the near future? What would you like to suggest to the EDB?

change of practices in normal school lives for all teachers, external support including financial resources, staff development programs, and in-house and consultancy services should be provided. In addition, most principals would like the SDA Framework to be implemented phase by phase, thus giving them more time and space to acquire new knowledge and skills in the matter. They reported that in the turbulent school environment where there were already many school reforms and innovations, further introduction of new concepts, such as school self-evaluation and external school review would inevitably lead to resistance. There were many specific factors that hindered the implementation of the SDA Framework in Hong Kong schools. These are summarized and classified below.

Hindrances at the system level

A loosely coupled system. The Hong Kong education system is loosely coupled. About 85 percent of schools in Hong Kong are aided schools, 5 percent are government schools, and 10 percent are private schools. While aided schools receive financial support from the government, they have their own school sponsoring bodies and management committees. Aided schools, by comparison with government schools, have greater autonomy and discretion to respond to requests for change and the implementation of education policies by the EDB. That is, resistance to change in the Hong Kong education system is perhaps much greater than that in education systems in other countries, where the state or government schools form the largest sector.

A too ambitious plan. There are approximately 1,200 primary and secondary schools in the Hong Kong education system. Conducting whole-school territory-wide inspections within a few short years was an unrealistic plan. Expecting most schools to be self-reliant in conducting self-evaluation and responding to external school review and to be able to raise their capacity for change within a year or so was again impractical and unattainable, especially at a time when the government was under great financial constraints and there has been a tremendous drop in the student population.

Too many existing reforms. There have been many new reform proposals for the education system in Hong Kong in the twenty-first century, in addition to those left over from the last decade. For the most part, implementation of these reforms and policies was attempted without good planning and coordination. Schools have been suffering from the great burdens and confusion arisen from these reforms (Law, 2003). Any introduction of new reforms and programs in schools would cause at best indifference and perhaps resistance, because of tremendous pressure and workloads already existing in schools.

Both SSE and ESR are complex processes. The implementation of the SDA Framework involves a change of school culture and a change of general practices in school lives. Such changes cannot be achieved only by directives issued by the education authority but need a well-planned, bottom-up strategy of initiation, which needs extra resources and supports from external sources.

At the shrinkage of the school system. Effective implementation of new reforms or initiatives needs a stable environment and extra resources and support. There has been a tremendous drop in student population since the Asian financial storm in 1998 and a number of schools have been urged to close down because of insufficient enrolment.

Hindrances at the school level

Implementation of the SDA Framework at the school level is not an easy task, given the present turbulent environment. Based on the research, the author was able to identify some factors that hindered the effective implementation of the SDA Framework. These factors are worthy of the special attention of school leaders and administrators in Hong Kong, though they are also of interested to policymakers and school practitioners in other contexts.

1. The plurality of categories of stakeholders and the diversity of views and opinions in schools might lead to many excellent reforms being opposed.
2. Past failed experience in the implementation of educational policy caused schools to take a passive approach to educational reforms.
3. Schools are inevitably political arenas and power struggles are common. These create resistance to educational change in the schools.
4. School leaders and the teachers in some schools might be embroiled in conflicts, which caused tensions, fears, and low morale among teachers, not conducive to introspection (Lee and Pang, 2011).
5. The communication breakdown between teachers and administrators found in some schools resulted in a very weak basis for professional collaboration and commitment (Lam and Pang, 2003; Pang 2007).
6. Some teachers and principals had little knowledge of or skills in SSE, and misconception of the SDA Framework was common.
7. There were no guidelines and criteria for measuring success that were commonly agreed for use in evaluation.
8. Most schools were either passive or reactive against change and there was a limited culture of organizational learning in schools (Pang, 2006b; Pang and Cheung, 2004).

Factors that facilitated the implementation of the SDA Framework

Though there is a predominance of factors that have hindered the effective implementation of the SDA Framework in Hong Kong schools, there are a few factors, at both the system level and the school level, that have facilitated the implementation of the SDA Framework at the school level.

Facilitators at the system level

A leaner, flatter governance structure of the central education authority. Based on the recommendations of the report on the review of the Education Department (Education and Manpower Bureau, 1998), the Hong Kong government successfully merged the Education and Manpower Bureau (EMB) with the Education Department (ED) in 2002. The governance and ruling structure for the school education system has changed from a three-tier structure (EMB-ED-Schools) to a two-tier structure (EMB-Schools). The interdependence between policymaking and policy implementation has been strengthened and reconciled the hindrance from a decoupled school education system. The central educational authority is now more interactive, and responsive to addressing the problems and difficulties that arise during the implementation of the SDA Framework.

An evolving model of quality assurance. The SDA Framework has been evolving in order to meet new needs of schools in the ever-changing external environment. The ESR procedures have been streamlined and they focus on how schools make use of the process of PIE for sustained development and self-improvement in the SSE cycle. Starting from the second term of the 2008/09 school year, ESR continues to be improvement oriented and is conducted in a school-specific and focused mode. Likewise, to facilitate SSE in a more focused manner and alleviate teachers' workload, the tools for the SDA Framework have been revised, based on the principles of simplification, reorganization, and refinement (Education Bureau, 2012b). The SDA Framework stresses the internal mechanism more than the external one and more resources have been put into the promotion of SSE.

Availability of tools for self-evaluation. After completing the first cycle of quality assurance in 1998, the revised Education Bureau has been successful in developing some sets of tools for schools' use in self-evaluation. These tools include performance indicators and key performance measures in the domains of management and organization, teaching and learning, school support and ethos, and academic and non-academic outcomes (Quality Assurance Division, 2002, 2008). They provide a balanced coverage and a common platform for assessment of different aspects of schoolwork and student performance for SSE and ESR and have built territory-wide norms against which school performance can be compared and assessed. Stakeholder questionnaires for teachers, pupils, and parents, and other tools in the social and affective domains for student well-being have also been developed for use in SSE, and schools are allowed to choose the relevant indicators for their own needs and uses.

Facilitators at the school organizational level

Some schools in Hong Kong successfully created a culture of self-evaluation and organizational change (MacBeath, 2008). The Quality Assurance and School-based Support Division of Education Bureau has provided guidance and essential supports over the years for school development, which has facilitated the implementation of the SDA Framework in these schools and enhanced their transformation into learning organizations. Factors that facilitated the implementation of the SDA Framework in these schools are summarized as below.

A transformational leadership. There was a transformational leadership in the schools that succeeded in implementing the SDA Framework and initiating organizational change. A transformational leader is a prerequisite for effective management of organizational changes. Some organizational components have a limiting influence on other organizational components because of the presence of multiple and often conflicting goals. The success in achieving effective organizational change in these schools was due to a transformational leadership that eliminated these tensions by deciding upon unified goals and clarifying technology (Bass and Riggio, 2006).

Shared values and missions. There were extensive commonly shared values among the staff members in the schools that successfully implemented the SDA framework. There were clearly stated school aims and missions, which were widely recognized by most teachers. Sharing values is the one fundamental basic that holds staff together and unified when faced with changes in short-term and long-term goals and visions (Pang and Wang, 2012). If organizations are determinate means-ends structures for attaining preferred outcomes, then agreement about preferences is the only source of order that is left.

Focused attention. There was special attention to human relations in the management system in the schools that had successfully implemented the SDA framework. Small step strategies within a confused, turbulent, and ever-changing environment may produce more effective, efficient, interesting, varied, and thoughtful organizational changes (Pang and Pisapia, 2012). Leaders in these schools compensated for multiple and conflicting goals by carefully selecting targets, controlling resources, and acting forcefully.

Good team spirit, high staff morale, and a strong sense of professionalism. The very successful schools in the implementation of the SDA Framework possessed a very strong teaching force that had good team spirit and high staff morale, as well as a strong sense of professionalism. The formation of the strong and professional teaching force was not an accident but the result of deliberate and careful selection during the recruitment of personnel (Pang, 2004). High teacher morale and strong team spirit were also the outcomes of the transformational leadership and effective management systems in the schools.

The above findings into the effectiveness of implementing the SDA Framework in schools and the factors that hindered and facilitated organizational change shed light on how school administrators can lead and manage organizational change for a school's continuous development and improvement, the details of which are delineated in the following sections.

Exploring possibilities of educational leadership in managing change in school

The main concern for organizational change is the social system of the organization, rather than task, technology, or structural dimensions (Gamage and Pang, 2003). In a social organization, it is the role of an effective leader to work with and through individual staff members and groups, towards achieving the goals of the organization. Involving staff members in identifying organizational problems is a complex task. It is difficult to act on a single front, so an integrated agenda for change is needed. For these reasons, a 'cocktail' approach to leading and managing change is proposed for the consideration of educational administrators and leaders (Gamage and Pang, 2003). In facilitating organizational change, a school leader needs to focus on flexibly and contingently mixing the following ten strategies: (1) create an appropriate climate for change; (2) adopt an appropriate leadership style for change; (3) share power and encourage participation in decision-making; (4) build a school-wide vision; (5) share values and culture building; (6) adopt a Kaizen approach to change; (7) continue professional development for teachers and principals; (8) use external consultancy services; (9) make reference to organizational research and theories; and (10) evaluate the progress of change.

Creating an appropriate climate for change

First, the leader needs to create an appropriate climate, where trust and confidence prevails. In preparing the ground for change, threat and fear need to be removed; communication should be made more effective, by increasing lateral communication by encouraging staff to express their ideas and opinions frankly. Staff energy and effort should also be channeled towards school goals through collegiality, since this breaks down barriers between departments and between teachers and administrators, encourages the kind of intellectual sharing that can lead to consensus, and promotes feelings of unity and commonality among the staff (Pang, 2010; Pang and Pisapia, 2012).

Adopting an appropriate leadership style for change

In school organizations, leaders should make use of different leadership styles in leading and managing change, e.g., transformational leadership (Bass and Riggio, 2006), cultural leadership (Cunningham, and Gresso, 1993; Driskill, and Brenton, 2011), or distributed leadership (Leithwood *et al.*, 2009; Spillane, 2006). The adoption of a certain leadership style is surely artistic and context-specific (Yukl, 2010). School leaders may consider the following views of leadership styles useful and helpful when adopting one, respective to their specific organizational contexts and the characteristics of subordinates. Classical organization (mechanistic, bureaucratic) theory tends to view leadership as largely a matter of hierarchical power over subordinates and almost wholly concerned with getting the task accomplished. In a human relations approach, leadership is an interaction between the leader and others in the group, which helps the social system to maintain itself (cohesiveness, productive group norms) and achieves the group's goal. Behavioral views generally accept that effective leaders exhibit high task-oriented and relationship-oriented behaviors. Contingency views of leadership posit that there is no single, 'best' leadership style suitable to all situations, and the criterion for leader effectiveness is the success of the organization or group in leading and managing change and in achieving its goals.

Sharing of power and participation in decision-making

School leaders should create an administrative environment that is democratic and open, in which the sharing of power and decision-making should be stressed. School leaders should encourage a high degree of cooperation among teachers and administrators and provide constructive feedback to each other. Teachers should be allowed to suggest the areas in which the school will be evaluated and to meet on a regular basis to learn from each other and to share their knowledge and experiences (Shapiro and Stefkovich, 2011). A kind of intellectual and power sharing, when created, will lead to consensus and will promote feelings of unity and commonality among the staff. It will help to break barriers between departments and among teachers and administrators and to reduce resistance to educational change.

Building a school-wide vision

A vision is 'what we are working towards?' and it gives direction to school development. It is hard for staff to pull together if there is no agreement as to which direction everyone wants to go in. A coherent vision specifies the particular values and beliefs that will guide policy and practice within the school. Not only does a school-wide vision give a school a direction for change, but also the excitement of trying something new. A school-wide and shared vision gives people the incentive to start and an impetus to sustain themselves in the early stages of educational change (Kowalski, 2010). It is important that schools not simply work on and then arrive at their collective vision. When the excitement brought by a collective vision begins to wane, schools need a larger vision to keep teachers motivated and excited.

Sharing of values and culture building

Organizational culture and the problem of change are highly associated. There have been lucid and persuasive discussions on the necessity for finding ways of altering the patterns of activities, group norms, and the temporal qualities that are characteristic of state schools, before we can initiate desirable educational change. Successful leaders should view their organizations' environment in a holistic way, that is, with a cultural perspective. An understanding of the school culture will give school leaders a broader framework for understanding difficult problems and complex relationships within the school and enable them to shape the values, beliefs, and attitudes that are necessary in the process of educational change and to nurture a learning environment (Schein, 2004). Definitions of organizational culture generally include references to shared values. The trappings of culture, the rituals, the stories, the myths, and the heroes are the expression of shared organizational values. The school leader who is able to adapt a vision to new challenges and share values with staff members will be more successful in building strong school cultures and achieving their goals in educational change.

Adopting a Kaizen approach to change

Masaaki Imai (1986) provides a general comparison of classification of change between Western ideas of large-scale 'innovation' and the Japanese notion of Kaizen or 'continuous improvement.' Kaizen improvement is quite different from innovation, the form of improvement that most Western policymakers are most familiar with. Innovation implies significant breakthrough and progress by only a limited number of trained professionals. Kaizen, by contrast, means a continual and gradual accumulation of small improvements made by all employees. To most Japanese, Kaizen means "the daily struggles on the job." (Japan Human Relations Association, 1992: 4) Whilst changes brought about by an innovation approach are fast, changes due to an improvement approach are quite slow. When educational reforms are introduced as innovations, they are usually dramatic, big-step-forward, intermittent, non-incremental, abrupt, and volatile. When educational reforms are introduced as improvements, they are usually long-term, long lasting, un-dramatic, small-step-forward, continuous, incremental, graduated, and constant (Pang, 1998).

Continuing professional development for teachers and principals

Both teachers and principals are the key to educational quality and excellence. Educational reforms always call for changes in learning processes, teaching strategies, and ways of managing schools. The quality of the teaching staff and school leadership is pivotal to bringing all these changes into reality (Harris and Jones, 2010). It is only through continuing professional development that encourages both principals and teachers to strive to further enhance school professionalism and leadership. Continuing professional development with updated and appropriate training programs allows schools' personnel to equip and develop themselves with the necessary knowledge, skills, and attitudes to become competent and confident in tackling the challenges arising from educational change (Education Department, 2002).

Inviting external consultancy

Even in instances where the leader is highly skilled, when sorting out difficult and complex problems it can be more appropriate to work with a consultant, who, ostensibly, has a neutral approach towards the staff and the organization. In the process of change, outside experts can provide consultancy, guide idea formulation, and offer temporary inputs of aid (Tsui *et al.*,

2010). In taking a problem-solving approach, the leader should not believe that engaging the services of a consultant is an admission of weakness. A leader, who identifies the strengths and weaknesses of an organization and engages the services of outside specialists, is creating opportunities for themselves to exercise more powerful leadership behaviours (Gamage and Pang, 2003).

Making reference to organizational research and theories

The ultimate objective of all scientific endeavors is to develop a body of substantive theory. Organizational theories are developed to explain the structure and dynamics of organizations and the roles of the individual in organizations. We surely need organizational theory to improve practices in organizations, because theories can help practitioners to describe and explain the regular behavior of individuals and groups within organizations and provide basic principles that provide a general understanding of structure and dynamics of organizational life. Making reference to organizational theories can directly benefit school practitioners in facing educational change at least in two ways: (1) to provide a general mode of analysis of the change and (2) to provide a frame of reference for decision making and developing alternative solutions to problem solving created in different phases of change (Hoy and Miskel, 2008).

Evaluation of the progress of change

The mechanism by which an organization translates its vision and values into reality will determine its long-term health. When adopting an integrated approach to change, the progress of change should be evaluated against performance and outcomes to ascertain whether it is running to plan (Kehoe, 2007). Organizational members need to develop their skills, knowledge, and behaviors continuously in order to cope with the demands at different phases of the change. When there are deviations and failures, the leader should take immediate action to amend and adjust the course of change, minimize wastage of human and financial resources, and put the change process back on a right and reasonable track (Gamage and Pang, 2003).

Conclusion

Evidence-based organizational change has become a very recent trend in the school reform and improvement movement, and the implementation of the SDA Framework in Hong Kong schools since 2003 is a case in point. The SDA Framework emphasizes the practice of SSE that allows school leaders to institutionalize a self-renewal strategy for daily managerial practices as well as to lead and manage change. ESR emphasizes how schools apply the PIE cycle in SSE to identify and meet their specific needs and facilitates SSE in a more focused manner. Ultimately, teachers' workload is alleviated. Owing to various hindrances at both the education system level and the school organizational level, the implementation of the SDA Framework may not be very successful in some Hong Kong schools. Nevertheless, the practical experience gained from some successful schools can shed light for other schools to transform into learning organizations through the implementation of the SDA Framework.

Beer and Nohria (2000) have suggested that a combination of Theory E and Theory O is more likely to produce better results in organizational change. Should ESR be implemented as a successful territory-wide educational policy, that is, adopting Theory E of change, the factors that hinder the effective implementation of the SDA Framework at the education system levels should be addressed. If Theory O of change is adopted, that is, to enhance schools' capacity of change at the organizational level, school leaders are urged to pay more attention to the hindrances found in this study. When the SDA Framework has been successfully institutionalized within the daily managerial practices, the school leader will be more able to initiate, lead, and manage organizational change effectively and efficiently.

In order to facilitate school change, administrators should have transformational leadership that: unifies the school's goals and clarifies the technology for achieving them; promotes the sharing of values among all members; and focuses attention by carefully selecting targets, controlling resources, and acting forcefully. Not only do good team spirit, high staff morale, and a strong sense of professionalism form the crucial basis for change, but they also help reduce the resistance to change. Since change is a complex and dynamic process and it is difficult for school leaders to act on a single front to initiate change, it is suggested that a 'cocktail' approach in educational leadership should be adopted to overcome the resistance during the change process. Among others, these approaches in leading and managing change include the ten possibilities mentioned above. Effective school leaders in Hong Kong are those who can adopt these approaches to change flexibly by coping with the requirements from the restructuring of the school accountability system since 2003, as well as challenges arising from the ever-changing external environment.

References

Bass, B.M. and Riggio, R.E. (2006). *Transformational Leadership* (2nd edn). Mahwah, N.J.: L. Erlbaum Associates.

Beer, M. and Nohria, N. (2000). Resolving the tension between Theories E and O of change. In M. Beer and N. Nohria (eds). *Breaking the Code of Change* (pp. 1–34). Boston, Mass.: Harvard Business School Press.

Cunningham, W.G. and Gresso, D.W. (1993). *Cultural Leadership: The Culture of Excellence in Education*. Boston: Allyn & Bacon.

Cuttance, P.F. (1994). Monitoring educational quality through performance indicators for school practice. *School Effectiveness and School Improvement*, 5(2), 101–126.
Driskill, G.W. and Brenton, A.L. (2011). *Organizational culture in action: A cultural analysis workbook* (2nd edn). Thousand Oaks, CA: SAGE.
Education and Manpower Bureau (1998). *Review of the Education Department*. Hong Kong: The Government Printer.
Education and Manpower Bureau (2002). *Education Statistics*. Hong Kong: The Printing Department.
Education and Manpower Bureau (2003). *Enhancing School Development and Accountability Through School Self-Evaluation and External School Review*. EMB Circular No. 23/2003. June 12.
Education Bureau (2012a). *External School Review: Information for Schools*. Hong Kong: Quality Assurance and School-based Support Division, Education Bureau.
Education Bureau (2012b). *Memorandum on SSE and ESR*. Available at www.edb.gov.hk/FileManager/EN/Content_6459/memorandum_on_sse_esr_e.pdf.
Education Commission (1997). *Education Commission Report No. 7: Quality School Education*. Hong Kong: The Printing Department.
Education Department (2002). *Continuing Professional Development for School Excellence*. Hong Kong: The Printing Department.
Gamage, D.T. and Pang, N.S.K. (2003). *Leadership and Management in Education: Developing Essential Skills and Competencies*. Hong Kong: The Chinese University Press.
Gamage, D.T. and Pang, N.S.K. (2006). Facing the challenges of the 21st century: Preparation of school leaders in Australia and Hong Kong. *Educational Research Journal*, 21(1), 21–46.
Harris, A. and Jones, M. (2010). Professional learning communities and system improvement. *Improving Schools*, 13(2), 172–181.
Hoy, W.K. and Miskel, C.G. (2008). *Educational administration: Theory, Research and Practice*. Boston, MA: McGraw-Hill.
Imai, M. (1986). *Kaizen: the Key to Japan's Competitive Success*. New York: Random House.
Japan Human Relations Association (1992). *Kaizen Teian 1: Developing Systems for Continuous Improvement Through Employee Suggestions*. Cambridge: Productivity Press.
Kehoe, D. (2007). *Leading and Managing Change: 25 Action-Based Articles Showing How to Lead and Manage Change*. North Ryde, NSW: McGraw-Hill.
Kowalski, T. J. (2010). *The School Principal: Visionary Leadership and Competent Management*. New York, NY: Routledge.
Lam, Y.L.J. and Pang, S.K.N. (2003). The relative effects of environmental, internal and contextual factors on organizational learning: the case of Hong Kong schools under reform. *The Learning Organization: An International Journal*, 10(2), 83–97.
Law, W.W. (2003). Globalization as both threats and opportunity for the Hong Kong teaching profession. *Journal of Educational Change*, 4(2), 149–179.
Lee, J.C.K. and Pang, N.S.K. (2011). Educational leadership in China: Contexts and issues. *Frontiers of Education in China*, 6(3), 331–341.
Leithwood, K., Mascall, B., and Strauss, T. (eds) (2009). Distributed leadership according to the evidence. New York: Routledge.

MacBeath, J. (2008). *The Impact Study on the Effectiveness of External School Review in Enhancing School Improvement Through School Self-Evaluation in Hong Kong: Final Report.* Hong Kong Quality Assurance Division, Education Bureau.

Macbeath, J., Schratz, M., Meuret, D., and Jakobsen, L. (2000). *Self-evaluation in European Schools: A Story of Change.* London: Routledge/Falmer.

Pang, N.S.K. (1998). Should quality school education be a Kaizen (improvement) or an innovation? *International Journal of Educational Reform,* 7(1), 2–12.

Pang, N.S.K. (2004). The effects of schools on teachers' feelings about school life: A multilevel analysis. *Hong Kong Teachers' Centre Journal,* 2, 64–84.

Pang, N.S.K. (2006a). Managing school change through self-evaluation in the era of globalization. In N.S.K. Pang (ed.) *Globalization: Educational Research, Change and Reforms* (pp. 293–313). Hong Kong: The Chinese University Press, the Hong Kong Educational Research Association and the Hong Kong Institute of Educational Research.

Pang, N.S.K. (2006b). Schools as Learning Organizations. In J.C.K. Lee, and M. Williams (eds) *School Improvement: International Perspectives* (pp. 65–86). New York: Nova Science Publishers Inc.

Pang, N.S.K. (2007). The continuing professional development of principals in Hong Kong SAR, China. *Frontiers of Education in China,* 2(4), 605–619.

Pang, N.S.K. (2010). Leadership forces in Hong Kong secondary schools. *School Leadership & Management,* 30(4), 351–365.

Pang, N.S.K. and Cheung, M. (2004). Learning capacity of primary schools in Hong Kong. In J. Lee, L. Lo and A. Walker (eds) *Partnership and change: Towards school development* (pp. 269–294). Hong Kong: the Hong Kong Institute of Educational Research and the Chinese University Press.

Pang, N.S.K. and Pisapia, J. (2012). The strategic thinking skills of Hong Kong school leaders: Usage and effectiveness. *Educational Management, Administration & Leadership,* 40(3), 343–361.

Pang, N.S.K. and Wang, T. (2012). Institutions' espoused values perceived by Chinese educational leaders. In N. Popov, C. Wolhuter, B. Leutwyler, G. Hilton, J. Ogunleye, and P.A. Almeida (eds) *International Perspectives on Education* (pp. 175–181). Bulgaria: Bulgarian Comparative Education Society (BCES).

Pang, N.S.K., MacBeath, J., and McGlynn, A. (2004). *Self-Evaluation and School Development.* School Education Reform Series No.19. Hong Kong: The Faculty of Education of the Chinese University of Hong Kong and Hong Kong Institute of Educational Research.

Quality Assurance Division (2002). *Performance Indicators for Hong Kong Schools.* Hong Kong: Quality Assurance Division, Education Department.

Quality Assurance Division (2008). *Performance Indicators for Hong Kong Schools with Evidence of Performance.* Hong Kong: Quality Assurance Division, Education Bureau.

Schein, E.H. (2004). *Organizational Culture and Leadership* (3rd edn). San Francisco: Jossey-Bass.

Scottish Office (2002). *How Good is Our School? Self-Evaluation Using Performance Indicators.* Edinburgh: the Scottish Office of Education and Industry Department.

Shapiro, J.P. and Stefkovich, J.A. (2011). *Ethical Leadership and Decision Making in Education: Applying Theoretical Perspectives to Complex Dilemmas* (3rd edn). New York: Routledge.

Spillane, J.P. (2006). *Distributed Leadership*. San Francisco: Jossey-Bass.
Tsui, A., Edwards, G., Lopez-Real. F., and Kwan, T. (2010). *Learning in School-University Partnership: Sociocultural Perspectives*. New York: Routledge.
Yukl, G. (2010). *Leadership in Organizations* (7th edn). Upper Saddle River, NJ: Prentice Hall.

9 School education and accountability in India
Mapping current policies and practices

Pranati Panda

With the expansion of globalization, marketization, and quality-driven reforms, there has been a shift towards a quest for excellence, accountability, and leadership in the education sector around the globe. Over the last two decades, low- and middle-income developing countries have increasingly invested in education as a mechanism for national development. Consequently, efforts for improving schools have taken center stage – increasing quality, access, enrollment, and equity.

School enrollment rates across South Asian countries at the primary level reached roughly 90 percent in 2011, witnessing a steep rise from 75 percent in 2000 (UNESCO, 2014). Though there is an increase in the percentage of school enrollment in the region, an analysis of household surveys showed that still a total of 27 million children (about 1.6 percent of the total population of South Asia) are out of school in Bangladesh, India, Pakistan, and Sri Lanka (UNESCO, 2014). This includes 17 million children of primary and 9.9 million children of lower secondary school age. In spite of a global commitment through initiatives like Education for All and the Millennium Development Goals by UNESCO in 1990 and 2000, respectively, developing countries are still grappling with the problem of out-of-school children and improving the level of learning of children who attend school. Similarly, a focus on human capital as a driver of economic growth for developing countries (Hanushek, 2013), by and large, does not seem to have improved educational quality. On the contrary, evidence is mounting that the level of learning is stagnating across school systems in developing countries (Pritchett and Banerji, 2013). Hence, the focus is to achieve universalization of quality education, which is a multifaceted and multidimensional notion. It ranges from extending access, reducing dropout, bridging gender disparity, improving learning attainment, and overall improvement of educational quality. According to Krishnaratne *et al.* (2013: 3):

> The international community has focused predominately on getting children into school. However, it is just as important to ensure that children are able to learn and acquire new skills when they do enter classrooms. Yet the quality of education in many schools is unacceptably

poor, and many children are leaving primary school without even basic reading, writing or numeracy skills.

This position underscores the importance of efforts in developing countries to both enhance resources and to address the weakness of the school system. Many developed countries have developed accountability and leadership standards and frameworks to lead the change process in the school education sector. The *World Development Report* 2004 (World Bank, 2004) recognized weak accountability frameworks as leading to poor motivation and inadequate incentivization for performance in many developing countries. However, while still not large, there has been a sizable amount of accountability-oriented reforms in the developing countries. In many instances, these reforms have been or are being evaluated. These reforms include different approaches (Bruns *et al.*, 2011). The *Global Initiatives* UNESCO report (2014) considers accountability as one of the important concerns linked to improving the quality of teaching and learning in school.

Context and purpose of school education in India

India, often characterized as having one of the longest continuums of cultures, values education as central to human development. The dynamics of education as a system are considered a powerful means for social change and nation-building. The purpose of education has strong historical roots. Steeped in Indian tradition, educational institutions were considered to be "temples of learning." In the ancient Indian education system, the "guru" (teacher) was the institutional answer for a socio-philosophical-historical context. Great importance was attached to the teachers in the ancient system of education. The guru was a person totally dedicated to the transmission of knowledge. The "*Gurukula* system" (a traditional institution of learning; etymologically G*urukula* means family of the *guru*) usually consisted of the teacher and the disciple living together in a common quest for spiritual bliss. There are two major characteristics of the pre-colonial period which are still relevant in the contemporary context: first, the accountability of the teacher; and second, the support, participation, and ownership of the community in matters of school education.

The subsequent colonial legacy of education brought significant changes. In short, the pre-independence education policy can be seen as a shift towards forming "good" citizens of the British Empire; central policy documents and reports on this matter are Thomas Babington Macaulay's *Minute on Indian Education* (1835), Wood's *Despatch* (1854), and the Sargent Report (Sargent Committee, 1944). Wood's *Despatch* (1854) was considered as the landmark development in the effort to spread English education and European knowledge, and to teach science. During this period, the state managed school system implemented a western style curricula, inspections, and examinations system. The responsibility of the state and the external evaluation of schools by inspectors became mainstreamed. The skills of the teachers, however, left much to be desired. The school system in independent India witnessed a political and constitutional commitment towards free and compulsory education and a move towards an expansionist approach, retaining many of its colonial characteristics.

Modern Indian thinkers have also had a significant influence on education and its purpose. In fact, the auspices the Indian education in the twentieth century is steeped in Mahatma Gandhi's (1937: 19) belief, "by education I mean an all-around drawing out of the best in child and man – body, mind and spirit." Patel (1953: 25) states:

> According to Gandhiji, if education is to fit the future citizen for playing its role in society, he should cultivate in school the character appropriate to a social being. He must be trained for his life. He must have an opportunity to practice civic virtues at school.

India, as a democratic country, has prioritized education within the political agenda since the adoption of the constitution of India in 1950. The strategic committees and commission reports on education in post-independent India demonstrated high aspirations regarding the role of education and the purpose of schooling for national development. One of the historic documents, *Education and National Development*, made the statement that "the destiny of India is now being shaped in her classrooms," (Government of India, 1966: 1) thus, placing the school as an institution of learning at the center stage.

Two National Policies on Education (NPE) (Government of India, 1968, 1986) have influenced the education system in India to a large extent through different schemes and programs of the government. The NPE (1986) states, "In our national perception, education is essential for all." (Government of India, 1986: 4) Three major initiatives towards reform in school education were institutionalized: (1) a national system of education based on a common educational structure (10+2+3, consisting of the first twelve years of school followed by three years of university), (2) a national curriculum framework, and (3) minimum levels of learning (MLL) standards.

The Indian school system is one of the largest and rapidly expanding school systems in the world. Since 1947, the narrative regarding the development of education in society has been very complex and indicative of the momentum towards massification, with a focus on equity and quality. According to the Unified District Information System for Education (U-DISE, 2013–2014), government maintained schools in India have grown significantly, from 23,000 in 1950 to all schools in 2014. The share of private school providers, currently at 18.76 percent (U-DISE, 2012–2013), is also growing immensely. The school system in India is witnessing increasing diversity among the student populations belonging to constitutionally recognized scheduled castes, scheduled tribes, and groups within castes that are officially considered to belong to disadvantaged sections of society. Even still, the path to achieving equitable education for all children in India is further challenged by the complexity of diversified contexts (rural, urban, and tribal), composition of schools (large and small) and structural conditions (provisioning relating to infrastructure, teacher quality, and other facilities in the school). Today, India employs more than 7 million teachers spread over more than 1.5 million schools to educate more than 200 million children (U-DISE, 2013–2014).

According to a study by the Public Affairs Centre in Bangalore (2007), as many as 76 percent of rural households send their children to government- or government-aided schools in India. This achievement, however, has not been accompanied by corresponding efforts towards improving staffing, maintenance quality, and learning attainment. Schools in India are constrained partly by an inadequate physical infrastructure, but also in terms of teachers' skills and motivation (PROBE, 1999). While India has made tremendous progress in enhancing schooling opportunities during the past six decades, regional, gender, and social disparities persist. According to ranking by the Education for all Development Index (EDI) (as cited by UNESCO, 2005), India is the 106th out of 127 countries in the low category. The EDI ranking of India is not much higher than that of other South Asian countries such as Bangladesh (107), Nepal (110), and Pakistan (123).

India has been flooded with reforms and policies over the last several decades with more emphasis on universalizing elementary education and up-scaling of secondary education for all children. In the contemporary policy regime, central government initiatives like Sarva Shiksha Abhiyan (SSA; or The Education for All Movement) and Rastriya Madhyamik Shiksha Abhiyan (RMSA; or National Mission for Secondary Education) are aimed at improving school performance (among other things). National Curriculum Frameworks (NCFs) (NCERT, 2000, 2005, 2009), both in school and teacher education, have placed schooling as a key driver for realizing students' potential. These frameworks are considered vital to bring change and improvement in the schooling practices in India. The NCF of 2000 states that "School education in recent times has emerged as an important segment of the total education system expected to contribute significantly to the individual as well as the national development processes." (NCERT, 2000: 4)

It is strongly believed and pronounced in various policy documents that school, as an institution, should be able to translate the national aspiration to build an equitable and inclusive society into action and that a quality of education can only be achieved through well-qualified teachers working in a high-accountability context. While acknowledging this, the NCF of 2005 (NCERT, 2005: 2) critiques the current state of affairs:

> Schools promote a regime of thoughts that discourages creative thinking and insights. The "future" of the child has taken center stage at the cost of the near exclusion of the child's "present," which is detrimental to the well-being of the child as well as society and nation.

Accountability and responsibility in education

Accountability, responsibility, and leadership have been prominent features among the educational landscape and discourses internationally for the past several decades. According to Lasley (2012: 11), "Educational accountability is a complex and highly debated topic." Desai (2012), in his book on accountability entitled *Angst, Awareness, Action*, stresses the importance of accountability in driving (good) governance. While arguing about accountability as a social construct, Desai's (2009) research on the power of public accountability indicates that low literacy level and high social diversity should not be significant barriers to high public accountability in India. As such, accountability is a social practice, defined by distinctive relationships and evaluative procedures (Ranson, 2003). There have been observations that the Indian state, its institutions, and the rules that govern them, are structured to avoid accountability altogether (Mehta, 2003; Saxena 2004). The term is often used synonymously with concepts of transparency, liability, answerability, and other ideas associated with the expectations of account-giving (Levitt *et al.*, 2008).

The term accountability is derived from the term account, which entails giving a description or justification of an action. Conceptually, accountability and responsibility are used interchangeably in India. While responsibility connotes the allocation of defined tasks or roles assigned by the authority or the system, accountability is often considered to be similar to the allocation of responsibility. According to Tucker (2012: 4), "accountability requires that public servants have clear responsibilities and are held answerable in exercising those responsibilities, and if they do not, face predetermined sanctions." In the Indian context, accountability can be understood as a personal concept, with people feeling an intrinsic sense of responsibility for individual children. For example to give an account, as the root of accountability, is seen as less personal, a more systemic concept (Mongon and Chapman, 2012).

The NCF of 2000 emphasizes that the "quality of a school or educational system should, in the real sense, be defined in terms of the performance capabilities of its students and graduates." (NCERT, 2000: 24). Thus, results of students' assessments are can be taken as an indication of the quality of an education system. As Hanushek and Wößmann (2007: 72) observe, "Little evidence is currently available about accountability systems in developing countries. This reflects the generally weak accountability in these countries along with a general lack of systematic measurement and reporting of student achievement." Of the developing countries, India is not an exception. In fact, the term accountability is only vaguely used in the educational sector of India and thus is difficult to interpret and analyze. Ouston *et al.* (1998: 15) note that although the term is widely used elsewhere, as if it were straightforward, it must be viewed as vague and incoherent.

Facets of school accountability

Accountability is one of the concerns touched upon in the NPE (Government of India, 1986: 25), pointing out that "the country has placed boundless trust in the educational system. The people have a right to expect concrete results. The first task is to make it work. All teachers should teach and all students should study."

The management and governance of school education in India has witnessed two significant shifts: in 1976, the Constitution of India was amended to allow for the states to have a significant degree of influence on matters of education. Second, the 73rd and 74th constitutional amendments provided institutionalized space for the participation of local communities in matters of education.

School education is governed and managed by both the government and private institutions. The schools run by the central, state and local governments comprise a clear "government sector." However, the private sector consists of three types of schools: government-aided schools receive grants from the government but are managed by a private body; private, unaided schools receive government recognition based on certain criteria outlined by the government and follow certain regulations but receive no government grants; and unrecognized schools are not recognized by the government and do not receive any state grants. The NCF of 2005 (NCERT, 2005: 9), reflecting on the hierarchical nature of school education, stated that "schools ranges from high cost 'public' (private) schools, to which the urban elite send their children to the ostensibly 'free,' poorly functional local body run primary school[s] where children from hitherto educationally deprived communities predominate." In all, school education is currently confronted with multiple issues and challenges such as multilayered hierarchical schools in terms of context (rural, urban, tribal, remote areas etc.), size of the school (large and small), quality concerns, and learning deficits among the children, particularly at the elementary level.

Learners' assessment and school accountability

Potential links between learners' performance and school accountability are at the heart of a critical discourse on educational quality in India. The testing of learners' achievement and alignment with students' academic growth is seen as an important practice of a functioning system of school accountability. According to Bruns *et al.* (2011: 29), "countries are increasingly carrying out national learning assessments, and more countries are participating in the regionally and internationally benchedmarked learning assessments." In 2009, two Indian states participated in the Programme for International Student Assessment (PISA) and ranked second to last among the 73 countries. Relatedly, Bahadur (2013: 3) explains, "the role of assessments have [sic] been accepted as a major factor in shaping how students learn and this has received due attention in numerous school systems across the countries." The 2005 NCF (NCERT, 2005) focuses on teaching-learning processes, assessing learners, and learning outcomes in an integrative framework. It states, "a good evaluation and examination system can become an integral part of the learning process and benefit both the learners themselves and the education system by giving credible feedback." (NCERT, 2005: 71) Over time, India has instituted various measures relating to mapping learners performance, some of which are described below.

One measure consists of high-stakes public examinations at the end of grades X and XII; these are considered vital to the school education system in India. The public examination results are seen as indicative of learning outcomes and are valued by the system, parents, and children at large. The high-stake examination in India is often associated with stress and anxiety. It is considered a basic parameter for admission into higher and professional education. However, in all of this, the focus lies on student-level accountability. There is hardly any accountability for the schools as the institution of education. Second, India also conducts a national level learning assessment called the National Achievement Survey (NAS) at the end of grades III, V, and VIII. The NAS report (NCERT, 2014) indicated that there is a critical relationship between school-related factors like leadership and management, governance and infrastructure, and learners' achievement. Third, many states in India also carry out their own assessments. It is hopeful that one day these states will used these assessments to develop a more fine-grained understanding of the strengths and weaknesses of their students and to adjust teacher training and other programs accordingly.

Similar to the NAS, a non-governmental organization called Pratham launched the Annual Status of Education Report (ASER) in 2005. ASER is an annual survey that assesses the ability of children to read simple texts and to do basic arithmetic. ASER (2012: 1) found that "fewer and fewer children in successive batches reaching 3rd and 5th standard are learning basics of reading and math." In comparison to its first report in 2005, it found that the performance of children is diminishing.

School inspection and supervision

The practice of school inspection was established on the recommendation of Wood's *Despatch* (1854) in India. The current practices vary across the states and are based on management of objectives rather than providing academic support to the schools. Public Report on Basic Education (PROBE, 1999: 91) noted that "faced with this work overload, inspectors and their superiors concentrate on what they see as the priority, such as the maintenance of school registers. Once again, the quality of teaching is out of focus." A series of studies, conducted by the National University of Educational Planning and Administration (NUEPA) on school education administration (1973 to 1981 and 1991 to 2001) also point to inadequate school inspection and supervision practices. The current inspection practices are seen as lacking precise criteria of assessment, clear written instructions on the process of evaluation, as well as mechanisms to improve inspection practices; in addition, the inspection reports are not considered sufficiently transparent (Joseph, 2012).

One notable impediment is the high workload for many school inspectors, whose numbers are deemed inadequate to cover the schools in India (Joseph, 2012; World Bank, 2009). Unsurprisingly, the Rajasthan secondary school survey (2005) demonstrated an infrequency of school inspections. It also showed that district education officers and inspectors tend to focus on compliance with regard to rules and regulations rather than capacity-building. Teachers tend to discuss problems with their colleagues or principals, rather than with district education officers (World Bank, 2009). Thus, school inspections in India become mere exercises to comply with norms and regulations rather than impulses for school improvement. Making matters more challenging, inspectors were found to have varying criteria for inspection (Joseph, 2012). The National Knowledge Commission (NKC, 2008: 44) suggests that:

> The system of school inspection needs to be revamped and revitalised, with a greater role for local stakeholders and greater transparency in the system. The solution does not lie in simply expanding the system, rather we need to develop systems to ensure meaningful monitoring, including provision of greater facilities to school inspectors, a separation of inspection of qualitative and administrative aspects, transparency in the criteria of inspection, and greater involvement of local stakeholders.

School performance evaluation

Considering the current practice for school inspection as outdated and having limited impact on school improvement, many provinces in India have been shifting towards instituting school evaluation and accreditation to improve the quality of school education. However, the evaluation of school performance remains a challenging concern in India. The various school evaluation models practiced across different states can be grouped into two models: school accreditation and school quality improvement.

School accreditation. This approach bears similarities to the practices of higher education. Though there are no formal accreditation standards for schools in India, there are a few initiatives for school assessment and accreditation. The Quality Council of India (QCI), through the National Accreditation Board for Education and Training (NABET), developed the Accreditation Standards for Quality School Governance in 2008 to provide a framework for the effective management of schools and the delivery of a holistic education program. Standards focus on establishing systems to enable learning, self-development, and improved performance. The standards for accreditation encompass three domains: (1) school governance,

(2) education and support processes, and (3) performance measurement and improvement. There are 50 parameters, which are measured on a five-point scale. Compliance and effectiveness of the respective parameters are rated on the five-point scale ranging from 0 to 5. The accreditation process includes both a self-review and external review, comprising ten steps. The consolidated score of all the parameters is used to determine the level of a school. The Accreditation Standard for Quality School Governance tool is mainly used by Kendriya Vidyalayas and Navyoug Schools (which are funded and managed by the federal government). NABET school accreditation is valid for the period of four years, with yearly progress review visits conducted onsite by NABET. The school also submits annual accreditation fees.

The Central Board of Secondary Education (CBSE) developed the School Quality Assessment and Accreditation (SQAA) in 2013. The goal of SQAA is to ensure that schools meet prescribed standards set by the CBSE. The SQAA is a mandatory accreditation scheme for schools affiliated to the CBSE. It consists of 74 indicators in 7 domains relating to infrastructure, scholastic, co-scholastic, human resources, management and administration, leadership, and beneficiary satisfaction. The schools have to apply to CBSE and pay a fee for the accreditation process. The CBSE allots one of currently 12 empanelled private agencies for the accreditation on the ground. The SQAA accreditation is valid for three years. The CBSE accreditation process is mandatory, where as that from NABET is a voluntary choice. However, both accreditation processes are similar and largely external driven.

One of the Indian states, Karnataka, established the Karnataka School Quality Assessment and Accreditation Council (KSQAAC) in 2005 (originally under a different name). The major objectives of the council are to assess and accredit primary schools and high schools across the state, to stimulate the academic activities for promoting the quality of school and schooling processes, and to foster the collaboration among all stakeholders. The KSQAAC aims at assessing the schools in five areas: local environment, learning environment, leadership, community participation, and innovative activities. The KSQAAC accreditation process includes self-assessment by head teachers and teachers, as well as a peer assessment by external evaluators. The KSQAAC issues an accreditation certificate containing the grade a school attained in the accreditation process; the grade is valid for a period of five years. Table 9.1 provides a comparative picture of school accreditation practices among NABET, SQAA, and KSQAAC.

School quality improvement. In the recent years, improving school quality, particularly at the elementary level, has been the central focus for many states. As part of the state initiatives, school assessment and monitoring efforts have gained traction in Gujarat, Odisha, Madhya Pradesh, and Rajasthan with different implementations. Table 9.2 analyzes the School Quality Improvement Models (SQIM) of the states of Gujarat, Odisha, and Madhya Pradesh (Pratibha Parv). It shows the different approaches to school evaluation for improving quality.

Table 9.1 School accreditation models

	KSQAAC	SQAA (CBSE)	NABET (QCI)
Purpose	- Promote quality of education - Promote collaboration among all stakeholders - Encourage school staff and school development - Promote community participation	- To assess and endorse that an institution/school meets established standards - To assess the effectiveness of an institution in creating the most innovative, relevant, and socially conscious, eco-oriented learning environment for all its staff and students - To involve the faculty comprehensively in institutional evaluation and planning for enhancing effectiveness of a school - To establish criteria for professional certification and upgrading of standards - To encourage continuous self-assessment, accountability, and autonomy in innovation in school education - To encourage continuous professional development and capacity-building of teachers	To achieve excellence through an education quality management system
Criteria	- Physical infrastructure: 20% - Learning environment (teaching, learning, and evaluation processes): 60% - Leadership: 10% - Community participation: 5% - Innovation: 5%	- Scholastics processes and products (25%) - Co-scholastic processes and products (15%) - Infrastructure: adequacy, functionality, and aesthetics (15%) - Human resources (10%), management and administration (10%) - Leadership (15%) - Beneficiary satisfaction (10%)	- School governance - Educational and support processes - Performance measurement and improvement
Grade	- 7 Point Grading: - A⁺, A, B⁺, B, C⁺, C and D	- For a school to be accredited, it must score over 60% overall and above 50% in each domain	
Use of result	Certification valid for 5 years	Certification valid for 3 years	The school can use the logo of NABET for 1 year

Table 9.2 School quality improvement models

	Gunotsav (Gujarat)	Samiksha (Odisha)	Pratibha Prava (Madhya Pradesh)
Purpose	• Raise teacher awareness for matters of educational quality • Provide educational evaluation and grading of schools and teachers • Assess quality • Facilitate improvement in school education	• The purpose of Sarva Shiksha Abhiyaan (SSA) and the Right of Children for Free and Compulsory Education Act, 2009 (RTE) is not only to ensure access to a school and completion of the elementary stage by all children but also to ensure a sufficient quality of education	• To assess the academic performance of students and track it at regular intervals at the elementary education level • To create an improvement in the quality of education in primary and upper-primary schools • To raise awareness of quality education among teachers and the general public • To assess the overall infrastructure of a school • To assess the state and use of school facilities • To provide a social audit opportunity and develop a sense of educational ownership in society
Criteria	• Learning in school 60% • Co-scholastic activities 20% • Use of resources and community participation 20%	• School environment • Curricular program • Co-curricular program • School community ties • School management • Midday meals	Learning and non-learning indicators
Grade	A, B, C, D, E, and F	Four-point grades	• Five-point grades A to E • Ranking of district, block, and school in state
Use of results	Formalizing/modifying policies in the field of primary education	Implementing appropriate interventions to improve school education	Special coaching and academic additional support to teachers

With support from the National University of Educational Planning and Administration (NUEPA), the central government has developed the National Programme on School Standards and Evaluation (NPSSE). The program aims to reach 1.62 million schools across the country by creating a sustainable and institutionalized system of school evaluation where each school takes ownership of its improvement and effectiveness. Therefore, it seeks to develop a common understanding of evaluation across stakeholders. The program emphasizes the importance of school evaluation as a cyclic process for formulating the school development plan. "Improvement" is considered to be the goal. Evaluations are seen as drivers to achieve this goal. The major objective of NPSSE is to establish an agreed set of key domains, core standards and processes, which all schools must strive to achieve.

Leadership and school accountability

Leadership and school accountability share a challenging relationship in India. Batra (2011: 8) argues that, "[A] lack of leadership training in combination with an amorphously defined position of the school head implies that there are no structured and reliable ways of developing accountability systems and practices." Thus, while leadership development may be a new terminology in the Indian school education system, the important role of head teachers has long been acknowledged by all the policy documents. With the increased attention to matters of schooling in the post-independence period, the role of the school head has undergone a significant transformation (Govinda, 2006). The overall goals of the school system, and consequently of a governmental school head teacher, are embedded in the Constitution, the legal framework, and government policies. As heads are part of a larger system, their duties extend beyond the school. Heads have roles and responsibilities related to caring for the education of students, developing pedagogical strategies, and managing academic staff for effective teaching-learning as well as non-academic staff for better school management. Acknowledging the increasingly complex role of school leadership, India has taken steps to introduce school leadership programs for the school heads. In this context Diwan *et al.* (2014: 1) call for a "paradigm shift in the way schools are managed and led. This positions the school head as the prime mover for initiating and implementing school-based change and development."

In the case study in primary schools in Tamil Nadu, Grover and Singh (2002: 11) conclude, "despite limited responsibility, the HMs' [school heads'] tasks are multifaceted and complex. In addition to teaching, day-to-day running of the school, which involves administrative and record-keeping tasks and maintaining the facilities, they are responsible for liaising with the community and parents." Despite the fact that policies have identified the school head to be a key position, their training is a matter of concern in India. Teachers are promoted to school heads on the basis of seniority.

Generally, teachers receive no formal training for this post. In this context, Grover and Singh (2002: 28) recommend:

> The role of the HMs should be redefined to completely separate them from the role of a teacher except in some extenuating circumstances. The advantages of this would be two-fold – the first being that it would free the time available to HMs to perform the tasks of school-based management more effectively, and the second being that it would create the distance necessary between him/her and the teachers to exercise supervisory authority over the teachers.

Teacher accountability

One of the most significant and recognized policy documents regarding teacher accountability in India is the report of the National Commission on Teachers (1985). The report states that "poor teacher performance is not a problem to be found in one or two states only; the disease, if one might use the term, is rampant and its spread so wide that hardly a segment of the nation's education services is exempt from the injurious effects." (National Commission on Teachers, 1985: 112f) The committee recommended a code of conduct to motivate and help teachers to perform better. A lack of professionalism among teachers, especially in the form of absenteeism is still a major concern.

The Right of Children to Free and Compulsory Education Act (2009) codifies teachers' professional responsibilities. Among other things, it lays out a mandatory professional conduct for tenured teachers, covering things such as regular attendance, completing the curriculum in the allotted time, assessing and helping the learning progress of children, and exchanging with parents and guardians. The Act also mentions disciplinary actions in case of failure to adhere to these.

Despite these policy developments, teacher accountability is still a work-in-progress at best, particularly at the elementary school level in India. In a study on the influence of teacher unions and teacher politicians on school governance in the state of Utter Pradesh (UP), Kingdon and Muzammil (2010, p.259f) found:

> A number of teacher accountability measures exist in UP, such as school inspections by the District Inspector of Schools; [the] Principal's annual entry into every teacher's character book/register; [a] system of teacher transfers as a disciplining device; and provision for suspension or withholding the salary increment of erring teachers and so forth ... However, evidence suggests that these accountability sanctions and probity procedures have not been effectively implemented because teachers resist them by pressurising [sic] the District Inspectors of Schools, both through their unions and via political pressure from teacher politicians.

Teacher absenteeism, as a major cause for economically poor students' achievement, has dominated the debate on teacher accountability. In their study on teacher and health care provider absence, Chaudhury et al. (2004) found that the frequency of teacher inspection in India correlated negatively with absenteeism, in other words a lower absenteesim rate was found in areas with a comparatively high rate of inspection. There are legal provisions for sanctioning teachers who have unexcused absences by withholding their wages or even suspending them, but this is difficult in practice. This may be linked to the fact that teachers' unions are typically strong and politically influential (Kingdon and Muzammil, 2001).

Community accountability

As a result of the 73rd amendment to the Indian Constitution, many Indian states have transferred aspects of control over public schools and their finances to local communities. The aforementioned Sarva Siksha Abhiyan, as well as the of Children to Free and Compulsory Education Act (2009), have acknowledged the increased accountability of schools through greater involvement of so-called village education committees (VECs), parent-teacher associations (PTAs), and school management committees (SMCs). A community can support a school in various ways and can "influence the content of subjects and add local, practical and appropriate examples," "monitor the realization of children's rights as well as violations of these rights," and "enable the village to become a learning environment for children realizing the concept of the 'village as a school'." (NCERT, 2005: 88) The SMC (and the local community as a whole) form an important part of the accountability chain as they complement inspections by higher-ranking officials, by way of regular monitoring (Tewary, 2013).

However, many community members in rural locations have never been to school. This can contribute to a lack of empathy towards schools and schooling (PROBE, 1999). Galab et al. (2013) conducted a study on community-based accountability for school improvement, where an approach called the "short route of accountability" (as described by the World Bank, 2004) was implemented. The findings indicate that the "short route of accountability" increased the pressure from parents on the schools to improve in several domains by strengthening the parental participation at SMC meetings and its influence. Furthermore, the schools responded to the increased pressure by improving. Galab et al. (2013: 6), found strong improvements over time with regard to "teacher attendance, student attendance, student performance and the quality of the midday meal as measured by the self-reported school scorecard results." The findings of the study corroborate the argument of Bruns et al. (2011) that pressures for better resource management and teacher effort to better influence school quality through increased parental. Consequently, they suggest that, "An alternative approach – using information for accountability – aims to change the relationships of accountability among the various actors in the education system to change behaviours and thus improve outcomes." (Bruns *et al.*, 2011: 29). In a study on the relationship between public participation in school matters, teacher accountability, and school outcomes, Pandey *et al.* (2010) emphasized that one of the reasons for the lack of accountability of teachers might stem from communities being largely uninformed about the levers available to them, especially in rural areas. The findings indicate that providing information in an effective manner to communities leads to improved learning outcomes and substantially more efficient spending of public resources by reducing teacher absenteeism and increasing teacher effort in classrooms.

Citizen monitoring can exact both transparency and accountability on the part of the providers, leading to better governance (Kapoor, 2010). Social accountability not only empowers citizens but also assigns responsibility to the community. Thus, one can draw the conclusion that community-led accountability can positively influence the performance of schools and learners in India.

Conclusion

The preceding context of school accountability begs the question whether the policies and practices described lead to school improvement and a functioning system of accountability. Inasmuch, different stakeholders have openly questioned public faith in schools in India. During the last decades, issues and challenges in schooling have been more prominent in literature, policy discourses, and planning documents. And yet, "There have been multiple 'silver bullets' offered by policy makers and pundits, but with all of the rhetorical flourishes, there still continue to be as many questions as there are answers." (Lasley, 2012: 1) This statement, originally written in reference to the US context, also holds true for the Indian context where policy statements are not always reflective of practices and where accountability mechanisms do not (yet) form a coherent system for school improvement.

For India, the absence of common standards in core subject areas across the states makes it difficult to compare learners' performances and establish a national educational accountability based on student performance. The NAS and public examination results have had limited utility for ensuring positive impact on the ability of the schools to foster student academic growth. While these are useful instruments to assess what students have or have not learned, they are so far used without having significant implications on improving teaching-learning processes and ensuring accountability of schools in improving learners' performance. Therefore, information generated through NAS, public examinations, and school-based examinations should be used for decision-making, the professionalization of teachers, and for school improvement. District- and state-level education officials could further use the assessment data to identify schools that require more support in terms of physical and human resources.

Accreditation and quality improvement models are currently dominating the school improvement practices in India. It is strongly believed that assessing a school's resources and assigning a grade to schools will build pressure to improve performance. However, the recent initiative of NPSSE is envisaged as a positive step to enable all schools to continuously engage themselves in self-improvement.

The central challenge for policy-makers in India is making teachers more accountable for students' leaning outcomes and improving their work ethic and performance. Many of the policy debates revolve around providing qualified teachers for all children. Although "teachers' moral, ethical values, character, conduct and accountability have been univocally pronounced since ancient times to the present education system," (Panda, 2011: 3) many professional development programs are organized by the state or under governmental supervision, working towards a better performance and improved teaching and learning, these have faced challenges. There are numerous constraints towards adherence to the codes of conduct by teachers.

However, the focus on school leadership programs has emerged as part of the ongoing discussion on how to improve schools and the corresponding initiatives. Considering the changing role of school leaders, capacity-building leadership programs have been instituted by different states. The major challenge for India is to lead teaching learning and managing change in a way that is mindful to the diverse context.

Furthermore, professionalizing school leadership for community participation, along with social accountability among community members and parents, is considered the nuclei to school improvement in India. It is strongly believed that community engagement though structured arrangements can improve school education and ensure a functioning chain of accountability between the communities and schools and teachers. There is still a lot of work to be done on this road.

In conclusion, the complexity of school accountability presents a perplexing situation. School accountability appears as a poorly defined notion and is rarely used or enforced by the stakeholders in India in a coherent manner. There is a need for developing a cohesive accountability framework for sustainable and progressive change in the school education sector in order to address the complexity of school accountability and the appropriate use of resources for improving school and learners' performance.

References

ASER (2012). *Annual Status of Education Report.* ASER Centre: New Delhi.
Babington Macaulay, T. (1835). *Minute on Indian Education.* Retrieved from www.columbia.edu/itc/mealac/pritchett/00generallinks/macaulay/txt_minute_education_1835.html.

Bahadur, A. (2013). Assessment and its Role in Learning. *Educational Assessment and Research – News and Views*, 1, 1.

Batra, S. (2011). The Construct and Scope of Educational Leadership. *Learning Curves*. 16, 7–12.

Bruns, B., Filmer, D., and Patrions, H. A. (2011). *Making Schools Work New Evidence on Accountability Reforms*. World Bank: Washington DC.

Chaudhury, N., Hammer, J, Kremer, M., Muralidharan, K., and Rogers, F. (2004). *Teacher and Health Care Provider Absence: A Multi Country Study*. Mimeo: World Bank.

Desai, J. P. (2009). The Power of Accountability. Retrieved from http://online.wsj.com/public/resources/documents/mum_accountability.pdf

Desai, J. P. (2012). *Accountability: Angst, Awareness, Action*. Pearson Education: India.

Diwan, R., Chugh, S., Awasthi, K., Subitha, G. V., Mythili, N., Tiwari, S, Singh, S., Negi, G. S., Malik, C. S., Bajaj, M., and Parween, D. (2014). *School Leadership Development: A Handbook*. National University of Educational Planning and Administration: New Delhi.

Galab, S., Jones, C., Latham, M., and Churches, R. (2013). *Community-based Accountability for School Improvement. A Case Study from Rural India*. Berkshire: CfBT Education Trust.

Gandhi, M. K. (1937). *Harijan*. Ahmedabad: Navajivan Trust.

Government of India (1966). *Education and National Development. Report on the Education Commission (1964–1966)*. New Delhi: Government of India.

Government of India (1968). *National Policy on Education*. Ministry of Human Resources and Development, Government of India: New Delhi.

Government of India (1986). *National Policy on Education*. Ministry of Human Resources and Development, Government of India: New Delhi.

Government of India (1992). *Programme of Action*. Ministry of Human Resources and Development, Government of India: New Delhi.

Govinda, R. (2006). *Role of Headteachers in School Management in India*. New Delhi: National University of Educational Planning and Administration.

Grover, S. and Singh, N. H. (2002). *The Quality of Primary Education: A Case Study of Madurai and Villupuram Districts in Tamil Nadu, India*. Harvard Graduate School of Education, Harvard University.

Hanushek, E. A. (2013). Economic Growth in Developing Countries: The role of Human Capital. *Economics of Education Review*. 37, 204–212.

Hanushek, E. A. and Wößmann, L. (2007). *The Role of Education Quality in Economic Growth*. World Bank Policy Research Working Paper 4122. Retrieved from http://adapt.it/adapt-indice-a-z/wp-content/uploads/2014/08/hanushe_w%C3%B6%C3%9 Fmann_the_role_of_education_2007.pdf

Joseph, A. M. (2012). *School Inspection System*. CCS Working Paper No. 276. Center for Civil Society: New Delhi.

Kapoor, R. (2010). *Essential Services: Community Based Management for Right to Education People as Change Makers*. Oxfam India working papers series.

Kingdon, G. and Muzammil, M. (2001). A Political Economy of Education in India, *Economic and Political Weekly*. 36(32), 11–18.

Kingdon, G. and Muzammil, M. (2010). *The School Governance Environment in Uttar Pradesh: Implications for Teacher Accountability and Effort*. RECOUP Working Paper 21, Faculty of Education, University of Cambridge. Retrieved from

http://r4d.dfid.gov.uk/PDF/Outputs/ImpOutcomes_RPC/WP31-GK.pdf.
Krishnaratne, S., White, H., and Carpenter, E. (2013). *Quality Education for All Children? What Works in Education in Developing Countries.* 3rd Working paper. Global Development Network, India.
Lasley, T.J. (2012). *Standards and Accountability in Schools.* Los Angeles: Sage Publication.
Levitt, R., Janta, B., and Wegrich, K. (2008). *Accountability of Teachers: Literature review.* Retrieved from http://dera.ioe.ac.uk/14020/1/1009_Accountability_of_teachers_ Literature_review.pdf
Mehta, P. B. (2003). *The Burden of Democracy.* Penguin Books: India.
Mongon, D. and Chapman, C. (2012). *High-Leverage Leadership: Improving Outcomes in Educational Settings (Leading School Transformation).* USA and Canada: Rutledge.
National Commission on Teachers (1985). *The Teacher and Society – Report Of The National Commission on Teachers-I: 1983–85,* National Commission on Teachers: New Delhi.
NCERT (National Council of Educational Research and Training) (2000). *National Curriculum Framework 2000.* National Council of Educational Research and Training: New Delhi.
NCERT (2005) *National Curriculum Framework 2005.* National Council of Educational Research and Training: New Delhi.
NCERT (2009) *National Curriculum Framework 2009.* National Council of Educational Research and Training: New Delhi.
NCERT (2014). *National Achievement Survey: Class V.* National Council of Educational Research and Training: New Delhi.
NKC (National Knowledge Commission) (2008). *Towards a Knowledge Society.* Government of India: New Delhi.
Ouston, J., Fidler, B., and Earley, P. (1998). The Educational Accountability of Schools in England and Wales. *Educational Policy.* 12(1–2), 111–123.
Panda, P. (2011). *Ethics, Conduct and Competency of Teachers.* Asian Network Training Research Institutions Educational Planning (ANTRIEP), New Delhi: India, 17(1), 1–3.
Pandey, P., Goyal, S., and Sundararaman, V. (2010). Public Participation, Teacher Accountability and School Outcomes in Three States. *Economic & Political Weekly.* 45(24), 75–83.
Patel, M. S. (1953). *The Education Philosophy of Mahatma Gandhi.* Ahmedabad: Navjeean Publishing House.
Pritchett, L. and Banerji, R. (2013, May). *Schooling Is Not Education! Using Assessment to Change the Politics of Non-learning.* Center for Global Development: Washington, DC.
PROBE (1999). *Public Report on Basic Education in India.* Oxford University Press: New Delhi.
Public Affairs Centre in Bangalore (2007). *India's Citizen's Charters: A Decade of Experience.* Retrieved from www.pacindia.org/uploads/default/files/publications/pdf/1264b6a536388591ba81aef60860abd6.pdf.
Ranson, S. (2003). Public Accountability in the Age of Neo-liberal Governance. *Journal of Educational Policy.* 18(5), 459–480.
Sargent Committee (1944). *Report of the Sargent Commission on Post-War Education.* British-run Government of India.

Saxena, N. (2004). *Improving Delivery of Programs through Administrative Reforms in India*. Retrieved from www.nac.nic.in

Tewary, V. (2013). *Community Participation Schooling: Evidence from DRC Survey Data*. Retrieved from www.accountabilityindia.in/accountabilityblog/2642-community-participation-and-school-functioning-evidence-drc-survey-data.

Tucker, S. (2012). *Accountability Initiatives*. Message posted to www.accountabilityindia.in/accountabilityblog/2541-enhancing-governance-education

U-DISE (2012–2013). *Unified District Information System for Education*. National University of Educational Planning and Administration, New Delhi: India.

U-DISE (2013–2014). *Unified District Information System for Education*. National University of Educational Planning and Administration, New Delhi: India.

UNESCO (2005). *EFA Global Monitoring Report. Education For All*. UNESCO.

UNESCO (2014). *Global Initiatives on Out-of-school Children. South Indian Regional Study Covering Bangladesh, India, Pakistan and Sri Lanka*. UNESCO.

Wood, C. (1854). *Dispatch Documents*. London.

World Bank (2004). *Making Services Work for Poor People*. World Bank: Washington DC.

World Bank (2009). *Secondary Education in India: Universalizing the Opportunity*. World Bank: Washington DC.

10 The promises and perils of school leadership for accountability
Four lessons from China, Hong Kong, and India

Moosung Lee and Misty M. Kirby

Research over the last decade has explored the elusive link between school leadership and student learning (e.g., Hallinger and Heck, 1996; Leithwood and Jantzi, 2008; Leithwood *et al.*, 2004). School effectiveness research has highlighted the importance of principal leadership and its impact on teacher practices and student outcomes (Blase and Blase, 1999; Hallinger and Heck, 1996; O'Donnell and White, 2005). While empirical studies have focused increasingly to the notion of instructional leadership, or its newly labelled reincarnation 'leadership for learning' (cf. Lee *et al.*, 2012a; MacBeath and Cheng, 2008), investigations of school leadership have also taken a number of angles. Among these is the role and impact of school leadership in a policy environment that demands increased accountability for student learning outcomes (Cooley and Shen, 2003; Heck and Hallinger, 2009; Lee *et al.*, 2012c). This research trend reflects the fact that externally imposed school accountability policies increasingly form a foundation of government education reform agendas, particularly in Anglo-Saxon countries. Accountability measures embedded in educational reform packages are often justified as a transparent means of improving student learning outcomes in the UK, and the US. Although accountability policies somewhat differ in form and emphasis between Anglo-Saxon countries and Asian countries, there is no question that they are changing the context in which leadership is exercised in schools (cf. Lee *et al.*, 2012c). The three preceding chapters written by Wang, Pang, and Panda provide abundant information and evidence about how accountability policies have reshaped the work of school principals in three Asian societies – i.e., China, Hong Kong, and India. Drawing from our close reading of the three chapters, our commentary chapter provides a number of important lessons for educators, policy makers and researchers in the region where school leadership practices have been considerably influenced by accountability policies and measures (cf. Lee *et al.*, 2012c; Walker, 2006; Walker and Ko, 2011).

The emerging landscapes of school leadership for accountability

Before going further, we wish to provide an overview of the emerging accountability systems in the three Asian societies in order to set the stage for our commentary chapter. Similar as reported in school accountability research in Western societies (e.g., Cooley and Shen, 2003; Holye and Wallace, 2007; Muijs and Harris, 2006; Plowright, 2007), the three chapters illuminate that there are two major mechanisms of accountability shaping school leadership: internal, self-regulating accountability, and externally imposed accountability. Specifically, Wang's Chapter 7 describes China's school accountability system as consisting of internal school-based evaluation with a focus on monitoring and external evaluation with a focus on differentiation. Similarly, Pang's chapter frames Hong Kong's school accountability system as featuring an 'external quality assurance mechanism ... achieved through the conduction of external school review', and an 'internal framework via quality assurance mechanism' relying 'on schools' own capability of school self-evaluation (SSE) in the process of continuous improvement'. Panda's chapter shows that India has a similar feature of externally driven accountability system (e.g., school accreditation, and school quality monitoring), whereas the school-based internal accountability mechanism does not appear to be developed as much as China and Hong Kong. This seems to be mainly because of India's relatively shaky infrastructure of K-12 schooling systems. Note that for India universal primary and secondary school education is still a core educational policy agenda.

At the same time, however, the three chapters illuminate varying features of accountability. Wang's case schools in North China appear to be placed in a very high accountability context. According to Wang, the Chinese government has implemented school and teacher evaluation measures, in which the critical portion is student testing scores. Notably, these measures are linked to determine teachers' pay and promotion nationwide since 2009. Wang expresses a concern that:

> High performing teachers are rewarded through promotions, salary increments, and awards. However, in some regions, and schools, the evaluations of schools and teachers are primarily based on student academic performance, and high stakes test results. The accountability policy has a narrow focus on obligatory and transactional function.

We know that a typical accountability measure in Anglo-Saxon countries is to build information platforms about school performance, which are usually based on standardised test scores, and share these with local community or the general public (e.g., UK's league tables, Australia's MySchool website, US's AYP website). A more proactive version of this approach is to make more customised information available (e.g., test scores by types of schools, by ethnic groups) to parents to inform school choice. The most radical (or controversial) version is to provide financial rewards or sanctions to schools in the name of school improvement, based on such performance information. The US implements such a measure, as does China. In this regard, the case schools in Wang's study are situated in a very high accountability policy environment.

Interestingly enough, Hong Kong is as competitive a society as China, but Hong Kong's school accountability foci seem to be a bit more diverse than China. Specifically, Pang in Chapter 8 shows how Hong Kong has implemented the School Development and Accountability (SDA) Framework through school self-evaluation, and external review. In so doing, schools have been given guidelines and tools of how they prepare school self-evaluation for external school review. Those guidelines and tools include the framework of performance indicators, the stakeholders' questionnaires to teachers, students and parents, key performance measures (KPMs), and the Assessment Program for Affective and Social Outcomes (APASO). Notably, APASO entirely focuses on affective and social outcomes beyond testing scores. That is, although teachers and principals in Hong Kong are placed in a high accountability context similar to China, teachers and principals are not evaluated by a sole measure focusing on standardised testing scores. Rather, Hong Kong's school accountability measures are more sophisticated, even though a certain level of distrust and tension around accountability systems has been forged between the government, and educators (cf. Mok, 2007). In addition, compared to India, Hong Kong's school accountability measures are more specific, and transparent. The guidelines and tools for quality assurance noted above seem to be relatively clear and specific, compared to India's case.

In sum, we note that there are commonalities in accountability policies at the macro level (or system level), whereas there are variations in accountability measures at the micro (or school level) across the three Asian societies. Specifically, the central (and local) governments in China and Hong Kong focus on building a solid legal and policy framework at the system level in order to regulate the accountability procedures at school in the name of decentralisation (e.g., school-based management, school-based evaluation). Although not elaborated at this stage, the Indian government seems to envision a similar approach to accountability, as shown in the Panda's Chapter 9.

In the contemporary policy regime, the centrally funded initiatives on SarvaSikhshaAviyan (SSA), and RastriyaMadhyamikSikshaAviyan (RMSA) for universalising school education are – among other things – aimed at improving school performance. We may call such a trend 'centralised decentralisation' – legal and policy platforms built by the central government for accountability, aiming to regulate accountability procedures at the school level in the name decentralization. This somehow oxymoronic approach seems to be interwoven by neoliberalist ideas of educational governance. For neoliberals, the state (or government) should play a 'reduced' role in education system to maximise the principles of market (e.g., competition, transparency, choice) in education governance but the state should also control the performativity of education system through an evaluative power such as accountability, and audit measures (Lee, 2007; Olssen et al., 2004). For readers who may wonder how China as a socialist country can accommodate and exercise neoliberalist ideas in public policy areas, we recommend that they should read David Harvey's work (2005) in general, and Kipnis (2007), and Lee and Zhu (2006) in particular. Based on our perspective of the contemporary accountability system as a core part of centralised decentralisation in the three Asian societies, in the following section we discuss what lessons can be learned from those societies.

Lesson 1: Both internal and external forms of accountability are implemented in the three societies. The two forms of accountability ought to be complementary but more often than not they are contrasting in shaping school leadership

As noted earlier, there are two common major mechanisms of accountability shaping school leadership in the three Asian societies. In theory, the two forms of accountability ought to be complementary to each other. For example, in the case of Hong Kong, although internal self-evaluation is conducted by schools according to the SDA Framework prescribed by the Education Bureau, external school review is conducted by an expert team to validate the exercise of school self-evaluation in order to maximise benefits from both an insider's, and an outsider's views of school practice, and performance. This is the idea of how the two forms of accountability are supposed to work. In reality, however, the two forms of accountability seem to generate tensions, conflicts and/or dilemmas in school leadership practices. For example, Lee et al. (2012c) report that externally imposed accountability requirements require school principals in Hong Kong to respond to the specific needs of their schools while at the same time adhering to common benchmarks, and complying with new (time-consuming) reporting mechanisms. Lee and Dimmock (1999) found that when Hong Kong principals focus too strongly on implementing practices associated with accountability and quality assurance, this increases pressure on teachers. That is, on the one hand, school leaders have to respond to externally imposed accountability measures. On the other hand, compliance to those external measures seems to generate negative school climates. Consistent with previous research, Wang's chapter reports, 'school leaders are facing a dilemma of how to cope with a test driven, performance-based education, and survive in a constrained space to allow teachers and students to enjoy autonomy and happy lives'. Note that the schools of Wang's case study are regarded as excellent schools due to high quality of teaching staff. In other words, even principals in such highly reputable and performing schools are pressured to address externally driven accountability measures in their school setting. Such tensions, conflicts and/or dilemmas stemming from external accountability are mainly because external accountability measures often reduce the moral agency of teachers, given the low trust in teacher professionalism premised in external accountability measures (Olssen *et al.*, 2004). In sum, the three chapters clearly tell us that maximising the benefits from incorporating the two forms of accountability is a daunting task for school leaders, given certain contradictory features between internal and external accountability measures.

Lesson 2: When accountability is dominated by external measures, teachers are busy, burning out, and continuously blamed

Wang's chapter illuminates how busy ordinary teachers are in China (although the case schools are not representative of all public schools in China). Wang states teachers' work life in her case schools as follow: 'They teach classes of 40–60 students for 10–12 hours per week. Besides lesson preparation, they spend 2–3 hours on marking and student consultation each day. A typical working day for a teacher is from 7 am to 4:30 pm with take-home work thereafter'. In addition to this routine workload, the evaluation system aggravates already heavy workload by demanding so-called 'hard evidence', and 'non-negotiable requirements' of their performance, including prescribed training courses, participating in professional development activities within, and across schools, such as class observations, open lessons, publishing a required number of articles related to teaching practices and action research, and achieving sustained quality teaching and student learning outcomes as evidenced by high-stakes test results, internal and external recognitions, and awards. It is not surprising to see why school leaders in the case schools expressed their concerns about teachers' stress, heavy workload, and burn out.

A similarly stressful and pressured situation for teacher work life is also found in Hong Kong. As Pang's chapter describes, there have been myriad reforms: 'too many existing reforms'. Various reforms in association with school accountability have been introduced since 1990s. For example, externally imposed accountability mechanisms first appeared in Hong Kong (e.g., School-Based Management) in the early 1990s (Cheng, 2009; Walker, 2004). Since then, Hong Kong schools seem to have the so-called 'Christmas Tree' problem (cf. Bryk *et al.*, 1998): too many disconnects within and between reforms bombarding schools (Walker, 2006). Under this circumstance, Pang's observation of 'tremendous pressure and workloads already existing in schools' is true. Indeed, our own investigation of the 2006 Progress in International Reading Literacy Study (PIRLS) revealed that Hong Kong primary school teachers indicated the lowest level of job satisfaction among teachers from over 40 participating countries. Despite this downside of teacher work life, reform failures are, more often than not, attributed to lower qualified and/or less competent schoolteachers, compared to tutors in Hong Kong's private education markets (cf. Morris, 2004).

A more serious problem related to teacher work life, when external accountability measures are dominated in education governance, is well presented in Panda's chapter. Considering major indicators of educational development and infrastructure in India (e.g., low enrolment rate, high teacher to student ratio, lack of school facility and equipment, low teacher salaries, low teacher qualifications, dearth of opportunities for professional development, etc.), Indian teachers would be a more disadvantaged group, compared to their counterparts in Hong Kong, and in Wang's case schools in North China. Given these conditions, teacher absenteeism seems to be almost inevitable. Despite this, teacher absenteeism is viewed as one of the critical impediments on school accountability in the Indian context. Ostensibly, it seems that teacher absenteeism is a cause of many educational problems in India. We think, however, that teacher absenteeism is not a cause of problems, but a consequence of problems, given the poor conditions of teacher work life. As such, an underlying problem seems to be that teacher absenteeism is utilised in making teachers the scapegoats of educational development in India. The following excerpt from the Report of the National Commission on Teachers, cited in Panda's chapter, shows how teacher absenteeism is used for blaming a victim:

> poor teacher performance is not a problem to be found in one or two states only; the *disease*, if one might use the term, is rampant and its spread so wide that hardly a segment of the nation's education services is exempt from the injurious effects.

The committee also recommended the broad parameters of a code of conduct to motivate and help teachers to perform better. The National Policy on Education (1986) envisages two important approaches for ensuring accountability and curbing professional misconduct for enhancing the dignity of teachers: (1) by way of a system of teacher evaluation through open, participative and data-based system, and (2) the preparation of a code of professional ethics for teachers.

Criticisms of teachers, as the source of reform failures, are also found in Hong Kong, and other countries. But criticisms of Indian teachers are more serious. They are described as a 'disease, impeding the process of building school accountability. Of course, this is a nefarious case of how accountability discourse is conveniently espoused with the discourse of blaming a victim. Given the poor educational infrastructure within which Indian teachers strive to work, attributing reform failures to teachers solely is obviously unfair. As Panda points out, the real problem is the fact that teacher absenteeism, as a cause for poor student achievement, overshadows the teacher accountability debate. In other words, the real problem is that accountability for the whole education system is reduced to the level of individual teachers. When this happens, and where there is a focus on compliance rather than quality education, teachers are blamed. Professional learning, which could be a powerful mediator in improving instruction, is often overlooked when the primary focus is compliance. In sum, drawing from the three chapters, we see that the quality of teacher work life can be worsened, and teachers can be easily targeted as a source of educational problems, especially when external accountability measures dominate in education reforms.

Lesson 3: External accountability measures would work positively when internal accountability mechanisms are willingly permeated in the everyday life of teachers and principals

Pang's chapter shows us the importance of internal or self-regulating mechanism for accountability. It suggests that continuous school improvement is possible only when self-evaluation is institutionalised for daily practice and is informed by valid and reliable performance indicators available for use in self-evaluation. Wang's case study of China's schools also shows that although principal and teacher evaluation for promotion was reviewed by external expert panels, in recent years principals and teachers have started to place more emphasis on school-based evaluation, and peer reviews regarding individual teachers' performance. Teachers in the case schools believe that they are on the right track.

According to Pang's description of Hong Kong's accountability model, it places more emphasis on internal accountability mechanisms than external accountability measures, which is somewhat different to China and India. In addition, Hong Kong's internal accountability mechanism seems to provide a more specific and elaborated model in building a solid school-based accountability mechanism:

> The SDA Framework has been evolving in order to meet new needs of schools in the ever-changing external environment. The ESR procedures have been streamlined and they focus on how schools make use of the process of PIE [planning-implementation-evaluation] for sustained development and self-improvement in the SSE cycle. Starting from the second term of the 2008/09 school year, ESR continues to be improvement oriented and is conducted in a school-specific and focused mode. Likewise, to facilitate SSE in a more focused manner and alleviate teachers' workload, the tools for the SDA Framework have been revised, based on the principles of simplification, reorganization, and refinement ... The SDA Framework stresses the internal mechanism more than the external one and more resources have been put into the promotion of school self-evaluation.

Panda discusses the role of community engagement as integral to a shifting of perspective as to who is held accountable. Using the World Bank's framework of 'short route of accountability', evidence is emerging to support an increase in teacher and student attendance, and performance when the community is engaged and leads school improvement. Coupling this idea with the experience of non-governmental organisations, where they have learned that communicating locally about the issues in the school and classroom dramatically shifts the manner in which these issues are addressed. According to Panda's chapter 'Social accountability not only empowers rights to the citizen, but also assigns responsibility to the community'.

There has been a policy convergence of external accountability (e.g., inspection, evaluation, governance by numbers, metrics, etc.) across Anglo-Saxon countries. A similar trend is identified in East Asian societies and India. While similar externally imposed accountability measures are often justified as a transparent tool, and are injected into different schools, Pang argues that 'School development cannot be copied and imposed from outside'. In this regard, the presence of well-defined internal accountability mechanisms and procedures, as in Hong Kong, appears to be a case that we need to further explore in terms of how (voluntarily), routinised internal accountability mechanisms can be synergised with external accountability measures.

Lesson 4: The role of principals in school improvement is critical in a high accountability context

In a high accountability context, ironically, government regulations or policies to enhance transparency of school performance and management seem to serve as another means of surveillance. Regulations for transparency of schools' performativity seem to play a role in surveillance by requiring schools to open and share performance data, and school management information with key stakeholders. Within this context, principals would shift the focus and allocation of their role behaviours in line with accountability requirements and regulations (Lee *et al.*, 2012c; Walker and Ko, 2011; Walker, Lee, and Bryant, 2014). More problematical and contrary to the primary aim of accountability (performativity with transparency), principals tend to be distracted from their educative function as accountability measures proceed (Walker, 2006). Indeed, Wang's chapter shows the principal's dilemma in such a situation:

> The school leaders review lesson plans monthly, observe classes from time to time, monitor and supervise teaching periodically. Therefore, we are under constant surveillance and need to take each class seriously. I cannot slack off. I feel this is like an invisible, ongoing evaluation, and monitoring.

Simultaneously, according to Wang, school leaders are facing a dilemma of 'how to cope with a test driven, performance-based education, and survive in a constrained space to allow teachers and students to enjoy autonomy and happy lives'. Interestingly, while most of teachers are pressured within the high accountability context, some teachers in Wang's study perceived that such a system is 'transparent and fair'. That is, some teachers believe that external recognition and evaluation (e.g., revised teacher rank systems, performance-based bonuses, open competition for promotion) forged by the current accountability system is at least transparent and fair. However, remaining questions surround whether or not such procedural transparency and fairness contribute to the fundamental change of schools or continuous school improvement. As Wang reports, some teachers simply strive in such a high accountability system to 'seek reputation', and not to 'lose face'.

In this regard, we believe that the role of principals is critical in buffering or mitigating negative pressures on teachers, and the narrow foci of school performance generated by external accountability measures. Principals should dilute evaluative and performance-oriented accountability through leadership practices. Indeed, Hoyle and Wallace (2007) document that school leadership practices could serve as a factor for moderating the drawback of school management in response to external accountability. This suggests that if principals do not play a role in buffering the negative effect of external accountability measures, teachers' perception of work pressures would be more exacerbated. Indeed, parallel findings have been reported in Hong Kong. Lee and Dimmock (1999) found that when principals focused too strongly on implementing practices associated with accountability, and quality assurance, teachers felt increased pressure. In a similar vein, Lee *et al.* (2012b) report that when principals in US schools accommodate local district use of targets and data (e.g., achievement data use for school improvement planning) into their leadership practices without pursuing other cultural changes or facilitating internal accountability mechanisms such as a school-based professional learning community, there actions have a significantly negative effect on teachers' focused instruction and student learning. Therefore, we think that principals should reshuffle and prioritise various accountability measures according to their schools' current organisational climate, condition, and capacity. In this regard, we also think that exercising instructional leadership is necessary but not sufficient. As India moves towards school improvement rather than system improvement, a particular leadership space will be created. As heads of school are slowly given autonomy in leading school-based change, creating 'a culture of school evaluation with accountability, and transparency' looks crucial.

In recent years, instructional leadership has been highly stressed by policy makers, educators and researchers, as it turns out to be the most significant type of school leadership in association with student learning outcomes; a recent meta-analysis of the school leadership effects research concludes that, among a number of competing leadership constructs (transformational, transactional, and other types of leadership), principal instructional leadership, on average, had the highest effect on student learning (Robinson *et al.*,

2008). However, caution should be exercised in interpreting this finding. In some school contexts, transformational leadership or other types of leadership were more effective than instructional leadership. Even in some school contexts, instructional leadership showed negative effects (cf. Robinson *et al.*, 2008). In sum, instructional leadership should not be used in the manner of one-size-fits-all. Despite this, instructional leadership has been overly highlighted in leadership development programmes in some countries (mostly high-performing countries in international testing) (cf. Bryant *et al.*, 2013; Walker *et al.*, 2013). By citing Yukl's (2010) work, however, Pang clearly suggests that exercising various types of principal leadership is critical for continuous school improvement, and adopting a certain type of leadership, best described as 'artistic and context specific'. In this regard, the call for 'cocktail leadership' is something that we need to further explore.

Conclusion

Research has documented how externally imposed accountability measures shape the role and impact of school leadership on student learning and many, though certainly not all, of the cases generate negative consequences.[1] For example, Lee *et al.*'s (2012b) recent study in the US using a nationally representative sample found that principals' reliance on student performance data following district accountability policies, which mandated target setting, and data reporting, had a negative influence on teachers' instructional behaviours and, indirectly, student achievement. Similarly, a body of research conducted in the UK has indicated that school accountability, and quality assurance practices are perceived primarily as burdens on teachers and school leaders (e.g., Hall and Noyes, 2009; Hoyle and Wallace, 2007; Muijs and Harris, 2006; Plowright, 2007; Rosenthal, 2004). Specifically, research has reported that teachers and school leaders felt stress in addressing the increasing number of Office of Standards in Education (Ofsted) inspections; preparing for such a significant increase in inspections generated extra administrative work (e.g., self-evaluation activities), and stressful working conditions (Hall and Noyes, 2009). Under these circumstances, 'teachers feel … professionally compromised, engaged in activity that is more about compliance than educational endeavor' (Hall and Noyes, 2009: 330). School leaders are also very sensitive to the self-evaluation form (SEF), and the Ofsted inspection, both of which seem to generate 'a galvanizing effect on school leaders' nervous systems' (Hall &Noyes, 2009: 312). Muijs and Harris's (2006) study points out that teachers in low-performing schools experience huge pressure with respect to accountability practices. The three chapters confirm all these problems facing principals and teachers in Asian societies (see Lessons 1 and 2). The chapters also provide some alternative ways for realising the promises of school leadership in the era of accountability (see Lessons 3 and 4). Building upon the three chapters, we await more alternatives to fulfil the promises of school leadership for accountability in Asia.

Note

1 We acknowledge that there are studies reporting positive effects of externally imposed accountability measures. For example, in the US Carnoy and Loeb (2002) found that students in states with high accountability measures had significantly greater gains in maths achievement than their counterparts in states with low or no accountability measures. However, other studies conducted in different societies have produced contrary findings.

References

Blase, J. and Blase, J. (1999). Principals' instructional leadership and teacher development: Teacher perspectives. *Educational Administration Quarterly*, 35, 349–378.

Bryant, D., Walker, A., and Lee, M. (2013). The impact of international, national, and local forces on the enactment of quality leadership preparation programs. In M. Brundrett (ed.) *Principles of School Leadership*. UK: Sage. (2nd edn) (pp. 221–243).

Bryk, A., Sebring, P., Kerbow, D., Rollow, S., and Easton, J. (1998). *Charting Chicago School Reform*. Bolder, CO: Westview Press.

Carnoy, M. and Loeb, S. (2002). Does external accountability affect student outcomes? A cross-state analysis. *Educational Evaluation and Policy Analysis*, 24(4), 305–331.

Cheng, Y. C. (2009). Hong Kong educational reforms in the last decade: Reform syndrome and new developments. *International Journal of Educational Management*, 23(1), 65–86.

Cooley, V. E. and Shen, J. (2003). School accountability and professional job responsibility: A perspective from secondary principals. *NASSP Bulletin*, 87(634), 10–25.

Hall, C. and Noyes, A. (2009). School self-evaluation and its impact on teachers' work in England. *Research Papers in Education*, 24(3), 311–334.

Hallinger, P. and Heck, R. (1996). Reassessing the principal's role in school effectiveness: A review of empirical research, 1980–1995. *Educational Administration Quarterly*, 32(1), 5–44.

Harvey, D. (2005). *A Brief History of Neoliberalism*. Oxford: Oxford University Press.

Heck, R. H. and Hallinger, P. (2009). Assessing the contribution of distributed leadership to school improvement and growth in math achievement. *American Educational Research Journal*, 46, 626–658.

Hoyle, E. and Wallace, M. (2007). Educational reform: An ironic perspective. *Educational Management Administration and Leadership*, 35(1), 9–25.

Kipnis, A. (2007). Neoliberalism reified: Suzhi discourse and tropes of neoliberalism in the People's Republic of China. *Journal of the Royal Anthropological Institute*, 13(2), 383–400.

Lee, J., and Zhu, Y.-P. (2006). Urban governance, neoliberalism and housing reform in China. *The Pacific Review*, 19(1), 39–61.

Lee, J. C., and Dimmock, C. (1999). Curriculum leadership and management in secondary schools: A Hong Kong case. *School Leadership and Management*, 19(4), 455–481.

Lee, M. (2007). Opening up the ideologies in learning: The treasure within. *KEDI Journal of Educational Policy*, 4(2), 17–36.

Lee, M., Hallinger, P., and Walker, A. (2012a). A distributed perspective on instructional leadership in International Baccalaureate (IB) schools. *Educational Administration Quarterly*, 48, 664–698.

Lee, M., Louis, K. S., and Anderson, S. (2012b). Local education authorities and student learning: The effects of policies and practices. *School Effectiveness and School Improvement*, 23(2), 133–158.

Lee, M., Walker, A., and Chui, Y. L. (2012c). Contrasting effects of instructional leadership practices on student learning in a high accountability context. *Journal of Educational Administration.* 50(5), 586–611.

Leithwood, K. and Jantzi, D. (2008). Linking leadership to student learning: The contributions of leader efficacy. *Educational Administration Quarterly*, 44(4), 496–528.

Leithwood, K., Louis, K. S., Anderson, S., and Wahlsttom, K. (2004). Review of research: How leadership influences student learning. Retrieved from www.wallacefoundation.org/KnowledgeCenter/KnowledgeTopics/CurrentAreas offocus/EducationLeadership/Pages/HowLeadershipInfluencesStudentLearning.aspx

MacBeath, J. and Cheng, Y. C. (2008). *Leadership for Learning: International Perspectives.* Rotterdam: Sense Publishers.

Mok, M. M. C. (2007). Quality assurance and school monitoring in Hong Kong. *Educational Research for Policy and Practice*, 6, 187–204.

Morris, P. (2004) Teaching in Hong Kong: Professionalization, accountability and the state. *Research Papers in Education*, 19(1), 105–121.

Muijs, D. and Harris, A. (2006). Teacher led school improvement: Teacher leadership in the UK. *Teaching and Teacher Education*, 22, 961–972.

O'Donnell, R. and White, G. (2005). Within the accountability era: Principals' instructional leadership behaviors and student achievement. *NASSP Bulletin*, 89(645), 56–71.

Olssen, M., Codd, J., and O'Neill, A.-M. (2004). *Education Policy: Globalization, Citizenship, and Democracy.* Thousand Oaks: Sage.

Plowright, D. (2007). Self-evaluation and Ofsted Inspection. *Educational Management Administration & Leadership*, 35(3), 373–393.

Robinson, V. M. J., Lloyd, C. A., and Rowe, K. J. (2008). The impact of leadership on student outcomes: An analysis of the differential effects of leadership types. *Educational Administration Quarterly*, 44(5), 635–674.

Rosenthal, L. (2004). Do school inspections improve school quality? Ofsted inspections and school examination results in the UK. *Economics of Education Review*, 23, 143–151.

Walker, A. (2004). Constitution and culture: Exploring the deep leadership structures of Hong Kong schools. *Discourse: Studies in the Cultural Politics of Education*, 25(1), 75–94.

Walker, A. (2006). Divided they stand, united they fall: Reform disconnection in Hong Kong. An unpublished manuscript.

Walker, A. and Ko, J. (2011). Principal leadership in an era of accountability: A perspective from the Hong Kong context. *School Leadership and Management*, 31(4), 369–392.

Walker, A., Bryant, D., and Lee. M. (2013). International patterns in principal preparation: Commonalities and variations in pre-service programmes. *Educational Management, Administration, and Leadership*, 41(4), 405–434.

Walker, A., Lee, M., and Bryant, D. (2014). How much of a difference do principals make? An analysis of between-schools variation in academic achievement in Hong Kong public secondary schools. *School Effectiveness and School Improvement*, 25(4), 602–628.

Yukl, G. (2010). *Leadership in Organizations.* Upper Saddle River, NJ: Prentice Hall, (7th edn).

11 Accountability policies and school leadership in Austria

Increasing competition and little accountability

Anna Kanape-Willingshofer, Herbert Altrichter, and David Kemethofer

The traditional Austrian system of school governance has been characterized as a model of "bureaucratic-professional double regulation" (Brüsemeister, 2004). This type of governance is based both on a comparatively high level of centralist state input regulation along the hierarchical lines of the administrative bureaucracy and on a high level of teacher self-control, in particular with respect to classroom teaching.

Since the beginning of the 1990s, however, there has been a growing debate about modernizing the governance of school systems in German-speaking countries (Brüsemeister and Eubel, 2003). This has resulted in various reform policies (Rürup, 2007). Altrichter and Heinrich (2007) have claimed that it is possible to distinguish three distinct phases of school modernization in Austria. In an *initial phase*, which in Austria started around 1993/94, *school autonomy* was the key word (Altrichter and Soukup-Altrichter, 2008). Legislation was passed and support measures were offered, which were meant to give room for in-school decision-making, with particular regard to curricular matters. This policy made it possible for schools to develop specific in-school curricula and so-called "Schulprofile" (school profiles). These school profiles are usually combinations of specific curricular elements (characterized by a thematic and/or methodological specialty) plus some additional features (such as extra-curricular learning opportunities, special features with respect to school culture and special services). With this profile, individual schools attempted to make themselves visible and attractive for target groups of students and parents and to attain sufficient student enrolment (particularly in times of decreasing student numbers). This is particularly relevant for private schools and secondary schools where parents have more freedom in their school choice. Recent studies show that the competition of schools (especially for above-average performing students) has led to differentiation and hierarchization within the school system; upholding their school's competitive capacity is a continuing concern of school leaders (see Altrichter *et al.*, 2014).

Only in a *second phase* of school modernization, during the second half of the 1990s, was the question of system governance explicitly raised. Concepts like school programs, self-evaluation, and quality management, new ways of school inspection, and coordination of classroom work through exemplary assignments and parallel tests ("Vergleichsarbeiten"; i.e. tests using identical items to compare the performance of different classes) became more prominent. These new measures were, however, not seen as a departure from the previous strategy of school autonomy nor as a step back to the old centralist models of regulation, but as a complement, which was supposed to provide top and intermediary levels of the school system with new options for control and intervention. Still, the idea of self-evaluation of schools through their teachers remained central; qualification and loyalty of teachers were seen as essential conditions for productive school development.

The *third phase* of this modernization debate was triggered by the results of the large-scale international assessments of Trends in International Mathematics and Science Study (TIMSS) and Programme for International Student Achievement (PISA), which were not favorable for the education systems of German-speaking countries (see Baumert, 1998; OECD, 2001). The 'PISA-shock' paved the way for new accents with regard to the modernization of the school system, such as demands for more, and more powerful *systemic instruments of governance* and, generally, *reinforced external governance of schools*. Therefore, in 2008 "performance standards" were introduced in Austria to form the basis for a more sophisticated evidence-based system of governance. Student performance, with respect to these standards, is regularly tested for system monitoring purposes; the results are to be used on all levels of the education system both as a stimulus, as well as an orientation for quality development, but not for comparison of students or schools (Altrichter and Kanape-Willingshofer, 2012). The first standardized testing took place in May 2012, with feedback results being made available only in January 2013. In March 2014, the Austrian Ministry of Education announced a stop to all students' assessments for 2014 (including field tests for PISA 2015 and national standard testing) due to information privacy issues. While the field tests for PISA 2015 were rescheduled to enable Austrian participation, a gap remains in the sequence of national standard testing. Thus, it is still too early to assess the effects of this new evidence-based system of governance.

Unlike the education systems of Germany (see Kotthoff and Böttcher, 2010), Austria has not introduced a national inspection system in which small teams of external inspectors evaluate individual schools according to predefined procedures and quality criteria (Ehren *et al.*, 2013). However, there have been experimental models of "team inspection" in some Austrian provinces (Altrichter *et al.*, 2013). In September 2013 a new legislation for a national system of quality management ("Nationaler Qualitätsrahmen") was introduced (BSAG Amendment, 2011; Altrichter, 2012). Based on this National Quality Framework (NQR) actors on all levels (e.g. individual schools, regional inspectors, the Ministry) are supposed to write a development plan, usually for a three-year period, based on central as well as local goals and assess its attainment by using all available evaluative data (e.g. national student performance data, but also self-evaluation). These various levels of stakeholders are linked by target agreements (e.g. between an individual school and its regional inspectorate). External development consultants, support schools, as well as a webpage with online self-evaluation instruments are provided.

In April 2011, the Austrian School Education Act (SchUG, 2015) was revised to strengthen the principal's role in the quality management of his/her school(s). Section 56(2) of the revised law now mentions school leadership and management, quality management, school and curriculum development, human resource development, as well as public relations management of schools as a school leader's main responsibilities. By including a requirement profile of school leaders, it is hoped to promote changes in school culture to reinforce the management side of the school principalship (Governmental Supplement, 2011).

Under the traditional model of bureaucratic-professional double regulation, school leaders were appointed from the ranks of experienced teachers. No prior training with respect to management competencies was required for application, but on-the-job training was provided after appointment. This situation may change in the near future, as three teacher-training institutions have been commissioned by the Ministry to develop master's level studies in school management. These programs began in 2013, but are presently not required for applying for a principalship.

In most school types there was a single principal with no deputy leaders and no middle management level between the principal and the teachers. In primary schools and in a type of secondary schools (Hauptschulen), there was no administrative support for the management and no ancillary educational staff at all. Also in the second type of secondary schools, the Gymnasium, there was limited support personnel. School leaders were an intermediate link in the administrative hierarchy meant to act as interpreter and gatekeeper between the external environment and the school. Inside the schools, they were expected to act as a "primus inter pares," which meant that they were expected to provide good organizational conditions for the work of the staff and to buffer the school against excessive outside interference, but not to interfere with the classroom autonomy of individual teachers.

The changes introduced by way of the three phases of school modernization have presented new demands on individual schools to act as semi-autonomous actors in their local environment and, thus, have certainly put pressure on the traditional concept of the role of school leadership. This new demand of school autonomy urged schools to quickly develop specific curricula and profiles responsive to their constituencies. School leaders were expected to stimulate development activities and to coordinate (sometimes heterogeneous) groups of teachers without being given new rights or instruments of leadership. More emphasis on internal conditions of leading emerged. New opportunities for the training of principals were developed by state agencies and made obligatory for new school leaders. The Ministry advocated for new instruments, such as school programs or school self-evaluation, which, in principle, offer some opportunities for internal coordination and development. These were also supported by official homepages and in-service initiatives. However, the use of these instruments has not been made obligatory for schools. The impact of PISA and TIMSS is still strongly evident in Austria's present attempt of establishing a data-based form of educational change and improvement (see also Specht and Sobanski, 2012, for an overview).

A uniform feature of these developments seems to be that demands have increased without being accompanied by a substantial reform of the legal conditions and of the rights and resources accorded to school leaders. Where attempts to change the system have been made, they were often implemented only half-heartedly; as an example, a new law on teacher employment that was meant to provide a (weak) basis for an in-school middle management was implemented in a way that did not reach its goals (see Seel *et al.*, 2006). The Ministry's attempts to introduce school programs as in-school coordination instruments were propagated by well-made support platforms and by regional in-service training. However, the law to make them binding was never passed due to opposition from the teacher union. There is an ongoing public discussion that calls for giving school leaders more voice in recruiting their staff, a right that is presently a prerogative of regional school administrations.

The practice of testing, accountability, and assessment in Austria's student assessment

The "Leistungsbeurteilungsverordnung" ("Decree on Student Assessment") (LBVO, 1997) is the legal document regulating student assessment in Austria. It leaves wide room for interpretation. As a consequence, there is an *in-school type of assessment* prevalent in Austrian schools; individual teachers use their own criteria, which might not be comparable to the assessments of neighboring schools. Often assessments vary across classes in the same school.

The lack of comparability of assessment and grading, as well as the lack of measurement quality (objectivity, reliability, validity) of in-school testing has often been criticized. To this point, there is a substantial group of students whose grades in mathematics do not correspond to their PISA results. According to Eder (2003), 7 percent of students who received negative classroom grades are in the top PISA-competence levels, while 10 percent who received the best grades are in the lowest PISA-competence levels. This has resulted in demands to use external student tests in order to make assessment more comparable and just (Eder *et al.*, 2009).

Contrary to these demands, the new law that introduced performance standards and student assessment (SchUG Amendment, 2008), also limited its use for system monitoring purposes and prohibited the use of these test results for grading. Nevertheless, the Ministry of Education expects that in the long run performance standards and external tests will gradually increase alignment and harmony among assessment requirements in schools (see Altrichter and Kanape-Willingshofer, 2012).

With regard to school graduation examinations of Gymnasium type and upper vocation secondary schools ("Matura"), a new format that includes more central elements and aims at higher comparability is being prepared. Its implementation has been postponed for one year due to teacher and parent protest and will be compulsory in grammar schools from 2014/15 and in vocational schools from 2015/16.

Teacher and school assessment

In Austria there are no formalized tools for teacher assessment. The appraisal of the quality of teachers' work is the task of their direct superiors, the school principals. The appraisal is usually non-selective and non-differential. Student performance is not used as an indicator of teacher quality in Austria.

However, federal officers called "school inspectors" exert supervision and control of individual schools. Inspectors are exclusively recruited from the ranks of experienced teachers and school leaders, as teacher qualification is a prerequisite for recruitment. Their work includes both the administrative organization of a school district and the control of individual schools with respect to legal compliance and educational quality (see BSAG, 2015). However, the strategies the school inspectors used for quality control varied between regions and also between individual inspectors due to a lack of common provisions. As a consequence, the media as well as the Austrian Court of Audit (see RH 2007, 2009) voiced concerns whether these traditional forms of inspection were up to the task of securing and advancing quality in schools. Some regional inspectorates reacted to this by experimenting with new types of school inspections, which were modeled after structures from the Netherlands and similar developments in the German "Bundesländer" (i.e. federal states) (see Altrichter *et al.*, 2013). With the new National Quality Framework, Austria seems to put even more emphasis on in-school development and internal evaluation and prevent the inspectorate from direct examination of schools.

On the whole, it seems fair to summarize that there has never been much accountability pressure on Austrian schools exerted by the authorities. This situation may change with the recently implemented instruments such as performance standards and external tests. These instruments could be used for assessing schools, teachers, and students. Presently, however, official statements, a range of provisions in the legal basis, and the implementation decrees state that external test data will only be used for system monitoring purposes, not for distinguishing between individual schools.

The role of school leaders in accountability and assessment

The following summarizes Austrian school leaders' view of various strategies of school development and provides some insights into principals' attitudes towards changes in the governance of schooling. The presented data were assembled from three different studies investigating Austrian school principals' opinions.

Principals' assessment of governance strategies

Data in this section are based on a questionnaire administered to school principals as Austrian national addition to PISA 2009. The population of the PISA 2009 study was defined by the age of their students (as a consequence principals of various types of lower and upper secondary schools from all over Austria were included) (see Altrichter *et al.*, 2012a; Schwandtner and Schreiner, 2010). Two-hundred and eighty-two principals were asked to assess a set of 15 different governance instruments and strategies for their appropriateness to improve school quality in Austria. A factor analysis distinguished four types of quality development strategies: through (1) instruments of evidence-based governance on a system level, (2) instruments of quality assurance on the level of individual schools, (3) qualification of educational staff, and (4) feedback from stakeholders (Altrichter *et al.*, 2012a, 2012b). Although all four strategies are considered as valid strategies for quality development by a majority of respondents, school leaders make clear differences in their assessment. As can be seen in Table 11.1, further "qualification of staff" is considered the most useful strategy for quality

Table 11.1 Comparison of different dimensions of system governance

Item	Mean	SD	t-value (df)	P
Evidence-based governance instruments	2.62	.60	−2.109 (257)	.036
Quality development strategies at school level	2.70	.53		
Evidence-based governance instruments	2.62	.60	−14.253 (260)	<.001
Qualification of staff	3.24	.51		
Evidence-based governance instruments	2.62	.60	−9.546 (257)	<.001
Feedback from stakeholders	3.05	.56		
Quality development strategies at school level	2.69	.53	−15.319 (259)	<.001
Qualification of staff	3.24	.50		
Quality development strategies at school level	2.69	.54	−9.352 (256)	<.001
Feedback from stakeholders	3.05	.56		
Qualification of staff	3.24	.51	4.905 (259)	<.001
Feedback from stakeholders	3.05	.56		

148 *Kanape-Willingshofer* et al.

development, followed by obtaining "feedback from stakeholders," employing "quality development strategies at the school-level," and using "evidence-based governance instruments" at the system level (paired differences are significant; $p<.05$ to $p<.001$). However, since there are substantial intercorrelations between the four factors (from $r=.20$ to $r=.45$; see Altrichter *et al.*, 2012b), they cannot be regarded as mutually exclusive strategies, but hint at a higher order factor underlying all four (e.g., an overall positive attitude towards reform in the school system).

Performance standards and external assessments

Performance standards have been implemented to improve school quality. They communicate clear competence descriptions in mathematics and German language proficiency (as well as English for lower secondary levels); attainment is annually assessed by external standardized testing for all pupils in the last year of primary education (fourth grade, since 2013, except 2014), as well as in the last year of lower secondary education (eighth grade, since 2012, except 2014). Results are solely used for feedback; that is, teachers receive aggregated results of their classes and principals receive aggregated results of their schools. Even though standardized national testing has now been introduced into the Austrian school system, the present form is one of low-stakes measurement for all stakeholders, including students, teachers, principals, and regional school authorities (see Pedulla, 2003). School leaders play a central role in effectively implementing an evidence-based governance regime since they are important gatekeepers. They may (or may not) stimulate and support staff to use the aggregated feedback, which the teachers receive based on the national performance tests for classroom and school development (cf. Altrichter and Kanape-Willingshofer, 2012).

The data discussed in the next paragraph are derived from a survey of principals whose schools participated in a pilot study of standardized student assessments in 2006 (Grabensberger *et al.*, 2008). It was shown that more than two thirds of school leaders reported to have gained many new insights through the feedback of the student performance test results. With respect to the transparency of test results, 69 percent of teachers wished to have access to the individual results of their students, but only 40 percent wanted their school leaders to be able to identify individual classes. The same situation emerged on the level of the school leaders: 60 percent wished to be informed about the results of individual classes, but only 46 percent thought it would be a good idea if the regional school board received the results of the individual schools. Moreover, a significant difference between school forms was found. Of school leaders in academic secondary schools ("Gymnasium"), 61 percent were in favor of local boards receiving individual school scores, compared to only 37 percent of school leaders in general secondary schools ("Hauptschulen"). These data reflect stakeholders' wishes for obtaining individualized information, but at the same time show their reluctance to share their own results with their superiors, especially when it may be expected that others have performed better (i.e. Gymnasium compared to Hauptschule).

External school inspections

The original legal basis for school inspections dates back to 1962 (Federal Act on School Supervision) (BSAG, 1962), but did not provide for a nationally uniform inspection model in Austria. The comparatively vague formulation of the law enabled the development of various regional inspection models such as inspecting in teams, standardization and formalization of inspection procedures, and use of data collection strategies modeled after social science research instruments (Altrichter et al., 2013; Kotthoff and Böttcher, 2010). As these school inspections have only recently been replaced by internal quality-management arrangements, future research is needed to show school leaders' evaluations of this new approach.

The subsequent data originate from questionnaire responses of 425 primary and secondary school principals in one province (Styria) as a part of the Austrian participation in the European project "Impact of School Inspection on Teaching and Learning" (ISI-TL, funded by the European Union) (see Ehren et al., 2013). In this province a new regional inspection model, the "team inspection model," was introduced in 2005/06.

The principals assessed most characteristics of this inspection model in a positive way, although a large group also indicated indifference towards the model. With respect to goals and effects of inspection (see Table 11.2) principals saw most effects on their staff. More than 60 percent thought that

Table 11.2 Evaluation of inspection goals

Team inspection ...	+	~	–	Mean	SD
helps to increase the quality and effectiveness of teaching	45%	43%	12%	3.37	.847
increases school work in legal, administrative, and economic criteria	43%	46%	11%	3.35	.817
helps to provide comparability between schools	16%	73%	11%	3.04	.659
helps teachers to become aware of what is important for a good school	47%	42%	11%	3.38	.831
increases the commitment of teachers with regard to seeing school development as part of their duties	61%	31%	8%	3.58	.841

Note: (+)... strongly agree and agree, (~) ... neither agree nor disagree, (–) ... disagree and strongly disagree.

team inspection helped to increase the commitment of teachers to understand that school development is one of their duties. Nearly 50 percent agreed that school inspections helped teachers recognize what is important for a good school and helped increase the quality of teaching. However, principals did not feel that school inspections offered a good basis for the comparison of schools.

Since inspection reports are to be published for the school community, they may insert new evidence into the relationship and negotiations between the schools' professionals and their stakeholders, such as parents, community representatives, and local politicians. Thus, school leaders were asked to assess the stakeholders' use of inspection results. The majority of principals indicated that neither the school board nor parents attended to the inspection criteria to a great extent. They estimated that four out of five parents used the inspection feedback to a minor extent or not at all, particularly when they had to choose a school or voice their opinion about a school. In addition, principals thought that the school board did not regularly consider the inspection feedback when making decisions (Altrichter *et al.*, 2013).

School leaders did not think that inspection data were appropriate for comparing schools and did not want inspection results to be published. When they were asked to rate different forms of publications, none of the options found support from a majority of school leaders. Reports to the school board ("Schulforum") were considered more favorably, possibly because respondents knew most about this obligatory established format.

School leaders' reluctance to have inspection results passed on to others was also reflected in their judgment about various forms of feedback. Although 60 percent agreed that it is useful to inform school partners about inspection results (vs. 7 percent in disagreement; 33 percent undecided or N/A), only 34 percent thought that handing the written report to the school board should be compulsory (vs. 27 percent in disagreement; 39 percent undecided or N/A).

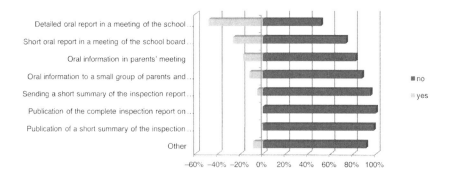

Figure 11.1 School leaders' (N=312) evaluation of the appropriateness of various forms of publishing inspection results

Overall, the recent modernization of Austrian school governance seems to leave stakeholders somewhat ambivalent. On the one hand, they regard evidence-based measures as useful to obtain feedback for instruction and school improvement and are interested in more detailed information about the performance of individual stakeholders. On the other hand, all of the analyzed data indicate stakeholders' strong wish to keep evaluation results private and to restrict public forms of accountability (such as public reporting).

Summary and outlook: New options for school leadership?

Austria has seen waves of reforms for school governance. These changes have provided more room for maneuver for local school development and have also increased competition between schools (see Altrichter *et al.*, 2014). Although performance standards for student performance and external performance testing have recently been introduced, the Austrian system is far from becoming a high stake accountability regime with clear performance threshold levels and sanctions for low-performing actors. By introducing performance standards, as well as a National Quality Framework, it is hoped that teachers and schools will be provided with clear goals and instruments for pursuing quality improvement in teaching and schools. The revised Austrian School Education Act (BSAG, 2015) strongly emphasizes school leaders' role in assuring that school quality is appropriately and regularly assessed, as well as that the obtained data are used for quality improvement not only at the classroom but also at the school level. Principals are now also formally responsible for quality control and human resource development, rather than mainly managing a school on an administrative level. This rationale still needs time to set in school leaders' (as well as teachers') minds, now that it is set in law. However, Austrian principals' challenge is not an easy one as they are responsible for quality improvement and human resource development, but at the same time have little freedom of decision when it comes to personnel selection and termination of contracts (at least in public schools).

The present scenario puts a lot of pressure on individual school leaders. As *gatekeepers* and *border managers* of the schools, they are informed about rising expectations by state authorities, inspectors, and community stakeholders, and it is expected that they translate ("recontextualize") (see Fend, 2006) these expectations into in-school communication, teacher motivation, development projects, and supportive work structures. This implies taking on leadership responsibility (to a larger extent than before when their tasks were restricted to in-school administration) and requires new developmental and managerial competencies, which they are usually not equipped with during their teacher education, the prerequisite experience for becoming a school principal. With one principal being the direct supervisor of all teachers in a school (due to the lack of deputy or middle managers) and a highly limited scope of action, the position was traditionally understood as an administrative managerial one, rather than a task of leadership by which common visions are established and implemented. Interestingly, leadership succession planning and leadership preparation is neither explicitly articulated as a principal's responsibility in the Revision of the Austrian School Education Act (see SchUG Amendment, 2011) nor in daily practice.

Due to increased responsibilities following recent changes, it does not come as a surprise that many school leaders have reservations about new governance policies and seem to long for a situation in which they are less accountable to their constituency and less transparency is requested. Conversely, they are still more open towards new governance instruments than their teachers (see Altrichter *et al.*, 2012a). Longitudinal data also indicate that, overall, Austrian school leaders have become more proactive and more in favor of development since 2000 (Altrichter *et al.*, 2012a). The next years will show whether and how school leaders make use of the newly introduced quality management and development instruments (i.e., performance standards, external student achievement test, and the National Quality Framework).

In the wake of recent reforms, governance structures have become more formalized and more demanding, and administrative actors have become more professional. In this situation of rising aspirations and demands, the traditional career and qualification paths from teaching into principalship are likely not to suffice for long. School leaders would be exposed to a more demanding situation without protection if they were not given the chance to expand their qualification and to professionalize their competencies. After years of resistance to special tertiary degrees for school leaders, the Austrian Ministry of Education has recently commissioned three teacher-training institutions to develop and run special study programs for school management at master's level. We hope that these academic programs will also boost research and development in the field of school management.

References

Altrichter, H. (2012). *Veränderungen von Schulaufsicht und Schulinspektion in Österreich*. Unpublished manuscript, Department of Education and Psychology, Johannes Kepler University, Linz, Austria.

Altrichter, H. and Heinrich, M. (2007). Kategorien der Governance-Analyse und Transformationen der Systemsteuerung in Österreich. In H. Altrichter, T. Brüsemeister and J. Wissinger (eds) *Educational Governance – Handlungskoordination und Steuerung im Bildungssystem* (pp. 55–103). Wiesbaden: Verlag für Sozialwissenschaften.

Altrichter, H. and Kanape-Willingshofer, A. (2012). Bildungsstandards und externe Überprüfung von Schülerkompetenzen: Mögliche Beiträge externer Messungen zur Erreichung der Qualitätsziele der Schule. In B. Herzog-Punzenberger (ed.) *Nationaler Bildungsbericht Österreich 2012, Band 2: Fokussierte Analysen bildungspolitischer Schwerpunktthemen* (pp. 355–394). Graz: Leykam.

Altrichter, H. and Soukup-Altrichter, K. (2008). Changes in Educational Governance

Through More Autonomous Decision-Making and In-School Curricula? *International Journal of Contemporary Sociology* 45(2), 33–49.
Altrichter, H., Kemethofer, D., and Leitgöb, H. (2012a). Schulentwicklung und Systemsteuerung. In F. Eder (ed.), *PISA 2009. Nationale Zusatzanalysen für Österreich* (pp. 228–253). Münster: Waxmann.
Altrichter, H., Kemethofer, D., and Leitgöb, H. (2012b). Ansätze der Systemsteuerung in der Einschätzung von Schulleitern. *Empirische Pädagogik*, 20(1), 12–32.
Altrichter, H., Kemethofer, D., and Schmidinger, E. (2013). Neue Schulinspektion und Qualitätsmanagement im Schulsystem. *Erziehung und Unterricht*, 163(9–10), 961–978.
Altrichter, H., Heinrich, M., and Soukup-Altrichter, K. (2014). School Decentralisation as a Process of Differentiation, Hierarchization and Selection. *Journal of Education Policy*. DOI:10.1080/02680939.2013.873954.
Baumert, J. (1998). *TIMSS – Mathematisch-naturwissenschaftlicher Unterricht im internationalen Vergleich*. Opladen: Leske-Budrich.
Brüsemeister, T. (2004). *Schulische Inklusion und neue Governance*. Münster: Monsenstein & Vannerdat.
Brüsemeister, T. and Eubel, K.-D. (eds) (2003). *Zur Modernisierung der Schule*. Bielefeld: Transcript.
BSAG (Bundes-Schulaufsichtsgesetz) (1962). *Bundesgesetz vom 25. Juli 1962 über die Organisation der Schulverwaltung und Schulaufsicht des Bundes*. BGBl. Nr. 240/1962. Available at www.ris.bka.gv.at/Dokumente/BgblPdf/1962_240_0/1962_240_0.pdf.
BSAG (2015). *Bundesgesetz vom 25. Juli 1962 über die Organisation der Schulverwaltung und Schulaufsicht des Bundes – aktuelle Fassung*. BGBl. Nr. 240/1962 revised through BGBl. I N5. 38/2015. Available at www.ris.bka.gv.at/GeltendeFassung.wxe?Abfrage=Bundesnormen&Gesetzesnummer=10009264.
BSAG Amendment (2011). *Änderung des Bundes-Schulaufsichtsgesetzes vom 20. Mai 2011*. BGBl. Nr. 240/1962 revised through BGBl. I N5. 25/2008. Available at www.ris.bka.gv.at/Dokumente/BgblAuth/BGBLA_2011_I_28/BGBLA_2011_I_28.html.
Ehren, M. C. M., Altrichter, H., McNamara, G., and O'Hara, J. (2013). Impact of School Inspections on Improvement of Schools: Describing assumptions on causal mechanisms in six European countries. *Educational Assessment, Evaluation and Accountability*, 25(1), 3–43.
Eder, F. (2003). Tests und Lehrerurteil. Wie gut stimmen externe Leistungstests mit Lehrereinstufungen überein? In E. J. Brunner, P. Noack, G. Scholz and I. Scholl (eds) *Diagnose und Intervention in schulischen Handlungsfeldern* (pp. 125–140). Münster: Waxmann.
Eder, F., Neuweg, G. H., and Thonhauser, J. (2009). Leistungsfeststellung und Leistungsbeurteilung. In W. Specht (ed.) *Nationaler Bildungsbericht Österreich 2009, Bd. 2: Fokussierte Analysen bildungspolitischer Schwerpunktthemen* (pp. 247–269). Graz: Leykam.
Fend, H. (2006). *Neue Theorie der Schule*. VS: Wiesbaden.
Governmental Supplement (2011). *Nr 1112 der Beilagen XXIV. Gesetzgebungsperiode*. Available at www.parlament.gv.at/PAKT/VHG/XXIV/I/I_01112/fname_210106.pdf.
Grabensberger, E., Freudenthaler, H. H., and Specht, W. (2008). *Bildungsstandards: Testungen und Ergebnisrückmeldungen auf der achten Schulstufe aus der Sicht der*

Praxis. *Ergebnisse einer Befragung von Leiterinnen, Leitern und Lehrkräften der Pilotschulen*. Graz: Abteilung Evaluation und Schulforschung.

Kotthoff, H.-G. and Böttcher, W. (2010). Neue Formen der „Schulinspektion": Wirkungshoffnungen und Wirksamkeit im Spiegel empirischer Bildungsforschung. In H. Altrichter and K. Maag Merki (eds) *Handbuch Neue Steuerung im Schulsystem* (pp. 295–325). Wiesbaden: Verlag für Sozialwissenschaften.

LBVO (Leistungsbeurteilungsverordnung) (1997). *Verordnung des Bundesministeriums für Unterricht und Kunst vom 24. Juni 1974 über die Leitungsbeurteilung in Pflichtschulen sowie mittleren und höheren Schulen (Leistungsbeurteilungsverordnung)*, BGBl. Nr. 371/1974, zuletzt geändert durch BGBl. II Nr 35/1997. Available at www.ris.bka.gv.at/;GeltendeFassung/ Bundesnormen/10009375/Leistungsbeurteilungsverordnung%2c%20Fassung%2 0vom%2025.05.2012.pdf.

OECD (Organization for Economic Co-operation and Development) (2001). *Lernen für das Leben. Erste Ergebnisse der internationalen Schulleistungsstudie PISA 2000*. Paris: OECD Publishing.

Pedulla, J. J. (2003). State-mandated Testing: What do teachers think? *Educational Leadership*, 61(3), 42–46.

RH (Rechnungshof) (2007). *Organisation und Wirksamkeit der Schulaufsicht*. Bericht. Available at www.rechnungshof.gv.at/fileadmin/downloads/2007/ berichte/teilberichte/bund/Bund_2007_02/Bund_2007_02_3.pdf

RH (2009). *Organisation und Wirksamkeit der Schulaufsicht; Follow-up-Überprüfung*. Report Bund_2009_13_5. Available at www.rechnungshof.gv.at/ fileadmin/downloads/2009/berichte/teilberichte/bund/bund_2009_13/bund_ 2009_13_5.pdf.

Rürup, M. (2007). *Innovationswege im deutschen Bildungssystem*. Wiesbaden: Verlag für Sozialwissenschaften.

SchUG (Schulunterrichtsgesetz) (2015). *Bundesgesetz über die Ordnung von Unterricht und Erziehung in den im Schulorganisationsgesetz geregelten Schulen (Schulunterrichtsgesetz – SchUG)*. BGBl. Nr. 472/1986, revised through BGBl. I Nr. 38/2015. Available at www.ris.bka.gv.at/GeltendeFassung.wxe?Abfrage= Bundesnormen&Gesetzesnummer=10009600.

SchUG Amendment (2008). *Änderung des Schulunterrichtsgesetzes vom 8. August 2008*. BGBl. Nr. 472/1986, revised through BGBl. I Nr. 117/2008. Available at www.ris.bka.gv.at/Dokumente/BgblAuth/BGBLA_2008_I_117/BGBLA_2008_ I_117.html.

SchUG Amendment (2011). *Änderung des Schulunterrichtsgesetzes vom 20. Mai 2011*. BGBl. Nr. 472/1986, revised through BGBl. I Nr. 112/2009. Available at www.ris.bka.gv.at/Dokumente/BgblAuth/BGBLA_2011_I_29/BGBLA_2011_ I_29.html.

Schwandtner, U. and Schreiner, C. (eds) (2010). *PISA 2009. Internationaler Vergleich von Schülerleistungen*. Graz: Leykam.

Seel, A., Altrichter, H., and Mayr, J. (2006). Innovation durch ein neues Lehrerdienstrecht? Eine Evaluationsstudie zur Implementierung des LDG 2001. In M. Heinrich and U. Greiner (eds) *Schauen, was 'rauskommt. Kompetenzförderung, Evaluation und Systemsteuerung im Bildungswesen* (pp. 9–111). Wien: Lit-Verlag.

Specht, W. and Sobanski, F. (2012). *OECD Review on evaluation and assessment: Frameworks for improving school outcomes. Country background report for Austria*. Available at www.oecd.org/education/preschoolandschool/49578470.pdf.

12 Top-down accountability and local management

Tensions and contradictions experienced by French principals as leaders

Romuald Normand and Jean-Louis Derouet

The issue of accountability is not much debated in the French educational world. The difficulty is semantic because there is no clear distinction in the French language between appraisal, assessment, and evaluation. Policy makers often translate the word "accountability" as a circumlocution: "obligation of outcomes," which can be seen as an indication of the importance of rules in the French educational system and the compliance with regulations expected from each citizen. But the idea of "making an account" or "being accountable" is not a common practice for French principals and teachers. As civil servants, they estimate they have to fulfill their legal duties, to apply the official curriculum guidelines decided by the Ministry of Education, and to defend the legacy of public services. People make some mental confusion between assessment and control, or assessment and inspection, which is amplified by a strong focus on teaching (at the expense of learning).

However, for several years, there have been some important transformations regarding the conception and the role of assessment by the Ministry of Education, particularly the creation of the Direction de l'Evaluation, de la Prospective et de la Performance (DEPP). This Directorate monitors the national assessments and develops statistics for the governance of the French education system. But despite the design of indicators and the development of national assessments, policy makers continue to have concerns about how to promote a "culture of accountability" across schools. For a decade, many reports from the inspection board and researchers have led to the same conclusions: there is a lack of assessment and accountability in the French educational system. Today, student assessment depends on grades and exams, without high-stake tests. There are no agencies or institutions that produce these tests and the assessment of teaching and learning, as well as leadership, is not really investigated by educational research in a practical way. Another explanation is the existence of several bodies of inspection, which dominates the administration of the educational system from the top to the bottom. Even though they have been criticized as excessive, hierarchical, and bureaucratic, the inspector's power is considered to be strong and decisive. The

Inspectorate has been developing audits and self-evaluation frameworks but these remain largely experimental and not systematic.

Despite a voluntary policy to promote a "culture of accountability" in the French educational system, the issue remains largely unquestioned by practitioners: inspectors, principals, and teachers. This response could be explained by ongoing, bureaucratic regulation in the absence of incentives at local levels that impedes any sustainable implementation of reform. Today, numerous voices among progressive policy makers and officials make a case for more devolution, more school autonomy, and less top-down bureaucracy. But the resistance to the introduction of accountability in the French educational system is not only a matter of structure due to the importance of centralization and bureaucracy. It also concerns the professional culture embedded in daily practices within schools, (e.g., the focus on teaching at the expense of learning, the loosely coupled relationship among staff members, the lack of vision and leadership among principals, the weakness of teacher self-development and creativity).

This chapter is developed around a study that aims to better understand the actions of principals in secondary education facing some dilemmas after the implementation of the French policy of accountability. The field of research on school management and leadership is not highly developed in France. Studies investigate the cultural and social characteristics of principals at work with respect to their social identity, professionalization, ethics, and deontology, but not really the multiple dimensions of their activities in schools (Elmore, 2004). The notion of educational management is not very popular among educators and academics. They consider the concept of management to be linked to business and economic views as opposed to values among public services. Professionals themselves use it rarely and prefer to speak about "controlling," "monitoring," and "steering" a school system or an organization rather than "managing" it. French principals view themselves as "administrators" or "representatives of the state" and they are very concerned about applying national legislation and Ministry directives. Under this bureaucratic top-down hierarchy, the idea of leadership encounters some limitations (Leithwood, 2001). Even if this notion is implicitly present within official instructions that define principals as "pedagogical and educative pilots" of schools, these executives lack real legitimacy to act on the teaching and learning issues, which remains in the hands of state inspectors (MacBeath, 2006). Therefore, principal leadership is recognized not as an official function, but rather through an implicit and blurred sense of professionalism expressed sometimes by principals and inspectors as "personal charisma," "sense of dialogue," and "proximity." On the contrary, "authority" and "responsibility" are the main social representations common to executives, allowing them to define their "missions" as public servants.

School principals' actions are largely framed by national regulations enacted by the Ministry and Parliament, which limit their autonomy and capacity to take initiative at the local level (Derouet and Normand, 2009). This presents several challenges for school principals. First, they have to be accountable through regular reports and interviews within the hierarchy (inspectors and superintendents) along administrative and bureaucratic lines. There is no link between school effectiveness and school improvement (Stoll, Fink, 1996). Additionally, principals face a challenge with regard to the policy of "individualization" of students' careers through the education system. This policy aims to adapt teaching to the learning and guidance needs of students. In 2005, the French government passed a reform (*Loi n° 2005-380 du 23 avril 2005 d'orientation et de programme pour l'avenir de l'école*, 2005) declaring the necessity of establishing certain minimum competence standards for students. As a response, a framework of basic skills and knowledge was published in 2006 by the French Ministry of Education to increase student performance at the end of compulsory schooling. However, it is more focused on guidance than on learning. This might be due to the tradition of the French system and the culture of educators who are mostly concerned with the equality of opportunities related to the transmission of knowledge and a fair access to education (Derouet and Normand, 2011). Indeed the system focuses more on tracking careers and modalities of access than modifying the relationship between teaching and learning. In addition, as teachers are accustomed to their "pedagogical freedom," they have historically decided in an individual manner what to teach (within the confines of the curriculum) and how to teach the curriculum in their classrooms. Inspectors visit them every five or seven years.

However the current implementation of the basic skills and knowledge framework has proven consequential to daily work of teachers in lower secondary schools. They are required by inspectors to work together to find ways to improve student success. Each student has to reach a certain level of skills in French, mathematics, and sciences at different stages of her or his scholarship. But curricula and courses are largely fixed by national instructions based on the number of teaching hours per school subject. Principals struggle to link these standards with the diversification required to promote personalized student learning and success (Hopkins, 2007). To strengthen cooperation in secondary schools, the legislation created a "pedagogical board" to help principals bring teachers together regularly in order to talk and to make decisions regarding school improvement and to facilitate teamwork; this took place as part of the aforementioned reform in 2005. But it remains difficult for principals to make these meetings effective for several reasons: opposition of trade unions, individualistic conceptions of teaching, lack of pressure and support, loose-coupled relationships in schools, etc.

The last challenge concerns the new accountability currently being implemented at the national level. Each principal has to design a school development plan to justify the use of resources and means, to fix targets related to national policy, and to be accountable for student achievement measured by national assessments and exams. But it is largely loose-coupled with what teachers do in their classrooms while there is not much cooperation between them.

School accountability in the French context: A loosely coupled environment

Before describing precisely the actions of principals, the French policy of accountability and its implementation will be briefly presented here. The policy is nascent in the French education context even though some frameworks and indicators were designed to support decision making and the evaluation of the education system (Cohen and Spillane, 1994). The Direction de l'Evaluation, de la Prospective et de la Performance (DEPP or Directorate of Evaluation, Forecast and Performance) has vast experience designing statistical data systems inherited from the expertise of the National Institute of Statistics and Economic Studies (INSEE). Over the years, it has developed a sophisticated system to gather data on the inequality gaps that have emerged between students from different social backgrounds.

The press typically publishes results of the (centrally administered) baccalaureate exams. This has, over time, led to a focus on exam results when comparing schools. Possibly to counterbalance this development, the Ministry of Education designed added value indicators for *Lycées* (high schools) in order to maintain, according to official discourse, a certain objectivity and neutrality with regard to the comparison of schools. Instead of only publishing raw test scores, two other indicators are also shared to provide a more well-rounded picture: the first one assesses the capacity of teaching staff to retain students during three years of schooling (an indicator of the pedagogical effectiveness of teaching teams); the second indicator assesses the capacity of the school to prevent students from dropping out (an indicator of the limitation of adverse selection and the maintenance of an equality of access).

A second type of evaluation has been implemented through national assessments or tests at the primary level (grades 2 and 5). These tests are designed to measure students' mastery of basic skills in French and mathematics (Normand and Derouet, 2004). Since their creation they have been considered as formative assessments to support teachers in their diagnosis of student learning needs. It was the intention of the DEPP that these tests distinguish themselves from tests developed by Anglo-Saxon countries in the hope that they would lead to higher acceptance by educators and trade unions. The tests were not oriented towards selection and certification but served as a tool to support teaching. However, based on our three-year study, these assessments are not really used by teachers to change their practices and to take the learning context into account (Derouet and Normand, 2004). Practitioners who participated in the study felt like these assessments were not apt to gain insights about student learning and students' cognitive processes. When looking at their actual use, we found that they were often used to group students into clusters (for example, according to academic achievement levels in a certain subject). Many teachers voiced their concerns regarding managing numerous students and heterogeneous profiles in classrooms. This can be seen as an indication that teachers are currently not sufficiently trained to develop assessments of their teaching practices.

In recent years, the Ministry has created a "booklet of skills" (*Livret de compétences*) for reporting student scores and attainments of basic skills at different stages. However, reports by the French General Inspectorate of Education (Houchot and Robine, 2007) indicate that this tool is not having a big impact: teachers fill out the "booklet of skills" in a quick and formal manner; it does not seem to lead to increased reflexivity on teaching practices. Teachers' assessments remain largely based on traditional marks; formative assessment does not seem to be a current practice in the profession (Normand and Derouet, 2011).

Bodies of accountability and inspection

Three bodies of inspection largely monopolize the evaluation of the secondary education system, its schools, and agents across three different areas: (1) accountancy and finances, (2) school administration, and (3) school subjects. Recently, the Ministry has encouraged audits. A lot of professionals are committed to the conception of "audits with participative aim," which means a principal is able, after a first diagnosis of the school, to call for a visit from a group of inspectors. These visits are different from traditional monitoring by inspection as they give the opportunity to build a constructive dialogue between the school management team and inspectors who provide recommendations. However, each principal is free to decide on the use of this information and its reporting among the staff. This kind of participative audit remains an exception in the inspection landscape and most visits by inspectors are imposed and not negotiated, even if they have uncertain effects on school achievement (de Wolf and Janssens, 2007). There are now two types of inspections. Individual inspections are carried out by a visiting inspector specialized in a discipline and school subject, who observes a teacher roughly every five years on average. A new type of inspection is the collective one. These are led by a group of inspectors specialized in the supervision of schools or finances, who collectively visit and evaluate the whole organization. This new type of inspection can be seen as an attempt to change the professional culture from one of control to one of control and support. For some inspectors, this paradigm shift has been difficult.

The 2001 Act, which modernized the laws of finances (Loi Organique relative au Lois de Finances), not only modified the public education accountancy system but implemented indicators of accountability through national programs of performance. According to new public management principles (Normand, 2012), the objective was to reduce costs and to increase effectiveness and efficiency of public services (state local authorities and schools in the education sector). When designing their school development plan and setting targets with their staff, principals have to take these new indicators into account. This is formalized through a contract of objectives linking the school with local authorities. In addition, a "letter of assignments" was created in 2011 (Ministère de l'Education Nationale, 2011). In this letter to the state local authority, the principal sets out targets related to national guidelines and the reduction of achievement gaps between students. On the surface, these measures suggest accountability coupled with autonomy (for example with regard to what goals to set and how to achieve them). However, principals do not have the authority to recruit staff and have very limited maneuverability in obtaining additional resources.

As authors, we examined this process of accountability and its consequences in the aforementioned study through interviews and a statistical survey. The aim was to better understand the vision of evaluation shared by principals in secondary schools and how they act daily with data to manage their school. The study also sought to explain challenges they were facing as leaders to promote school improvement and performance in a loose-coupled environment.

Methods

The study was conducted in the district of Lyon over the course of three years. It consisted of an extensive document analysis of matters of evaluation in the French education system and 30 interviews with secondary school principals. The interviews revolved around various aspects of data driven school leadership: *the information system* (use of data, design of tools, objectives, limitations, conveniences, degrees of complexity, and remaining needs); *the supporting role of data in coordination and management* (data sharing and dissemination, team work, discussion, and negotiation); *the role of data in relation to the external environment* (inspectorate, families, state and local authorities, relationships/partnerships, and exchanges/strategies); *and principals' professional background in the use of data* (training, experience, professional identity, and personal interest in evaluation and assessment issues). The interviews were complemented by observations in school. In addition, the interviews formed the basis for a quantitative study that was sent out to 1500 school principals (with 400 participating). In this chapter, the main research findings related to matters of accountability are presented. They are derived from a subset of data from the main study.

Findings

According to official guidelines, a diagnosis is to be undertaken in regular intervals. The diagnosis is used to inform the "assignment letter" of principals and it also serves as a basis for a development plan containing objectives for the schools. Each principal is supposed to analyze the characteristics of the school, its evolution, strengths, weaknesses, and potentials; official guidelines provide a frame of reference for this. Besides a demographic analysis (number of students, pedagogical structures, class sizes, etc.), indicators are clustered into different categories: guidance (careers of students), students' scores (exams and national assessments), and care (sanctions, retention, attendance). In theory, this could lead to an increased exchange between the principal and staff as the school is "diagnosed." However, our findings suggest it is more used as a means to justify the actions of principals to their hierarchy than to communicate with the staff. The data collected often does not include data on teaching and learning conditions. Indicators are mainly used to measure inequality gaps between students according to their social background. However, these indicators only provide very little information regarding possible areas of development, as they are not very detailed. Although principals are encouraged by the local authorities to design "steering tools," or to define "targets for progress" through "contracts of objectives," the use of indicators reveals a formal planning of actions. The school board discusses the school development plan but our findings indicate that, so far, it does not have a big impact in changing the school culture.

Principals in our study were of the opinion that the results of a diagnosis should not be imposed on teaching staff and parents, but that they had to be carefully introduced to avoid the emergence of hostile reactions from the teaching and parental community. One the one hand, they feel and see a need to base the diagnosis on "hard data" to avoid assessments based on feelings or subjective views. On the other hand, there is an expectation of trust between principals and teachers and an expectation that the concerns of the latter are taken into account. Principals therefore generally look for a balance between objectivity of data and the maintenance of trust with teachers and parents.

Our study indicated that some of the data generated through the various evaluation and diagnosis instruments are useful in reassuring teachers their concerns are taken seriously. This concerns areas (e.g., rates of promotion and retention, and indicators related to the student–teacher ratio) are part of the diagnosis. While to some extent data use has had a positive impact on limiting selectivity and elitism among select teachers, data are scarcely used to assess the effectiveness of plans and actions. Data provided by the local authority are not really used while other fields of assessment are not really developed. In addition, principals manipulate the indicators and other data through minor negotiations with teachers.

Data help principals to objectivity inform their acts, but the school context remains complex and can hardly be analyzed by the existing indicators and a global diagnosis. This means that currently each principal has to invent his or her own way to manage data to support decision making, leadership, and relationships with the staff and the state local authority. Some of them design specific indicators, for example to anticipate the closing of a course or the decline in the number of students, to study local dropouts, or to compare data across time. Data are also gathered and combined to check hypotheses about school attractiveness or strategies of parents circumventing the regulations of the catchment area. Most of the principals from the study try to share their analysis with other persons and choose only a few relevant indicators for their decision making. They are aware that statistics can create some interpretative problems and can bring about a belief in a false objectivity with a negative impact on judgment. Principals from the study were firmly opposed to the rankings between schools.

Principals use data to argue about their strategies with teachers and the state local authority. They also use data to reassure teachers, but also to demonstrate the urgency and the need for action. They report data on slides and papers in order to reduce their complexity and to produce an acceptable discourse for the teaching community. Principals also employ statistics to promote discussions on equality of opportunities. Some of the principals from the study "cheated with data" by declaring a false number of students vis-à-vis the local authorities to obtain additional teaching hours in their budget. In addition, statistics are used to share information on student achievement and guidance.

Principals organize meetings to present the school development plan and different actions, often supported or expressed by statistics, in other words data. However, as teachers lack training in reading data and making data-based decisions, principals can be misunderstood by teachers who might feel stigmatized. Despite these presentations, many teachers feel ill informed, which does not facilitate the dialogue between school leaders and teaching staff and the sharing of responsibilities. Teachers, and to a lesser degree, principals are not really involved in data-driven development, research development, or professional development. Additionally, the current professional culture of teachers in France is not conducive for a climate of identifying and reflecting on problems and towards concepts of instructional effectiveness and school improvement. Many teachers reject the idea of rankings and neglect data, which could challenge their practices. Many teachers consider themselves not to be responsible for student achievement. As a consequence, principals often limit collaborative efforts in data sharing and school development to a few voluntary teachers who agree to work in teams or to be involved in the school development plan. However, as mentioned before, matters of accountability regarding teaching and learning are not really present. Most of principals limit their role to providing data on achievement, guidance, and retention without challenging teachers' judgment on students.

Apart from this type of use, principals generally prefer using data related to their school and pedagogical issues, even if it remains challenging to talk about it with teachers. The local authority is interested by data on local governance and administrative accountability. The support of the inspectorate remains rare, even if its audits are actually much appreciated. Principals in the study criticized the local "policy of statistics," which they felt did not take into account the local context of schools. Objectives and targets were also not clear for them and they did not feel supported within the hierarchy. The exchange of information among principals during local meetings did not seem to impact the coordination of actions among schools. They remained isolated units and did not cooperate as a network. The share of knowledge and skills and the promotion of a same "culture of accountability indicators" did not help to compensate for the split between professional bodies and between the secondary and the primary education sectors. Administrative regulation seemed to override possible teamwork on school development plans and indicators.

Conclusion

The information presented in this chapter highlights a gap between the design of accountability by the French Ministry of Education and its implementation within the daily life of secondary schools. Because the system of gathering and using data is not adjusted to teaching and learning issues, principals are condemned to manage them externally along the priorities defined by the local authorities. Statistics are mainly used for reporting but not for school improvement and teamwork. The idea of being accountable is at present far from the mind of teachers who maintain an individualistic vision of teaching. As a consequence, it is difficult for a French principal to act as a transformative leader using data because of the approach's elusive influence, despite the school development plan and the creation of a "pedagogical board" (Leithwood and Jantzi, 1991, 1999). However, there are signs of change. The Ministry and the general inspectorate are increasingly interested in the development of self-evaluation of schools, while the need for intermediary functions of support and coordination both inside and outside schools is getting recognition by policy makers. The development of a coherent accountability policy system requires placing evaluation and assessment at the center of school improvement in order to transform the internal and pedagogical organization.

What is at stake is also the modernization of the national data system to convert it into a tool that helps teachers support student achievement and progress. For these changes to be implemented effectively, the role and functions of principals and inspectors would have to be revised to be less hierarchical and more focused on management and leadership. It would mean a profound change in their professional culture. But what is also at stake is the capacity of the Ministry of Education to provide better tools and resources to support schools and to sustain continuous professional development at the school level. A move towards more autonomy and decentralization is also likely to help simplify the bureaucratic scaffolding that impedes to develop transversal relationships and networking between schools. The challenge is to better recognize leaders, even within the teaching profession, to further open spaces for innovation and creativity, and to promote an intelligent accountability system beyond traditional, hierarchical, and unproductive controls.

References

Cohen, D. K. and Spillane, J. P. (1994). National education indicators and traditions of accountability. In OECD (ed.), *Making Education Count: Developing and Using International Indicators* (pp. 323–337). Paris: Centre for Educational Research and Innovation.

Derouet, J.-L. and Normand, R. (2011). The hesitation of French policy makers in identifying a third way in education, *Journal of Educational Administration and History*, 43(2): 141–163.

de Wolf, I. and Janssens, F.J.G. (2007). Effects and side effects of inspections and accountability in education: an overview of empirical studies. *Oxford Review of Education*, 33(3): 379–396.

Elmore R.F. (2004). *School Reform from the Inside Out*, Cambridge, MA: Harvard Education Press.

Hopkins, D. (2007). *Every School a Great School*, London: McGraw Hill/Open University Press.

Houchot, A. and Robine, F. (2007). *Les livrets de compétences: nouveaux outils pour l'évaluation des acquis; Inspection générale de l'éducation nationale*, Rapport n° 2007-048 – juin 2007, http://media.education.gouv.fr/file/50/0/6500.pdf

Leithwood, K. (2001). School leadership in the context of accountability policies, *International Journal of Leadership in Education*, 4(3): 217–235.

Leithwood, K. and Jantzi, D. (1991). Transformational leadership: how principals can help reform school cultures, *School Effectiveness and School Improvement*, 1(3): 249–281.

Leithwood, K. and Jantzi, D. (1999). The effects of transformational leadership on organizational conditions and student engagement with school, *Journal of Educational Administration*, 38(2), 112–129.

MacBeath, J. (2006). *School Inspection and Self-evaluation: Working with the New Relationship*. London: RoutledgeFalmer

Ministère de l'Education Nationale (2011). *Note de service n° 2011-201 du 20-10-2011*. Paris: Ministère de l'Education Nationale.

Normand, R. (2012). The teaching profession put to the test of new public management: The third way reform in Bezes, P., Demazière, D., Le Bianic, T., Paradeise, C., Normand, R., Benamouzig, D., … and Evetts, J. New public management and professionals in the public sector. What new patterns beyond opposition? *Sociologie du travail*, 54 : 1–52.

Normand, R. and Derouet, J-L. (2004). Le développement d'une culture de l'évaluation. Comment les enseignants utilisent les résultats des évaluations nationales en CE2 et 6ᵉ, Rapport pour le Commissariat au Plan et la Direction de l'Evaluation et de la Prospective, http://ep.enslyon.fr/EP/ressources/diffusion_culture_evaluation/enseignants_evaluations_nationales/view

Normand, R. and Derouet, J.-L. (eds) (2011). Évaluation des élèves, développement professionnel des enseignants, et transformations de l'organisation scolaire. Réflexions autour d'expériences anglo-saxonnes, *Revue Française de Pédagogie*, 174: 5–20.

Spillane, J. P. (2006). *Distributed Leadership*. San Francisco: Jossey-Bass.

Spillane, J., Halverson, R., and Diamond, J. (2004). Towards a theory of leadership practice: a distributed perspective, *Journal of Curriculum Studies*, 36(1): 3–34.

13 Accountability in the German school system

More of a burden than a preference

Stephan Gerhard Huber, Bettina-Maria Gördel, Selin Kilic, and Pierre Tulowitzki

The Federal Republic of Germany is comprised of 16 federal states, known in German as "Länder" (singular is Land, plural Länder). As a federal principle, matters of education and culture lie with each state. This means that each of the 16 states has its own school system framed by individual jurisdictional and administrative laws, encompassing its own educational policy goals, school structures, school types, curricula, etc. Therefore the 16 school systems in Germany feature different educational and governing traditions. Despite these differences, the governing of each state is organized according to a rather traditional bureaucratic governing model (see Table 13.1).

The minister of a state usually represents the top of the governing structure (macro level) with a succession of subordinate institutions (meso level), and the schools themselves functioning as the lowest units (micro level). In larger states like Bavaria, North Rhine-Westphalia, and Baden-Württemberg, there is a four-level administrative organization, which includes the Ministry, a state office for education and/or school quality and the regional school supervisory administration, the school supervisory offices at the level of counties or county-independent cities, and finally school leadership at the school level. In the smaller states (like Bremen, Hamburg, Berlin) the structures are simpler. In Hamburg, for example, only two levels of administration exist (see Maurer, 2006).

Despite varying school types the states share a relatively similar structure: a common compulsory elementary school until fourth or sixth grade and secondary schools that are differentiated into compulsory technical or vocational schools, secondary modern schools, and grammar schools.

The system of accountability through mechanisms of quality assurance or quality control

In order to bring the educational policies of the 16 states into greater alignment, the Standing Conference of Ministers of Education and Cultural Affairs (in German "Kultusministerkonferenz" or KMK) was established. However, the KMK does not have the authority to make binding decisions.

Table 13.1 General governing levels of an education administration within a German Land

	Administrative level	Functions and competences
Macro level	Education Ministry	• Governmental and administrative tasks for the respective Land • Strategic management and coordination of tasks • Organization and structure of administrations • School supervisory authorities at the macro level
Meso level	State Office for Education/School Quality	• Support of the Ministry in its strategic and conceptual tasks for the respective Land
	School supervisory authorities at the middle level	• Operative tasks at the regional level: implementation of governmental, administrative, and conceptual decisions at the macro level
Micro level	School supervisory authorities at the lower level	• Operative tasks: advice and control of schools at local level
	Schools	• Teaching and schooling, self-management of schools

Source: Maurer (2006)

It can only suggest and provide recommendations that in return need to be approved by the parliaments of the states. Therefore, although the KMK may reach consensus regarding nationwide educational policies, the states may choose not to adopt these policies.

The actual influence of the KMK varies depending on the political climate regarding education. For example, its influence in matters of quality control has increased since the results of the Programme for International Student Assessment (PISA) 2000 because these results sparked national concern and manifold discussions among the German public about the federally structured school system. Since then, studies of transnational organizations have not only influenced German policy development by raising political and social awareness about problems in the school system, but also their findings about the characteristics of successful school systems have served as a yardstick for the reform process. PISA 2000 revealed not only the mediocre performance of German pupils, in general, in comparison to other states in the Organization for Economic Co-operation and Development (OECD) (see Schümer *et al.*, 2004), but also considerable differences in school quality among the German states themselves. In particular, pupils from immigrant or socially deprived families were found to have significantly fewer chances to achieve a sound educational career than those with a "stable" background (for more details see Baumert *et al.*, 2001). In response, the KMK has been aiming to align the educational policies of the states according to the key features of successful PISA countries by, for example, setting national education standards for all states, agreeing on a system of regular, national monitoring, and setting standards for teacher professionalization (see KMK, 1997, 2001a, 2001b, 2002a, 2002b).

As in many other Western countries, there has been a trend towards decentralization in the German education system. All German states have been undergoing this paradigm shift towards a decentralized and more output-oriented system of quality control. The shift has given schools increased responsibilities in matters of curriculum and instruction, human resources, finances, organization, and (self-)evaluation (see Huber and Gördel, 2006; Rürupp and Heinrich, 2007). Thus, schools are being reformed under a policy that can be characterized as "decentralized centralism" (see Karlsen, 2000) or as "autonomy based on (central) evaluations" (see Heinrich, 2007). It is a mixture of "top-down" stipulations to prescribe, evaluate, and control quality standards, and "bottom-up" school development processes based on a greater number of competencies ascribed to schools (see Table 13.1). Since PISA 2000, new regulations regarding means of quality and accountability control have been added. Among them are instruments such as education standards, large-scale assessments, school inspections, and education reports, which form a broad monitoring system.

Due to the federal constitutional system, the 16 states have progressed independently towards an output-controlled steering system of school quality and the characteristics are varied. Nevertheless, in all states five shared structural components can be found: (1) the traditional school supervisory authorities, (2) external school inspections, (3) internal self-evaluations, (4) assessment tests for system monitoring combined with regular reports about the education system (called "Bildungsbericht Deutschland" or German education reports), and (5) teacher and school principal professionalization.

Systems of quality assurance and control

School supervisory authorities. The traditional assessment system of school quality in Germany consists of school supervisory authorities that supervise public as well as private schools (general education and vocational schools). Subordinate school supervisory authorities ("Schulämter," similar to local education agencies on the level of local authority) are given the power to check a school's compliance with regards to regulations of quality oversight. These oversight regulations cover three areas of the teaching profession and school administration. Schools are supervised by (1) an academic supervision ("Fachaufsicht") over teaching and educational work; however, supervisory authorities are not permitted to interfere with the pedagogical responsibility of the individual teacher, specifically relating to matters of classroom teaching, (2) a supervision of the staff at public sector schools ("Dienstaufsicht"), and (3) a legal supervision ("Rechtsaufsicht"). Although the oversight regulations of the 16 states are similar in their stipulations, the organization of the oversight system differs from state to state.

The role of this supervisory system is evolving as the states have introduced an accountability system of self-responsible schools that uses both self-evaluations and school inspection systems. Therefore, the states must identify and separate the oversight responsibilities of the inspectorate and the school supervisory authority. Overlapping tasks of their work are the consulting and support services for inspected schools. Hence, they have to transform into authorities on school support or school improvement. Whereas the inspectorate is responsible for evaluating and advising the schools, the new school supervisory authorities will have take on the position of "quality institutes" that support the self-responsible school in its improvement measures. Thus after an inspection, public schools will be obliged to seek the approval of their school supervisory authority in regards to potential development measures.

Inspection. Inspections are mandated to evaluate self-responsible schools in their educational and organizational matters. A team, often coming from a quasi-independent institute of the respective state, conducts the inspections. In all states, inspectors not only observe the relevant areas of school quality and report the results to the Ministry of the respective school supervisory authority and/or the legal body in charge of the maintenance of the school, but they also discuss problems and possible areas of school development with the head teacher and the teachers. Thus, they seek to combine two roles: namely to provide evidence for the purposes of accountability and to facilitate school improvement. All states are similar in that although the inspection is a public process, the results are not published (nor do official pupil achievement tables or league tables exist).

In the following section, the inspection system of Lower-Saxony is presented as an example for common practice in Germany. In general terms, the official aim of the inspections in Lower-Saxony is to focus on the school as a systemic organization, organized in a similar way, based on comparable evaluation criteria (see Arbeitsgruppe "Schulinspektionssystem," 2005). Inspections are meant to serve as a monitoring system for the school system of Lower-Saxony. The inspectorate, on the one hand, fulfils the task of evaluating the quality and needs of schools, and, on the other hand, surveys certain areas of the school system in Lower-Saxony in order to identify which demonstrate an urgent need for improvement, as well as those that will require work in the future. Once a year, the inspectorate reports to the Ministry so that the latter is able to identify options for steering strategies aimed at improved quality management in the school system. The focus of the inspection is always on the quality of instruction. Schools and practitioners are assessed based on a quality framework, which varies according to school type, as well as on inspection manuals. The quality framework of Lower-

Saxony contains 16 quality criteria and approximately 100 sub-criteria, which vary according to the school type. During the inspection itself, the inspectors contextualize the school and they evaluate teaching according to the evaluation criteria of the relevant quality framework. The inspectorate emphasizes that only quality of instruction of the school as a whole is evaluated.

Inspections are carried out in four phases: (1) procuring of information regarding the school and preparation of the inspection team, (2) school inspection, (3) distribution of the report to the various stakeholders (school supervisory authority, school administration, teachers, the staff council, the parent and student council, and the legal body in charge of the maintenance of the school), and (4) if necessary, instructions for the school principal to improve certain areas of schooling. If a school is assessed as "below standard," the principal is required to consult with school supervisory authorities. Within one year, the school will be reinspected.

Self-evaluations. The latest changes in the school legislations of the states reflect the transition of supervisory systems, moving away from centralized and external assessments and towards cooperative and internal means of quality assurance. In return for the higher degree of administrative and academic self-responsibility granted to schools, schools have to set up school-specific profiles, in which the values and pedagogical principles and the objectives and measures of classroom and school development are laid out. By means of this document, schools demonstrate their obligation to regularly evaluate their work in their self-defined programs, knowing they will be held accountable for this work to themselves, to the supervisory authorities, to pupils and parents, and to the public.

This approach to self-evaluation within the quality control system demands a change of the role (and duties) of the school supervisory authorities: external check-ups are replaced by internal self-evaluations and by external evaluations such as meta-evaluations of the school reports on self-evaluation, as well as by inspections. As mentioned before, the task of the school supervisory authorities in the future will increasingly be to assist schools in the interpretation of the results of tests, evaluations and inspections on school quality, as well as to advise and support schools in their efforts towards school and classroom improvement. Moreover, the states are establishing support systems consisting of further training and development opportunities, counselling, supervision, etc., to help school leaders and teachers fulfil their new responsibilities in the field of quality control and quality development. Without external assistance, the implementation of a system with self-assessment would probably fail because of the potential resentment of teachers and school administrations (see Hopkins and Lagerweij, 1996; Wenzel, 2000).

Assessment tests. Before 2004, the German school system was an input-oriented control system based on political and administrative regulations for school education. However, in 1997, the 16 states agreed to introduce an output-oriented control system in order to improve and standardize the quality of school education, as well as to make it comparable among the states. By the school year 2004/05, all 16 states had started to implement nationally binding education standards in schools. Based on competence areas of the respective subjects, students were to be assessed against these education standards regarding the knowledge, abilities, and skills expected at a certain stage within their school careers. Any areas identified as performing below standard—both individual (of classes and schools) and general (of regions, states, or certain pupil populations)—are used to provide the respective state with a starting point for specific areas requiring quality development in its classrooms, schools, and education system overall.

Each Land is in the process of establishing its own evaluation system. Additionally, in 2004, the Standing Conference KMK founded the Institute for Quality Development in the Education System (Institut zur Qualitätsentwicklung im Bildungswesen or IQB), a scientific quality institute at the federal level linked to the Humboldt-University in Berlin. The IQB aims to work closely with the respective institutions of the states in order to assist them in their efforts to improve school quality, to further develop, standardize, and evaluate their progress in adhering to the national education standards, as well as to scientifically survey the implementation of these standards in the states.

There are teachers, along with school supervisory authorities, who question the overall benefits of student assessment tests. They argue that while standardized assessment tests would likely foster cognitive competences in classroom teaching because these are easily measurable, the teaching of other important competences such as methodological skills, critical thinking, or taking responsibility for oneself and for society would be neglected. However, representatives of the business world, parents, politicians, and the public demand more transparency of the processes in schools and classrooms, and they are looking for easily visible assessments of school quality, as well as of the education system as a whole. Many educationalists therefore favor standardized tests, citing their objectivity or at least comparability. Moreover, a common argument is that inspections and self-evaluations provide further information about the aspects of education that are not readily measurable. Hence, system monitoring should also take into account the "soft" criteria and social components.

There is a broad consensus that school leaders and teachers need to receive specific training in order to derive meaningful conclusions from test results for classroom and school development measures, as well to be able to benefit individual students. At the moment, the vast majority of German teachers and school administrators do not possess these statistical skills. Professional development institutes are just beginning to qualify school personnel in these areas. Moreover, Germany has not yet established a finite knowledge base— an understanding of how the system level can use results from education monitoring in order to run the education system effectively and to adjust policies according to specific problems in individual schools (see Böttcher, 2003; Döbert, 2003).

Classification of the German system of quality control and the distribution of authority: Politics and motives

At the moment, three general kinds of quality control categories can be identified, which vary according to the overseeing institution: (1) the inspection-based system (regulatory controlled), (2) the monitoring-based system, and (3) the professionally controlled system. All three systems can be organized in various ways, and they can be combined in various ways in order to complement one another. Out of these different configurations and combinations, various types of accountability may emerge, depending on the specific emphasis. Differences can be observed between bureaucratically-, politically-, legally-, ethically-, professionally-, or market-oriented types of accountability (see e.g. Moos, 2005). At least one of these types prevails in any given quality control system. The respective emphasis reveals to a considerable extent not only how authority is distributed among the institutional players but also which politics, objectives, and interests shape the control system.

The German oversight system can be classified as a system that combines all three types of quality control systems. Whereas aspects of regulatory and professional control defined by the state previously dominated, it is now shifting towards more of a monitoring and support-based system run by the state. As a consequence, schools are accountable for the quality of their work to school supervisory authorities. Schools assess their quality based on a variety of internal and external assessments. This system can be described as a combination of a bureaucratic and a legally-oriented type of accountability control. Moreover, the aspect of professionalization plays a considerable part in the German systems of quality control. However, this professionalization is highly dependent on state legislation and regulation. There is no pressure from the free market for the modernization of schools and teaching methods, or for continuous professional development, as there is, for instance, in the case of the medical and legal professions. The monitoring system described depends on two poles: centralization and decentralization.

Political motives for the new balance in the German oversight systems between centralization and decentralization are the economic and bureaucratic overloads of the central state institutions. Their policies and actions do not seem to be as successful in terms of quality assessment, improvement, and innovation as those pursued at the grassroots level. This is shown by the results of two studies conducted by the German Institute for International Educational Research Frankfurt a.M. (DIPF) on the school systems of successful PISA countries (Döbert and Sroka, 2004; Döbert *et al.*, 2004).

Kogan (1986, 1996) classifies systems of quality control with regard to the stakeholders (rather than, for example, the institutional configurations): (1) state control and accountability by bureaucratic means and legal regulations,

(2) professional control and accountability, and (3) consumer control and accountability. These models can be realized and combined in various ways. However, the essential aspect of this classification lies with the question of *where* the locus of control over evaluative decision processes is located. In looking at this issue, Altrichter and Heinrich (2005) created the matrix of accountability control shown in Table 13.2.

School leadership in Germany

In comparison with their peers in many other countries, school leaders in Germany have limited authority, in part due to Germany's bureaucratic traditions. They have authority over staff employment and dismissal, they have little influence on the schools' curricula, and they have limited control over financial resources. Nevertheless, school leaders are responsible for enforcing national and school regulations and for the daily management of school life. Above all, they are in charge of administrative tasks. Furthermore, they are responsible for representing the school, which includes maintaining contact with neighboring schools and institutions, as well as the community. Further school-based responsibilities have emerged as a result of the decentralization of decision-making processes, usually shifting them from federal state system level towards the school level (as described earlier in this chapter). School-based management has been implemented in nearly all federal states over the last ten years. However, the degree of decision-making power and the resources allocated to the schools vary from state to state. Hence, the influence of school leaders is restricted while teachers are relatively free to make didactical and methodical decisions

Table 13.2 Models of accountability

Dominant actors	Decisions on evaluations are primarily made	
	Internally	*Externally*
State	School leaders (as legal/bureaucratic superiors)	School supervisory authorities, inspection teams, external achievement tests, accreditation
Profession	Self-evaluation (school leaders as considerate coordinators)	Peer review
Consumer	Participation of the parents/pupils (e.g. decisions in school councils, partaking in the evaluation process as independent observers [school leaders as consumer oriented managers])	Competition, consumer decisions (e.g. voucher system, transparent information about the schools' performances, private schools)

Source: Altrichter and Heinrich (2005) (translated by the authors)

under the culture of the "institution of pedagogical freedom." Furthermore, it can be argued that the true decision-making body in schools is actually the staff conference (or the school community conference, which consists of teachers and parents), as the school leader is obliged to implement and follow decisions made in the staff conference.

In most of the different types of schools, the school leader now conducts the regular, official assessments of teachers. The school leader's teaching obligation depends on the type of school, the number of classes, and the number of pupils in her or his school. In a grammar school with over 1,000 students, the teaching obligation of a school leader is at least two lessons per week (the maximum is 11 hours a week in certain states); teachers at grammar schools teach, depending on the state, 23 to 27 hours a week. School leaders in elementary schools have considerably more lessons to teach. In Bavaria, for example, 50 percent of elementary school leaders teach 18 hours or more. School leaders are supported by vice-school leaders and by other staff who take over specific tasks, such as devising lesson plans, school career counseling, and extra curricular tutoring.

Vacant school leadership positions are posted publicly. Applicants' backgrounds are checked, including an assessment of their past achievements and their teaching skills. A basic prerequisite for being appointed as a school leader is teacher training and teaching experience in the respective school type; additional qualifications are an advantage. These could include previous experience as a deputy school leader, experience on senior management teams, or experience as an instructor in charge of the induction phase of teacher training. Mostly, however, the state examinations after teacher training, as well as the regular official assessments by superiors, are the deciding factors. The candidates who are evaluated as most suitable are appointed school leaders for life, with a tenure track, civil servant position.

Preferences and strains in school leadership practices and the importance of accountability

The study presented in this section was conducted in Germany, Switzerland, Austria and Liechtenstein in 2011 and 2012 (Huber, 2013a, 2013b, 2016a; Huber and Schwander, 2013; Huber and Wolfgramm, 2013a, 2013b; Huber et al., 2013a, 2013b;). It aimed to gain empirical insights into the work setting of school leaders. Its goal was to demonstrate which professional activities school leaders like to do (preferences) and which are a strain on them (strains). Moreover individual factors (e.g. aspects of one's professional biography), as well as institutional factors (e.g. conditions of the work setting), were tested as predictors of job strain. For operationalization purposes, Huber's (2012, 2013c, 2016b, Huber et al., 2012) model of school leadership practices was used and Böhm-Kasper's (2004) model of school-related strain was adapted to the contextual specifics of school leadership.

The School Leadership Study was conducted as follows:

1. An exploratory study comprised of 20 individual interviews with school leaders of all school types was conducted to identify relevant factors that were to be further explored in the written survey.
2. A general inquiry using a web-based questionnaire was conducted. It focused on, for example, participants' career history, school-related work setting, and general and specific stressful work life conditions.
3. The daily professional practices and activities of school leaders were recorded via an end-of-day-log covering three work weeks distributed throughout the school year (in which the participants entered their daytime activities every evening, indicating what they had done, when, with whom, where, and for how long).
4. Interviews were conducted with school leaders focusing on the one hand on areas of pressure and tension in school leadership practice, which may lead to increased experiences of high levels of stress, and on the other hand on the interrelations of stress patterns of highly strained school leaders.
5. Job profile analyses were conducted, to investigate national and regionally specific (i.e. federal states or cantons) demands on school leadership.

Altogether 5,394 school leaders participated in the general inquiry (representing a response rate of 49 percent). The sample consisted of 3,764 school leaders from Germany, 741 from Austria, and 889 from Switzerland and Liechtenstein. The school leaders were between 25 and 66 years old (M=52.45; SD=7.75) at the time of the study. For the analysis of quantitative data, structure equation modeling and path analysis were used.

The analysis of the specific strain experiences, which is the strain associated with specific activities, types of activities, and areas of practice gives clear evidence that organizational and administrative activities are perceived as particularly stressful and most disliked. Activities closely connected with teaching and education (such as teaching in a class, talking with students, exchanging ideas with colleagues, and pursuing one's own professional development) proved to be very popular and were perceived as only slightly stressful. The same pattern can be found in the analysis of the following types of activities: those close to education, close to classroom teaching, and close to professional exchange with colleagues are seen as less stressful than other types of activities.

Figure 13.1 illustrates the stress of and preferences for the nine different fields of activities for the three German speaking countries: Germany, Austria, and Switzerland. The two fields of activities involving accountability activities are highlighted with gray boxes. These two fields are quality development and quality assurance. Quality development includes items like contributing to the school development plan, making important information available for relevant actors, and developing plans for continuous professional development. Quality assurance includes items like conducting school

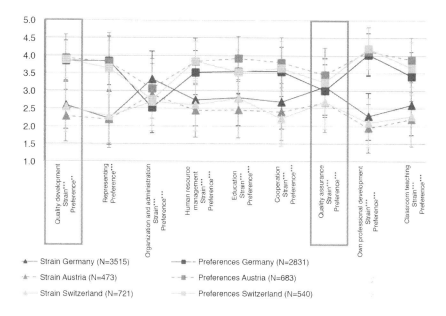

Figure 13.1 Strain by and preferences for the different activity fields by German, Austrian, and Swiss school leaders

Note: $*p < .05$; $**p < .01$; $***p < .001$.

evaluations (surveys), analyzing evaluation results, and giving feedback to the staff about external evaluations.

The mean strain levels of the activity field of quality development for German and Swiss school leaders lies in between the means of the other activity fields. This indicates that quality development is not seen as highly straining, but nor is it seen as not straining at all. Nevertheless, the means for German and Swiss school leaders are slightly above average. There is a significant difference for the Austrian school leaders who are less strained by quality development. Like the other activity fields, aside from "organization and administration" and "quality assurance," school leaders rate their preferences higher than their perceived strain for this activity field. The same pattern can be seen in the activity field "quality assurance" for Austrian and Swiss school leaders but not for German school leaders. German school leaders are, in general, more highly strained by all activity fields than their colleagues from Austria and Switzerland.

In general it can be stated that school leaders who experience an activity as stressful do not like to perform this activity as much as activities perceived as not (or less) stressful, which, in turn, are more popular. However, there are also some exceptions, which theoretically speaking makes sense because even enjoyable activities can lead to stress.

However, the following tendency has become obvious: tasks that belong to the traditional range of tasks of teachers are more popular among school leaders and are experienced as less stressful than tasks that have been recently added to school leadership responsibilities through changes in the school system as a consequence of decentralization (new public management). Compared to their Swiss colleagues, German school leaders demonstrate a lower job satisfaction and a higher level of occupational stress and emotional exhaustion.

The findings of the end-of-day log show that organizational and administrative activities take up most of a school leader's work day (see Figure 13.2). School leaders invest on average one-third of their time in these activities. About one-quarter of their time is used for activities concerning one's classroom teaching, with huge variations seen according to the size and type of school (elementary/secondary). Education and guidance and personnel matters are in the mid-range.

Table 13.3 shows correlations between the stress and preferences of the two fields of quality development and quality assurance and the variables of job satisfaction and job strain. This correlation table shows that both of the activity fields and both strain by and preference for those activity fields correlate negatively with work satisfaction and positively with job strain. The same pattern can also be seen with the strain of the other types of activities. Strains of all types of activities correlate negatively with job satisfaction and positively with job strain. There are also strong correlations between the

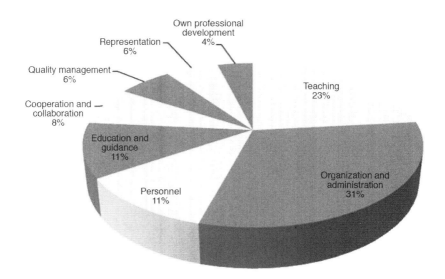

Figure 13.2 Distribution of work time of school leaders (percentage)

Table 13.3 Correlation between activity fields and job satisfaction and job strain for German school leaders

		Job satisfaction	Job strain
Strain: Quality development		−.319***	.380***
	Number	3,512	3,513
Strain: Quality assurance		−.253***	.339***
	Number	3,503	3,504
Preferences: Quality development		.297***	−.278***
	Number	2,828	2,829
Preferences: Quality assurance		.262***	−.325***
	Number	3,503	3,504

Note: */**/*** denotes significant differences on the 5/1/0.1% level.

evaluations of the perceived strain across the different types of activities. In other words, if someone perceives one type of activity as stressful, that person usually sees the other types of activities as straining as well and vice versa, since the correlations are causally omnidirectional.

In the evaluation of the preferences of the different types of activities, a similar picture can be discerned. Each type of activity correlates positively with job satisfaction and negatively with job strain. But in this case not all types of activities correlate with each other. There are no significant relations between organization and administration and education, nor between organization and administration and classroom teaching.

The scales used represent three different levels of accountability activities, or accountability between three different groups. On the first level students are accountable to school leaders. This level shows the perceived stress from or the preferences of school leaders for activities such as *grading student's papers*, *enforcing disciplinary measures*, and *enforcing the fulfilment of compulsory education*.

The next level looks at accountability between teachers and school leaders and how stressful or preferable school leaders perceive activities in this domain. This scale includes activities such as *evaluating teacher lessons, critically reflecting on teaching practice together with the teachers*, and *advising teachers in their work*. On the third level school leaders are accountable to the public/community, which in this context also means representing the school in public. This last scale includes items such as *managing school and student data, writing reports for educational authorities*, and *analyzing evaluation results*. Figure 13.3 shows that on both the student and the teacher levels of accountability, the preference for those activities are higher than the perceived strain (this pattern is also seen in Figure 13.1 with regard to the different fields of activities). In Germany, activities regarding accountability to the public are seen as more straining than preferred.

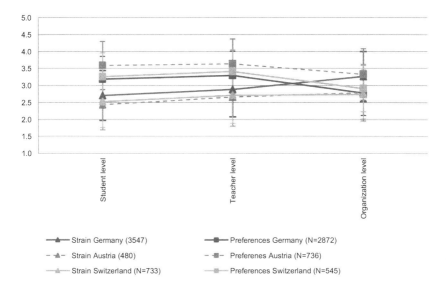

Figure 13.3 Strain and preferences on different levels of accountability for German, Austrian, and Swiss school leaders

Note: $*p < .05$; $**p < .01$; $***p < .001$.

To analyze the predictors of job strain and job satisfaction, two regression models were conducted. In this modelling the levels of accountability described were used as independent variables. In this case, significant predictors for job satisfaction are the strain of accountability activities on the teacher and organisation level and the preferences of accountability activities on the teacher and organisation level. With regard to job satisfaction, the level of strain rated by school leaders for activities on the student level is less important.

In the second model with job strain as the dependent variable, all levels of accountability concerning the perceived strain are revealed to be significant predictors for job strain. Within the preferences both the teacher and the organization level are significant predictors. The rated level of preference for activities on the student level by school leaders does not have a significant effect on their job strain. The strongest factor in both models is the perceived strain of accountability activities on the teacher level (see Table 13.4).

In a different model with the same dependent variables, the preference for and strain of quality development and quality assurance were used as predictors. Correlations can be found between job satisfaction and job strain and the fields of activities. The strongest correlations in both models are between the dependent variable and the strain caused by quality development. An adjusted correlation with job satisfaction as the dependent variable reveals that there is no significant correlation. It can be stated that unlike the other

Table 13.4 First regression model for job satisfaction and job strain

	Job satisfaction R^2 .114	Job strain R^2 .222
Strain: Student level	−.004	.106***
Strain: Teacher level	−.113***	.160***
Strain: Organization level	−.071*	.136***
Preferences: Student level	.033	.000
Preferences: Teacher level	.100***	−.090**
Preferences: Organization level	.111***	−.124***

Note: *$p < .05$; **$p < .01$; ***$p < .001$.

variables, strain caused by quality assurance is not a predictor of job satisfaction of school leaders. The second model (see Table 13.5), however, shows a different result. The strain stemming from quality assurance is a significant predictor for the school leaders' job strain, whereas the preference for activities in the field of quality development has no significant effect on job strain.

Table 13.5 Second regression models for job satisfaction and job strain

	Job satisfaction R^2 .133	Job strain R^2 .185
Strain: Quality development	−.191***	.262***
Strain: Quality assurance	−.050	.109***
Preferences: Quality development	.116***	.002
Preferences: Quality assurance	.089***	−.145***

Note: *$p < .05$; **$p < .01$; ***$p < .001$.

Discussion

In summary, it can be stated that school leaders prefer activities they do not experience as stressful and do not like activities they find highly stressful. This pattern is found within the activity fields quality development and quality assurance. An interesting finding here is that the link between these two fields of activity appears to be fairly weak. However, both fields contain, as previously mentioned, important singular activities in the field of accountability. Whereas quality development is not seen as highly stressful compared to the other activity fields, quality assurance is a big stressor for school leaders and not a preference. Taking a closer look at these two activity fields, which in theory and also in practice belong together, it becomes obvious that quality assurance contains more activities in which school leaders are controlled. Their range of autonomy is more limited than in other activity fields including quality management. Quality management, by contrast, includes more activities concerning school development, thus requiring more internal than external accountability. Quality development is regarded more positively and promises a higher benefit in the cost benefit ratio for school leaders. Quality assurance, however, promises a lower benefit and higher costs for school leaders and their schools since those activities are primarily geared towards reporting to authorities, and school leaders do not see a big gain for their school's development. These results are emphasized in the second part of the study, where accountability was measured on three different levels. On these levels accountability on the organizational level was clearly rated as the highest strain and lowest preference, especially for German school leaders.

All in all, the results show that accountability in general is not always a major strain for school leaders in Germany. There are aspects of accountability that school leaders enjoy and that they do not find significantly more stressful than other activities. However, when it comes to accountability involving a high degree of control from local authorities or the community, which minimizes the school leader's range of action, accountability is experienced as highly straining. These types of activities belong to the least preferred activities out of all activity fields.

Looking ahead

In order to improve the educational effectiveness of individual schools in the current context of accountability demands, school leaders should not be afraid to make use of the autonomy they do possess. A factor that supports this is the aforementioned transition of school *supervisory* offices into school *advisory* offices. According to this policy of school accountability, both schools and school leaders and also the school supervisory/advisory offices are held accountable for their work. The area of accountability for the advisory offices is to be an effective support system at the school level. Thus, school leaders should perceive themselves as equal partners with the senior hierarchy level(s). They should actively demand these levels' support. Only then might school supervisory offices, ministries, and especially politics provide the necessary time-consuming and expertise-requiring "tailor-made" support.

References

Altrichter, H. and Heinrich, M. (2005). Schulprofilierung und Transformation schulischer Governance. [School Profiles and the Transformation of Governance] In Xaver Büeler, Alois Buholzer, and Markus Roos (eds) *Schulen mit Profil. Forschungsergebnisse – Brennpunkte – Zukunftsperspektiven* [Schools with Profiles – Research Findings – Hot Issues – Perspectives] (pp. 125–140). Innsbruck: Studien Verlag.

Arbeitsgruppe "Schulinspektionssystem" (2005). *Abschlussbericht* [Final Report of the Task Force "School Inspections"] February, 21. (http://cdl.niedersachsen.de/blob/images/C8892332_L20.pdf, 6.02.06).

Avenarius, H. (2004). *Die Reform wird Zeit und Geduld brauchen. Die Reform der Schulgesetze läutet eine neue Ära in der Bildungspolitik ein.* [The Reform Will Need Time and Patience] May, 12 (www.forumbildung.de/templates/imfokus_inhalt.php?artid=308, 23.01.2006).

Avenarius, H. (2006). "Standard-Konzepte" und "Qualitätsrahmen" für "Eigenständige Schulen" – ein Widerspruch? In *GFPF-Nachrichten/Gesellschaft zur Förderung Pädagogischer Forschung* 2, 21–33.

Baumert, J., Artelt, C. and Klieme, E. *et al.* (2001). *PISA 2000 – Die Länder der Bundesrepublik Deutschland im Vergleich. Zusammenfassung der zentralen Befunde.* [PISA 2000 – Summary of the Central Findings of a Comparison of the German 'Länder'] Berlin: MPIB.

Böhm-Kasper, O. (2004). *Schulische Belastung und Beanspruchung. eine Untersuchung von Schülern und Lehrern am Gymnasium.* Münster: Waxmann. (Pädagogische Psychologie und Entwicklungspsychologie Vol. 43).

Böttcher, W. (2003). Schulreform durch Standards? [School Reform by Means of Standards?] In Hans Döbert, Botho von Kopp, Renate Martini and Manfred Weiß (eds) *Bildung vor neuen Herausforderungen. Historische Bezüge – rechtliche Aspekte – Steuerungsfragen – Internationale Perspektiven* [Education Facing New Demands. Historical References – Legal Aspects – Steering Issues – International Perspectives] (pp. 160–168). Neuwied: Kriftel.

Döbert, H. (2003). Neue Steuerungsmodelle von Schulsystemen in Europa. [New Steering Models of School Systems in Europe] In Hans Döbert., Botho von Kopp, Renate Martini and Manfred Weiß (eds) *Bildung vor neuen Herausforderungen. Historische Bezüge – rechtliche Aspekte – Steuerungsfragen – Internationale Perspektiven* [Education Facing New Demands. Historical References – Legal Aspects – Steering Issues – International Perspectives] (pp. 287–303). Neuwied: Kriftel.

Döbert, H. and Sroka, W. (eds) (2004). *Features of School Systems. A Comparison of Schooling in Six Countries.* Münster: Waxmann.

Döbert, H., Klieme, E. and Sroka, W. (eds) (2004). *Conditions of School Performance in Seven Countries. A Quest for Understanding the International Variation of PISA Results.* Münster: Waxmann.

Heinrich, M. (2007). *Governance in der Schulentwicklung. Von der Autonomie zur evaluationsbasierten Steuerung.* Wiesbaden: VS.

Hopkins, D. and Lagerweij, N. (1996). The School Improvement Knowledge Base, in D. Reynolds, R. Bollen, B. Creemers, D. Hopkins, L. Stoll and N. Lagerweij (eds) *Making Good Schools: Linking school effectiveness and school improvement.* London: Routledge.

Huber, S.G. (2004). *Preparing School Leaders for the 21st Century. An International Comparison of Development Programs in 15 Countries.* Lisse (Netherlands): Swets & Zeitlinger.

Huber, S.G. (ed.) (2010). *School Leadership: International Perspectives.* Dordrecht: Springer.

Huber, S.G. (2011). Research on Principals in the German Speaking Countries. In O. Johansson (eds) *Rektor – En Forskningsöversikt 2000–2010* (pp. 230–254). Stockholm: Vetenskapsrådet.

Huber, S.G. (ed.) (2012). *Jahrbuch Schulleitung 2012. Befunde und Impulse zu den Handlungsfeldern des Schulmanagements.* Köln: Carl Link.

Huber, S.G. (2013a). Forschung zu Belastung und Beanspruchung von Schulleitung.

In S.G. Huber (ed.) *Jahrbuch Schulleitung 2013. Befunde und Impulse zu den Handlungsfeldern des Schulmanagements* (pp. 222–240). Köln: Wolters Kluwer Deutschland.

Huber, S.G. (2013b). Schulleitung heute: Zwischen Begeisterung und Belastung? *b:sl Beruf Schulleitung.* Allgemeiner Schulleitungsverband Deutschlands e.V. (ASD) (eds). 7/2013, Berlin.

Huber, S.G. (2013c). *Handbuch Führungskräfteentwicklung. Grundlagen und Handreichungen zur Qualifizierung und Personalentwicklung im Schulsystem.* Köln: Carl Link.

Huber, S.G. (2016a). *Schulleitung – Forschung in den deutschsprachigen Ländern: Belastungs und Beanspruchungserleben im Schulleitungshandeln.* Münster: Waxmann.

Huber, S.G. (ed.) (2016b). *Steuergruppenhandbuch. Grundlagen für die Arbeit in zentralen Handlungsfeldern des Schulmanagements* (4th edn). Köln: Link-Luchterhand."

Huber, S.G. and Gördel, B. (2006). Quality assurance in the German school system. *Eu* school system. *European Educational Research Journal, Public education, democracy and supra- and transnational agencies in Europe,* (5), 3–4, 196–209.

Huber, S.G., Schneider, N., Gleibs, H.E. and Schwander, M. (2012). *Leadership in der Lehrerbildung: Entwicklung von Kompetenzen für pädagogische Führung.* Stiftung der deutschen Wirtschaft.

Huber, S.G. and Schwander, M. (2013). Arbeitstagebuch: Wie verteilt sich die Arbeit von Schulleitungen? *b:sl,* 03, 8–9.

Huber, S.G. and Wolfgramm, C. (2013a). Das Kollegium als soziale Ressource. *b:sl,* 3, 7.

Huber, S.G. and Wolfgramm, C. (2013b). Was bedingt Unzufriedenheit und hohe Belastung? *b:sl,* 3, 17.

Huber, S.G., Wolfgramm, C. and Kilic, S. (2013a). Vorlieben und Belastungen im Schulleitungshandeln: Ausgewählte Ergebnisse aus der Schulleitungsstudie 2011/2012 in Deutschland, Österreich, Liechtenstein und der Schweiz. In S.G. Huber (eds), *Jahrbuch Schulleitung 2013. Befunde und Impulse zu den Handlungsfeldern des Schulmanagements* (pp. 259–271). Köln: Wolters Kluwer Deutschland

Huber, S.G., Wolfgramm, C. and Kilic, S. (2013b). Tätigkeitsvorlieben. *b:sl,* 3, 10–11.

Karlsen, Gustav E. (2000). Decentralized centralism: Framework for a better understanding of governance in the field of education. *Journal of Educational Policy,* 15(5), S. 525–538.

Kogan, M. (1986). *Educational Accountability.* London: Hutchinson.

Kogan, M. (1996). Monitoring, control and governance of school systems. In OECD (ed.) *Evaluating and Reforming Education Systems* (pp. 25–45). Paris: OECD.

Kultusministerkonferenz KMK. (1997). *280. Sitzung der Kultusministerkonferenz. Konstanzer Beschluss zur Durchführung länderübergreifender Vergleichsuntersuchungen zum Lern- und Leistungsstand von Schülerinnen und Schülern.* [Agreement on the Conduction of Comparative Testing of Pupil Achievement among the Länder] Konstanz. October, 23, 24.

Kultusministerkonferenz KMK (2001a). *Weiterentwicklung des Schulwesens in Deutschland seit Abschluss des Abkommens zwischen den Ländern der Bundesrepublik zur Vereinheitlichung auf dem Gebiet des Schulewesens vom*

28.10.1964 i.d.F. vom 14.10.1971. [Development of the Education System in Germany Since 1971] Bonn. May, 10.

Kultusministerkonferenz KMK (2001b). *296. Sitzung der Kultusministerkonferenz. Definition von sieben vorrangigen Handlungsfeldern als Konsequenz aus PISA.* [Definition of Seven Relevant Fields of Action as Consequence of PISA] Bonn. December, 5, 6.

Kultusministerkonferenz KMK (2002a). *Bildungsstandards zur Sicherung von Qualität und Innovation im föderalen Wettbewerb der Länder.* [Education Standards to Assure Quality and Innovation in the Federal Competition of the Länder] Bonn. May, 23, 24.

Kultusministerkonferenz KMK (2002b). *Bewertung der bundesinternen Leistungsvergleiche (PISA-E).* [Assessment of the Comparison of the PISA Results of the German Länder] Berlin. June, 25.

Maurer, H. (2006). *Allgemeines Verwaltungsrecht.* 16., überarb. u. erw. Aufl. München: C.H. Beck.

Moos, L. (2005). How do schools bridge the gap between external demands for accountability and the need for internal trust? *Journal of Educational Change*, 6(4), 307–328.

Rürup, M. and Heinrich, M. (2007). Schulen unter Zugzwang – Die Schulautonomiegesetzgebung der deutschen Länder als Rahmen der Schulentwicklung. In Herbert Altrichter, Thomas Brüsemeister and Jochen Wissinger (eds) *Educational Governance. Handlungskoordination und Steuerung im Bildungssystem* (pp. 157–183). Wiesbaden: VS.

Schümer, G., Tillmann, K.-J. and Weiß, M. (eds) (2004). *Die Institution Schule und die Lebenswelt der Schüler. Vertiefende Analysen der PISA-2000-Daten zum Kontext von Schülerleistungen.* [Analysis of the PISA-2000 Data] Wiesbaden: VS Verlag für Sozialwissenschaften.

Wenzel, H. (2000). Qualitätssicherung und Schulentwicklung. [Quality Assurance and School Development] In Heinz-Hermann Krüger and Hartmut Wenzel (eds) *Schule zwischen Effektivität und sozialer Verantwortung* (pp. 111–123). Opladen: Leske + Budrich.

14 Swinging between two platforms

Accountability policy in the Netherlands and educational leadership in and around schools

Jeroen Imants, Yvonne Zwart, and Peter Breur

In the Netherlands, accountability is a topic of fast-growing interest in education as well as in the public sector in general. Dutch schools, as well as other public organizations, are expected to be accountable for the spending of public resources, and for the economic, societal, institutional, and personal benefits of these resources. This pressure towards accountability manifests itself in two ways and promotes the development of two platforms for accountability policy and practices in education. One platform for accountability policy in education is built on two public needs. One public need is that resources that are meant for educational purposes should be spent in schools on the intended purposes. The second public need is that generally aspired standards for student learning should be realized by the employment of these public resources. The second platform for accountability policy is built on the belief that when schools are held publicly accountable, improved quality of teaching and better student learning will result. With the first platform, the focus is on control, while with the second platform the focus is on improvement. Within daily school practice, a tension is often reported between the control perspective and the improvement perspective of accountability (Hofman *et al.*, 2005).

The Dutch educational system is strongly decentralized and is sometimes called the 'world champion in autonomy' (Jaap Scheerens as cited in Inspectie van het Onderwijs, 2012). Because of its decentralized characteristics, the Dutch educational system might be a special case with respect to the relationship between control and improvement perspectives on accountability. The first aim of this chapter is to explore how the two platforms for accountability policy relate within daily school practice in the Netherlands. Relatedly, the sub-aim is to explore opportunities for Dutch schools and school boards to position themselves in relation to the two aforementioned platforms.

The decentralized Dutch context of accountability policy and practice can be expected to have a specific impact on educational leadership in and around schools. Educational leadership potentially has a strong impact on how accountability policy is implemented. On the one hand, accountability policy is steering educational leadership in and around schools towards specific directions through emphasizing data-driven work in classrooms and schools and through the administrative procedures for inspection from the national Inspectorate. On the other hand, accountability policy is creating new opportunities for educational leadership in the Dutch context. These opportunities occur because school boards and schools are autonomous to interpret accountability policy to promote value-driven, data-informed, and data-inspired teaching in schools. The second aim of this chapter is to explore the role of educational leadership in and around schools in developing site-specific interpretations of accountability. Two questions are central in this chapter: how is accountability policy implemented in a decentralized national and local policy context? And which role does educational leadership in a decentralized national and local policy context play in positioning the school towards accountability policy?

To answer these questions, attention will be paid to the policy context that informs school accountability in the Netherlands, the role of the national Inspectorate in the practice of testing, accountability, and assessment, and the role that school leaders and school boards play regarding accountability and assessment practices in Dutch primary schools. To this end, three recent year-end reports of the national inspectorate will be analysed. Case studies of schools under a decentralized school board will be examined to identify opportunities for and restrictions on the implementation of school-specific strategies for accountability and assessment practices and to explore the role of educational leadership in and around these schools. In the concluding section, we discuss lessons learned from the analysis to inform new possibilities for school leadership for educational effectiveness and improvement.

Conceptual framework

Accountability

According to Hoy and Miskel (2008), systems of school accountability generally include three components: (1) standards, (2) tests aligned with the standards, and (3) consequences related to varying levels of goal attainment. By prescribing that standardized student learning outcomes become the content of the tests, the alignment between standards and student assessment in schools is strengthened. To realize a substantial impact on improved student learning, many complex and contentious jobs and practices must be completed for standards-based approaches to influence classroom instruction (Hoy and Miskel, 2008).

Two aspects characterize recent Dutch accountability policy. These are a statewide or national scope and a systemic approach, in which an alignment in and between levels of the educational system is sought. However, an analysis of accountability practices shows that this national, systemic, and aligned approach is not easily implemented. In the Netherlands, the national scope is clearly present in accountability policy by the specification of national standards. A relatively strong steering mechanism for the government prescribes precise and detailed standards for education for students from Years 4 to 18. However, the national government only has weak steering mechanisms to promote (or to enforce) a systemic approach to accountability and alignment in and between levels. To this end, Dutch accountability policy focuses on two instruments: (1) results-oriented teaching, and (2) holding school boards accountable for the quality of teaching and student learning results (Inspectie van het Onderwijs, 2010, 2011). The national Inspectorate plays a key role in controlling if and how these policy instruments are implemented. In this section results-oriented teaching will be discussed. The position of the school boards will be discussed in the section on decentralization.

According to the Inspectorate, results-oriented teaching is the most important key to educational improvement (Inspectie van het Onderwijs, 2010, 2011, 2012). School boards, principals, and teachers all play their role in this strategy via alignment. Results-oriented teaching is strongly recommended by the national government, though it is not obligatory because of autonomy. However, in the year-end reports by the Inspectorate of education, results-oriented education is a priority. The impact of inspection on schools and school boards is large, because of the regular school visits and public reports produced. This pressure of the Inspectorate toward results-oriented teaching can be regarded as an indirect but strong enforcement of government policy to promote a systemic and aligned approach.

Results-oriented teaching is the systematic and purposive effort to maximize the learning results of students. According to the Inspectorate (Inspectie van het Onderwijs, 2010, 2011) elements of results-oriented teaching encompass the inclusion of the following:

- Clear goals for all students;
- Teachers who know what to teach in their classrooms;
- Alignment of instruction with the needs of students;
- Diagnosis of problems of students with stagnation in learning;
- Adequate help and assistance for students with stagnation in learning;
- Yearly monitoring progress of groups of students;
- Promotion if improvements in case of stagnation in learning progress of students.

In 2008–2009 about one quarter of the primary schools adhered to these elements of results-oriented teaching. At the primary education level, teachers, principals, and schools are more familiar with these practices than teachers and principals at the secondary and vocational levels. In primary schools where results-oriented teaching has been implemented, students show better learning results for mathematics (Inspectie van het Onderwijs,

2010), with room for improvement in result-oriented teaching for all the parties involved (Inspectie van het Onderwijs, 2012).

Educational leadership

Educational leadership defined

As Leithwood and other internationally recognized specialists in school leadership state, "School leadership is second only to classroom teaching as an influence on pupil learning." (Leithwood *et al.*, 2006: 4) In this chapter teachers are positioned as central *actors* instead of teachers as *factors* that can be steered in a passive way. This active role of teachers implies that leadership is executed in interactive processes. Classroom and school factors play important roles in effective instruction and sustained school improvement. The effects of these classroom and school factors are mediated to a considerable extent by how teachers make sense of these factors in their daily school and classroom practice (Easley, 2010; Luttenberg *et al.*, 2013). Traditionally, in professional development programs, teachers have been regarded as 'passive participants,' lacking knowledge and skills. More recently, however, teachers have been increasingly regarded as 'active learners,' and as agents in co-determining their working and learning goals, contents, processes, and outcomes (Imants and Van Veen, 2010). The effectiveness of educational leaders not only depends on individual leader's characteristics and behaviours, but also on how teachers enact the educational leaders' strategies and behaviours regarding the development of school and classroom factors and the professional development of teachers.

In this chapter leadership is regarded as distributed through the school. Distributed leadership is defined as an organizational and social practice or activity that can be performed by many different actors in diverging organizational contexts and situations (Spillane, 2005). *Educational l*eadership is defined as all the leadership activities in and around schools that are intended to affect and structurally change the process and results of teaching and learning. Educational leaders collectively apply and use a set of steering functions and mechanisms that are distributed across the school at the levels of the classroom, the school, and the board, or district (Leithwood, 2007). As a consequence, teacher leaders execute some of these educational leadership functions. These teacher leaders can play important roles in improving the effectiveness of teaching and student learning results in the school (Muijs and Harris, 2003). An example in Dutch primary schools is the role of the special services coordinator. Initially, the tasks of these coordinators were twofold: (1) to coordinate the services for students with specials needs including the links with local school networks, and (2) to support teachers and to act as a consultant for colleagues during their work with students with special needs (Imants *et al.*, 2001). In the last decade this role has expanded in many schools to a specialist role in monitoring quality of education. A related strategy of school leaders is to strengthen and formalize this teacher leadership role.

These insights into the distributed and interactive character of educational leadership are summarized in Figure 14.1 The practices and positioning of teachers are placed in the center, according to the key role they play in effective teaching and school improvement and as learners in professional development.

Educational leadership and accountability

In accountability policy and practice, the role of school administrators is complicated because accountability systems call for simultaneous and systematic changes in organizing, teaching, and administering in schools. Two main strategies to develop educators and educational systems towards standards-based reform have been identified as professional development and comprehensive school reform (Hoy and Miskel, 2008).

For professional development to be effective several key features like reform type, duration, collective participation, active learning and content focus should be aligned,. Professional development is often rolled out as one-shot, in-service workshops delivering prepackaged information, and such an approach is not adequate (Imants and Van Veen, 2010). The sustained effectiveness of complex professional development programs in schools depends strongly on how these programs are initiated, supported and integrated by school leadership (Leithwood, *et al.*, 2006). Moreover, central office personnel in school boards play powerful roles in determining the impact of professional development on teaching (Leithwood, 2010).

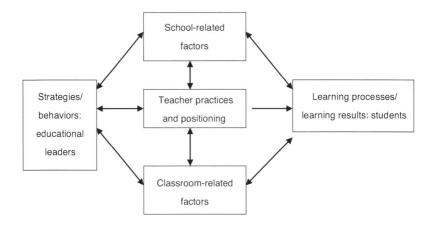

Figure 14.1 Educational leadership, teacher practices, and student learning
Source: Imants (2009)

Comprehensive school reform often consists of unified freestanding packages of reforms with goals and standard protocols for adoption and use. These initiatives are systemic only if they promote coherence and reduce fragmentation, align with the standards and assessment of the national accountability system and focus on academic achievement (Hoy and Miskel, 2008).

It can be assumed that top-down and all-inclusive comprehensive school reform models do not fit well into the Dutch tradition of board and school autonomy. In daily practice in and around Dutch schools, such comprehensive models cannot be identified. However, especially in primary education, many instruments and methods to help schools, school leaders, and teachers to implement result-oriented teaching and to enhance alignment among classrooms, schools, and their boards are diffused. An example of these strategies is the implementation of diagnostic tools that test student learning progress according to the national standards independent of the specific methods for student instruction. Another example is the so called 'quality cards' that supply teachers and schools with practical examples of how to work in a data driven way, and how to differentiate instruction. These instruments are implemented on voluntary base and implementation presupposes the professional development of teachers and school leaders. Professional development is a widely applied strategy in Dutch education to develop schools towards standards-based reform. The focus on effective professional development creates a need, as well as an opportunity for educational leadership in and around schools.

Given the systemic character of accountability and assessment practices in schools and the need for alignment of multiple factors at different levels, it is assumed that for effective educational leadership to occur, aligned educational leadership practices and activities in school and around schools should be distributed at three levels: the school board, principals, and teacher leaders.

National context of the study

Decentralization in the Dutch context

In the Dutch language, the words 'accountability' and 'control' are closely associated (*verantwoordingsplicht*). However, the association between the words 'accountability' and 'improvement' is not as self-evident. Strong control can be regarded as a hindrance to improvement. For a profound understanding it is important to note that this specific Dutch meaning of the word probably is not only a matter of language. This meaning might also find its origin in the history and culture of decentralization of Dutch education. The Netherlands is a unique context for studying accountability policy and educational leadership. In the Dutch constitution, freedom of education has been guaranteed by the national government since the nineteenth century. School boards are free to establish schools, and government is obliged to subsidize these schools, as long as the boards and the schools meet formal requirements and quality standards. As a result, Dutch education has been strongly decentralized for decades. Until recently, hardly any intermediate hierarchical administrative structures between the national government and schools, and their often-small (and unprofessional) boards, have played a prominent role in educational policy and management. Additionally, most catholic and protestant school boards were small and populated with volunteers, and occasionally by the local priest or the minister, who was co-opted from the community and church. In public education, the publicly elected community council was the school board.

Within the policy context of educational freedom, the national government is responsible for guaranteeing the quality of education. That is, the content of what constitutes education for students and the levels at which these contents are educated are defined by the state through national standards. Besides these national standards, schools and boards are free to present additional content to their students, for example in the field of religious education. As a result of the growing pressure towards accountability during the last 20 years, the government has been continually defining and redefining, broadening, sharpening, and promoting educational standards.

Pedagogy and instruction remain the responsibility of autonomous school boards and schools. They are free to conceptualize the means to realize learning performances of students, as long as these performances meet the national standards. It can be observed that the elements of results-oriented teaching not only regard the national standards. The practice of inspection controls and evaluates some central element of the pedagogy and instruction in schools as well. In this respect, inspection practice is double-barrelled. On the one hand, inspectors promote schools to enhance self-evaluation on the quality of pedagogy and instruction, and on the other hand, inspectors evaluate schools in their reports on elements of pedagogy, instruction, and classroom climate.

Besides accountability policy, during the last three decades two dominant Dutch educational policies have been recognized: deregulation policy and scale enlargement policy. Together, these three policies have promoted the merger of small school boards into large and medium-sized boards. As a result of the interplay of these three policies, school boards as intermediate hierarchical administrative structures between government and schools have developed and expanded. It is now normal that administrative and staff work for school boards are fully paid; these activities are regarded as professional or managerial jobs. Not only in structure (scale enlargement and building up of the hierarchy), but also in culture and with regard to the relationship with the schools and the local community, the position and work of school boards has changed dramatically.

School boards implement policies for school personnel evaluation, monitor the quality of education in schools, and control the budgets of schools.

Some school boards put pressure on schools to standardize curriculum, for example to reduce budgets that are spent on instructional methods. Although this tendency is characterized as bureaucratization in national discussions, it might be more appropriate to consider it as local centralization within a national decentralized context. Schools and school boards are, by and large, free in how they realize learning performances of students. As a result of the national accountability policy, school boards are held accountable by the Inspectorate for meeting the national standards in the schools that reside under the board. For this reason, school boards interfere much more with education and pedagogics in schools as compared to 20 years ago. Notwithstanding this tendency, schools and teachers are still considerably autonomous. For Dutch teachers, their individual autonomy is an important characteristic of work in education, and an important influence on whether or not they stay in the profession (Vogels and Bronneman-Helmers, 2006).

Local centralization in a decentralized national context

Principals and school boards play a central role in results-oriented teaching, because they have the task and responsibility to initiate and steer this process in their schools (Inspectie van het Onderwijs, 2012). More and more, school boards are held accountable for the learning results of the students in their school and for the quality of results-oriented teaching. Principals play the key role in the implementation of results-oriented teaching in their schools. One of the priorities in the work of the Inspectorate of Education is to investigate how school boards promote the implementation of quality assurance in the board and their schools (Inspectie van het Onderwijs, 2012). Moreover, the boards are responsible for the proper use of public resources, and for the compliance of national laws and rules. School boards are the employers of teachers and principals with control to hire and fire. School boards are expected to undertake activities in the field of human resource management and development, related to local educational and financial policy. It is up to the school boards to promote a systemic and aligned practice of quality policy, personnel policy, educational policy, and financial policy in the schools and the board. According to these tasks and responsibilities for school boards and principals, in 2013 the focus of the inspectorate was on four aspects of the quality of education: 1) satisfying educational results, 2) the handling of stagnant student learning, 3) quality professional development for teachers, and 4) quality assurance, administration and finance management (Inspectie van het Onderwijs, 2012).

An essential role of educational leadership in schools and school boards is to focus financial, personnel, and quality policies on improvement of student learning and learning results. Specific and complementary forms of educational leadership are required at the three levels of the local educational system: the board, the principal, and the teachers.

In the next sections of this chapter one specific school board will be analyzed to answer the two research questions. The analysis shows how accountability policy can be implemented in a decentralized national and local policy context. Further, the margins for educational leadership in and around the schools will be explored via the context of this improvement-oriented school board aimed at developing site-specific interpretations of sustainable result-oriented teaching.

The context of the school board

Vision and policy of the school board

The board is a catholic foundation for the education of 4–12-year-old students in an industrialized small city in the east of the country. The board administers 10 primary schools and 1 school for special primary education, divided over 17 locations. In total, about 4,300 students attend the schools. The board employs 420 adults (many teachers in primary education work part time in the Netherlands). Although the schools are doing well, it is the ambition of the board to continuously improve. In the period 2011–2015 the focus is on improvements in student results for math, reading, and language.

The vision of the board for sustained improvement in teaching and learning can be realized by creating alignment through and within the layers of the organization, and by appreciating diversity between and within schools. Creating ownership among teachers and principals is a corner stone of the board's strategy, entitled The Teacher Central. Two principles under this board strategy are: (1) a method for quality assurance that has already been implemented, in which global indicators for school quality are monitored and discussed, and (2) a survey used to measure outcomes among all schools administered by the board. It should be noted that this survey was executed by a teacher of the board in the context of her master in education dissertation.

Three elements are central in the specification of steps in the board's strategy toward the schools: (a) the implementation of result-oriented teaching in a tailor-made fashion for the teachers and the schools; (b) the implementation of a specific method for planning, performance, and evaluation of classes that is informed and inspired by student learning data to make result-oriented teaching work for teachers in their classrooms; and (c) the implementation of teaching strategies, in which teachers deal with a diverse student population in their classroom to create opportunities for extra care for students with delays or stagnation in learning.

For each of these three elements, practical methods for teachers and principals are made available by the educational advisor of the board. During implementation of these three elements, schools and teachers adapt these methods to make them fit within their own vision and practice. While implementing these elements in schools, the strategy of the board is further elaborated and explicated in recurring conversations between diverse actors in and between layers.

Informed by the board strategy, every school plans a school development trajectory. Three priorities are: (1) the coupling of data on student learning results and student learning activities to the planning of teaching and instruction by teachers; (2) the introduction and implementation of seven characteristics of effective instruction; and (3) the strengthening of educational leadership by the principal and teachers. Essentially, the most important shift that is aspired for in the strategy for 2011–2015 is to couple data on student learning results with specific instruction and the development and execution of concrete and practical group plans to be executed in the classroom. A shift within schools is made from evaluating and structurally streaming students based on incidental test scores, towards monitoring student progress and taking instructional and grouping decisions that directly affect teaching and learning. Educational leadership by the principal and the special services coordinator (a teacher who is specialized in diagnosing stagnation in student learning and behavioural problems and in monitoring quality of education in the school) is focused on creating opportunities for teachers to develop professionally, on serving as a role model, and on communicating a clear and inspiring vision.

Educational leadership in school board policy

In every school a steering committee is installed, in which the principal, the special services coordinator, and one or two teachers participate. Direct participation of team members in the committee is regarded as essential for finding the balance between alignment and diversity, and for the development of ownership among teachers.

At the board level, a project team is installed, in which representatives of the principals, the educational director of the board, a staff member of the central office, and the external advisor participate. On a yearly basis, a staff member of the central office and the external advisor organize several plenary sessions for all the principals and special service coordinators and for central office staff and board members to discuss the progress of the strategy and to select priorities for the next period. The strategy for the introduction of results-oriented teaching in the board and the schools is dynamic during the implementation. New experiences and insights are used to actualize the strategy. The ongoing discussions in the steering committees in the schools and the project team in the board play a central role in that process.

The peer review method

The board strategy has a strong focus on development of result-oriented teaching practices in schools. In the course of the first year, the project team developed the need to stay informed about the progress in the schools by monitoring the process. Besides, the project team aspired to strengthen the role of the principals as educational leaders and the active participation of teachers in the result-oriented teaching. For these reasons, a peer review method has been developed regarding the quality of result-oriented teaching in the schools. No ready-made procedure was available for the review. For assistance during the design and execution of the review, a senior researcher of the School of Education at the regional university was assigned to the project team.

The principals in the project team have played a central role in the design and the content of the review. According to the board strategy, all principals contribute to the realization of the review. The review's aim is to monitor the process of the introduction and implementation of result-oriented teaching and to identify opportunities for improvements in result-oriented teaching, including the active role of teachers, as well as improvements at the level of the board and external assistance.

According to the general strategy of the board, the project team was the designer of the peer review. In a period of six months, about five meetings of the project team with the senior researcher from the university were held to design the review and to develop support among the principals in the board. The process can be described as an ongoing process of sharpening the aim of the review along with the further specification of the questions and procedures for the review. In this process the senior researcher made notes and proposals after a project team meeting and combined these notes with general methods for review and critical reflection. During the subsequent meeting, the proposal was further elaborated and tested against the aims of the review. Afterwards, the senior researcher again streamlined and completed the content procedure for the review. This cycle was repeated four times.

Before the review was executed, the concept, method, and content of the review were discussed in a plenary session with all the principals and special service coordinators. The method builds on the insight that the educational leaders in the school should play a central role in data collection and interpretation of the results. This is conditional for complete and correct collection of data, and for a representative image of the state of affairs regarding result-oriented reform within schools. Besides, an active contribution to the review process promotes systematic reflection on their role as educators for implementing result-oriented teaching. In line with this insight, all of the principals played a central role in the execution of the review. As a result, the principals were the owners of the review data.

During the five meetings, the project team formulated four questions for the review:

1. How can communication between classrooms, schools, and the board be optimized regarding the effective use of data that are collected for result-oriented teaching?

2. How does use of these data contribute to sustained improvement of teaching and learning?
3. How does use of these data contribute to ownership at the three levels?
4. What is a productive balance between autonomy and steering from an upper layer regarding the execution of the project?

Each question was further analyzed into more specific, sub-questions. For example, analysis of the third question yielded four sub-questions:

a. Do teachers, principals, and central office staff and administrators take responsibility for the preparation and execution of result-oriented teaching (at their level of functioning in the organization); do they actively contribute?
b. Do teachers, principals, and central office staff and administrators have a recognizable voice in the preparation and execution of result-oriented learning (at their level of functioning in the organization)?
c. Which measures are taken to create optimal opportunities for all actors to contribute actively to the process?
d. Can a development towards shared responsibility for result-oriented working be identified and do contributions of different actors show growing convergence?

To answer these review questions a method has been developed by the project team consisting of two guidelines: (1) a matrix for data collection and analysis, and (2) a procedure for diads of principals to work with the matrix.

Guideline for collecting and analyzing review data

The guideline for collecting and analyzing review data is a matrix. In this matrix, the questions of the project team are operationalized in themes for the rows and the columns. In the rows of the matrix four themes are displayed that focus on the technical quality of result-oriented teaching in the school:

- Data collection, data display, and dissemination of data displays;
- Data use;
- Result-oriented working in school;
- Result-oriented working in board.

In the columns three themes are displayed that focus on the cultural and organizational context of result oriented teaching in the school:

- Performance, communication, and coordination;
- Ownership;
- Sustained improvement of teaching and learning.

The combination of entrances of columns and rows leads to specific questions for the review in the cells. As an example, the two questions in the cell of the matrix row 1 x column 2 ('data collection, data display and communication' x 'ownership') are presented: (1) who in the school/in the board is familiar with the data? And (2) do all teachers in the school know these data and data displays?

The matrix is designed for collection and analysis of the review data. During the review the answers on the questions in the cells can be immediately recorded into the cells. A hindrance to success that might emerge during the review is the time-consuming character of analysis and reporting of the data. This potential problem is anticipated by offering the opportunity to set down the results immediately during and after the review into the cells of the matrix.

Guideline for executing the review

The collegial review is executed via diads of principals of different schools (critical friends). For data collection each principal in the diad asks the other principal about her or his school the questions that are depicted in the cells of the matrix. Questions are asked in a non-evaluative way. The basic attitude under these review interviews is unlimited curiosity with regard to how the other school works, without coupling any positive or negative evaluation at these insights. One principal interviews the other principal until the point is reached that the picture seems complete, and no more new information is found. The interviewer reports the answer according to the structure of the matrix. More specifically, the matrix is used to write down the answers in the cells. The interviewee controls and eventually corrects or completes the data. Both principals together are responsible for two reports of school reviews.

After the work of the diads is finished and the reports are completed, all the school reports are discussed in the project team, and in the annual meetings with the principals and special services coordinators. Principals have the school report at their disposal for internal use.

Research methods

The two questions in this chapter are: how is accountability policy implemented in a decentralized national and local policy context? And which role does educational leadership in a decentralized national and local policy context play in positioning the school towards accountability policy?

This section reports on a comparative case study that was executed to evaluate the implementation of the peer review on result-oriented teaching in the schools (question 1), and to explore the role of educational leadership in and around the participating schools (question 2). To answer these questions on the implementation of the peer review method every participating school is regarded as a case.

Data collection for research purposes

The school reports of the peer reviews served as the raw data for the case study. The school reports of the peer reviews of eight primary schools were collected and analysed. The special education school did not participate in the peer review and the results of two schools were not available for the research. Before the data of these school reports could be used for answering the research questions, a systematic selection of valid data was needed. The senior researcher inspected the raw data of the school reports. The aim was to select those data (1) that were reported in a complete and unequivocal way, and (2) that directly related to the research questions and the categories of the analysis of the peer review. For the analysis of the peer review data, 3 main categories and 13 subcategories were distinguished. The raw peer-reviewed data were selected and summarized according to these 3 main categories and 13 subcategories:

- Data collection, making displays, and diffusion of displays
    - which data are collected
    - from which resources
    - is display made and by whom
    - how and by whom are displays diffused
- Task performance, communication, coordination, and data use
    - which data are used/not used; role of data in external accountability
    - taking responsibility at own level of work
    - coupling decisions based on data to characteristics of effective instruction
    - coupling decisions based on data to instruction of teacher and learning goals of students
- Result-oriented teaching in school and board
    - coupling result-oriented teaching, student-centered teaching, and care for special needs students
    - teacher voice in result-oriented teaching
    - shared vision on result-oriented teaching
    - putting result-oriented teaching in context of quality assurance for school and board
    - result-oriented teaching at board level

The results of the step of data selection and organization were critically discussed with the external advisor and the staff member of the central office. Data on leadership practice were derived from self-reports that were collected during a plenary session for principals and special service coordinators. These data were controlled by the external advisor and the staff member of the central office, and evaluated as reliable.

Data analysis for research purposes

During the data analysis, all selected data were summarized into three matrices that were organized according to the three main categories and the subcategories. Moreover, these data were related to additional observations regarding the leadership practices in the schools.

The comparison of cases results in two patterns of result-oriented teaching in the eight schools. One pattern is restricted, because the implementation of result-oriented teaching is superficial. The other pattern is extended, because of the deeper implementation of result-oriented teaching (Fullan, 2007). Differences between superficial and deep concern are as follows:

- the passive or active role of the teachers,
- a formal orientation to the procedures or an orientation at the meaning of the procedures,
- instrumental improvements in instruction or improvements that are directly related to perceived differences between students,
- the distributed character of leadership activities,
- the role of a shared vision,
- the perception of school members of the role of the board.

The two patterns of result-oriented teaching were the starting point for analyzing the self-reports of the principals and the special services coordinators, especially the two patterns regarding the distributed character of leadership activities and the passive or active role of the teachers. Four themes for analysis were: (1) the role of the teachers, (2) the role and position of the special service coordinators, (3) the role of the principal, (4) and the role of the board and the project team.

Results

The restricted and extended patterns are summarized in Table 14.1. Four schools fit into the extended mode, although there still is a risk of losing the active participation of the teachers, and a shared school-specific vision on result-oriented teaching is only in an early stage of development. Two schools fit into the restricted mode, one school is in between the two modes and the eighth school only recently started result-oriented teaching.

Result-oriented teaching in the schools

The content of the rows 'collection of data' and 'interpretation of results' is self-evident. In the restricted schools, the collection and discussion of data at the levels of classroom and school are steered by the special service coordinator. The focus of data interpretation and use is on formal procedures and

Table 14.1 Restricted and extended modes of result-oriented teaching

Category	Restricted	Extended
Collection and analysis of data	Collection and discussion of data at classroom and school level steered by special service coordinator	Active engagement and ownership of teachers in collection and discussion of data in classroom and school
Interpretation of results	Focus on formal procedures and instruments for data collection and static representation of results; instrumental use and individual responsibility for one's class	Focus on professional discussion based on results, and on meaning of displays of data; meaning oriented use (questions and examples of colleagues trigger thinking about students and instruction), collective responsibility for student results in school
Instructional implications (group plans)	Formal data-driven group plans as a final result (three levels of students) to apply differentiated levels within class; supply of teacher to three fixed levels central focus	Group plans as starting point for data inspired differentiated instruction; diverging learning needs students central
Instructional implications (instructional behavior)	Low impact on varied instruction within three levels; more instruction on lower levels (repeated instruction) instead of varied instruction	High impact on varied instruction, search for variety in instruction according to differences between students within and between levels
Steering roles and hierarchical levels	Central role special service coordinator as a middle manager and owner, teacher as implementer of school leader's policy; three hierarchical levels within schools	Distributed leadership among teachers, special service coordinator, school leader and board; two hierarchical levels within schools, special service coordinator as an advisor, teacher as owner, and school leader as over all responsible
Vision	Vision externally imposed, ownership only with school leader and special service coordinator	Start of a discussion that promotes the development of a shared vision
Perception of board by team members	Formal division of responsibilities and tasks at four hierarchical levels	High engagement and ownership by all actors at three levels: teachers, school leadership, and board

instruments for data collection and on a static representation of results; data are used instrumentally for the individual responsibility at the class level, not the team. In extended schools, an active engagement and ownership of teachers can be observed for the collection and discussion of data among classrooms in the school. The focus is on professional discussion of the results and on meanings of the displays of data; use of data is meaning oriented (questions and examples of colleagues trigger thinking about the learning of students and instruction), and a collective responsibility for student results can be observed.

More complicated is the content of the cells in the rows regarding instructional implications. The main image is that in the restricted mode, teachers mainly have an instrumental interpretation of the results of data. They divide their classes into three groups of students according to the outcomes of the tests, and they give more instruction or less instruction according to the level of the groups. It seems that these teachers do not really look for the more specific needs of their students that should be identified at a deeper level, beyond the test scores. They do not adapt their instruction to the students' specific needs apart from superficial adaptation across the three levels. Their instruction remains within the narrow boundaries of the standard methods that are available for instruction in the school.

In the extended mode, instruction is not ideal, but teachers look for opportunities to adapt instruction to individual needs of students across/within the levels, based on data. They use the instruction method and additional resources to differentiate for the learning processes of diverging students. In one school, a visit by the inspector made a radical shift happen towards the extended mode of result-oriented teaching. Although student results were not too favorable for the school, the school escaped from a negative inspection report. Nevertheless, all team members were alarmed by this narrow escape. Within a period of four months, instruction became better differentiated for students with diverging learning needs and student results significantly improved. This incident shows that a first step from restricted toward extended can be made in a relatively short period.

Another interesting difference is expressed in the rows 'steering roles' and 'vision.' In the restricted mode, teachers, as well as the principal, put the special services coordinator central in result-oriented teaching. As a result, three hierarchical levels emerged in these schools: the principal, the special services coordinator, and the teachers. Only the principal and the special services coordinator share the vision. Teachers are not actively engaged in sharing and developing the vision. In the extended mode, the principal keeps full responsibility of result-oriented teaching in the school; the special services coordinator is a coach, coordinator, and collegial consultant, and the teachers are actively involved and have specific full responsibilities in data interpretation and planning of adapted instruction. In these schools, a school-wide discussion on the vision on result-oriented teaching has started (in the actual stage of development without sustained results).

Although all the eight schools in this comparative case study share the same board, the perception of the board significantly differs among the eight schools. In the restricted mode, the board is regarded as the upper level of hierarchy and as a source of top-down steering processes towards schools. In the extended mode, the board is regarded as a partner that is positively steering and stimulating favorable conditions.

Educational leadership

The differences in the two images of the eight schools were also identified in the self-reports regarding educational leadership in and around the schools. They include:

1. The roles that teachers play can be distinguished in more or less instrumental executers versus teachers as critical interpreters of result-oriented teaching;
2. The special service coordinator serves as a middle manager with delegated responsibilities, versus serving as a coordinator, coach and collegial consultant for teachers with responsibility for result-oriented teaching as a task;
3. Some principals delegate the responsibility for result-oriented teaching towards the special services coordinators while other principals remain actively engaged in leading results-oriented teaching and keep full responsibility for the results. Emerging problems in schools illustrate the importance of smart and clear positions for principals and special service coordinators. In a school with the restricted mode the development of result-oriented teaching stops when the position of special services coordinator is vacant. In the school that is starting up result-oriented teaching, a significant problem occurs when the role of special service coordinator is not clearly worked out. And for the school that is positioned in between restricted and extended, a formal interpretation of positions and tasks within the steering committee is characteristic. In the blueprint of this school teachers are actively involved, while in daily practice principal and special service coordinator do most of the work;
4. Three points regarding the role of the board and the project team include: (a) steering the implementation of result-oriented teaching by the board and the project team is experienced as open. Emergent progress is made in the process instead of precisely defined steps forward, with opportunities for schools and principals to take their course within the global vision that has been formulated by the board; (b) trust has developed among the members of the project team and the principals within the board that everyone will be kept in line and that the shared vision will be elaborated in a more concrete way by every practical step forward; and (c) the board reports that from this period the central question at the board level will be: what are the needs of the students in our schools and how can aligned and systemic accountability policy practices promote successful learning?

Discussion and conclusion

In this chapter we reported on a school board and the schools under that board developing result-oriented teaching within the Dutch decentralized educational system. The school board was central in this chapter, showing that within the context of the Dutch educational system, a local interpretation of accountability policy is possible and potentially productive. The interpretation of accountability policy by this school board can be characterized as the search for a balance: balance between improvement and control, with a strong focus on improvement, as well as a balance between autonomy and steering, and between diversity and alignment. The assumption of the board is that quality is not realized at one of these platforms; quality is realized by swinging between the platforms like trapeze artists.

For the moment it is not clear if this trapeze work will lead to better teaching and learning, or to leadership ownership. The first outcomes of the collegial review are promising, with regard to ownership of all actors involved and sustained improvement and capacity building. Regardless, the fact that the extended project team has succeeded in designing an instrument and a procedure for collegial review that has been received with open arms by all principals and special service coordinators is a serious indication that steps have been made forward within the board regarding the ownership of results-oriented teaching.

In this comparative case study, educational leadership is active at all levels in the system: the board, the principals, the special service coordinators, and in some schools, teacher leaders as steering committee members. During the process, educational leadership has become more aligned. This alignment is not a given at the start of the process. Sustained and enhanced alignment asks for continuous, thoughtful, and careful interventions from the central staff and the project team members. A serious risk is that the principals delegate responsibility for result-oriented teaching towards the special services coordinators and three hierarchical layers are created within relatively small primary schools.

After two and a half years, it can be said that a solid educational leadership base has been created at the levels of school board, principals, special services coordinators, and teacher leaders. This educational leadership base is a result of the results-oriented work previously accomplished and the conditions established for further success to come.

The Dutch educational system is characterized as a strongly decentralized system, with a recent tendency toward local centralization. In Dutch accountability policy, a strong focus is placed on the definition and assessment of standards. How these standards are reached is the responsibility of school boards and schools. Standardization of output and the introduction of assessment instruments and procedures by the national government indirectly impact the school curriculum and teacher instruction in classrooms. Nevertheless, within the Dutch educational system, there is a lot of space and a strong necessity for school boards and schools to develop their own bottom-up approach of results-oriented teaching and quality assurance, in which the development of ownership among all actors, and first of all professional development of teachers, is strived for. The term 'chain responsibility' is introduced for this systemic approach (i.e., the aligned and complementary responsibilities for quality of education and student learning results among teachers, principals, and school boards).

New possibilities emerge for educational leaders to swing between the control platform and the improvement platform. A productive approach for educational leadership is to view control and improvement as two complementary forces in the hands of boards, principals, and teacher leaders. In policy and daily school practice, both perspectives of control and improvement are strongly intertwined and incompatible. In such cases, safety and balance are found in swinging between the two platforms in a smart, elegant, and inspiring way.

References

Easley II, J. (2010). *The Audacity to Teach!: The Impact of Leadership, School Reform, and the Urban Context on Educational Innovations.* Lanham MD: University Press of America.
Fullan, M. (2007). *The New Meaning of Educational Change* (4th edn). New York: Teachers College Press.
Hofman, R., Dijkstra, N, De Boom, J. and Hofman, W. (2005). *Kwaliteitszorg in het primair onderwijs.* (Quality control in primary education). Groningen: GION.
Hoy, W. and Miskel, C. (2008). *Educational Administration: Theory, Research, and Practice* (8th edn). Boston: McGraw-Hill.
Imants, J. (2009). Teachers' research, professional development, and educational leadership. In: M. Khine and I. Saleh (eds) *Transformative Leadership and Educational Excellence: Learning Organizations in the Information Age* (pp. 103–121). Rotterdam: Sense Publishers.
Imants, J. and Van Veen, K. (2010). Teacher learning as workplace learning. In: P. Peterson, E. Baker, and B. McGaw (eds) *International Encyclopedia of Education* (3rd edn, vol. 7) (pp. 503–510). Oxford: Elsevier.
Imants, J., Van der Aalsvoort, G., De Brabander, C. and Ruijssenaars, A. (2001). The role of the special services coordinator in Dutch primary schools: a counterproductive effect of inclusion policy. *Educational Management and Administration* 29(1), 35–48.
Inspectie van het onderwijs (2010). *Onderwijsverslag 2008–2009.* Utrecht: Onderwijsinspectie.
Inspectie van het onderwijs (2011). *Onderwijsverslag 2009–2010.* Utrecht: Onderwijsinspectie.
Inspectie van het onderwijs (2012). *Onderwijsverslag 2010–2011.* Utrecht: Onderwijsinspectie.
Leithwood, K. (ed.) (2007). Special issue: the leading edge of distributed leadership research. *Leadership and Policy in Schools 6,* 1–125.
Leithwood, K. (2010). Characteristics of school districts that are exceptionally effective in closing the achievement gap. *Leadership and Policy in Schools 9,* 245–291.

Leithwood, K., Day, C., Sammons, P., Harris, A. and Hopkins, D. (2006). *Seven Strong Claims about Successful School Leadership*. Nottingham: NCSL.

Luttenberg, J., Van Veen, K. and Imants, J. (2013). Looking for cohesion: the role of search for meaning in the interaction between teacher and reform. *Research Papers in Education 28*(3), 289–308.

Muijs, D. and Harris, A. (2003). Teacher leadership: a review of the literature. *Educational Management & Administration 31*, 437–449.

Spillane, J. (2005). Distributed leadership. *The Educational Forum 69*(2), 143–150.

Vogels, R. and Bronneman-Helmers, R. (2006). *Wie werken er in het onderwijs?* (Who works in education?). Den Haag: Centraal Cultureel Planbureau.

15 Emerging accountability policies and practices in education
The case of Norway

Guri Skedsmo and Sølvi Mausethagen

In this chapter, we explore questions about educational accountability within the Norwegian context, with a particular focus on recent policy changes and implications for principalship. In Norway, initiatives to monitor and improve educational quality have intensified over the last decade in particular (cf. Skedsmo, 2009). However, by comparison with other countries in the Western world, Norway has been characterized as reluctant to implement monitoring practices and accountability policies. In addition, there has been limited implementation of incentives to mobilize teachers and principals' motivation and work efforts. One explanation for this is that the ideologies behind such policies represent a break with prevailing values and traditional notions of schooling, and they imply a loss of trust in the profession's ability to meet its societal mandate through a national, compulsory curriculum. The Norwegian case sheds light on how accountability policies are enacted in a context where the profession has historically enjoyed a relatively high degree of status and autonomy, where ideas about inclusion and social equality have been crucial and where society has been and continues to be characterised by a relatively high degree of trust.

In this chapter, we explore how this context influences educational accountability in Norway. We first define accountability policies and practices. Second, we outline the historical education context, including the reforms implemented during the 2000s. Third, we review studies of accountability in Norway, with a particular focus on principalship. Finally, we discuss how accountability policies are variously perceived and enacted, and what we see as typical features of educational accountability in Norway.

Perspectives on accountability

As a global trend, educational accountability introduces new monitoring systems to enhance quality in education (Fuller, 2008; Ranson, 2003). This policy's underlying theory is that holding municipalities, schools, and teachers accountable through measures such as tests and evaluations boosts student achievement because teachers and schools work to adopt more effective teaching methods (Heilig, 2011; Mintrop, 2004). Accountability policies typically emphasize performance management, quality indicators, the use of incentives and sanctions, and competition as key drivers of improvement (Gunter and Fitzgerald, 2013; Sahlberg, 2007).

These elements are included in what is broadly defined as performance-based managerialism (Clarke and Newman, 1997), and it can be argued that this performance-based approach represents the dominant form of accountability. Several researchers refer to this as managerial accountability (Romzek and Dubnick, 1987; Sinclair, 1995), arguing that there are other forms of accountability that refer to different aspects of the work in schools and thus different coordination processes. Indeed, referring to managerial accountability as educational accountability would imply a rather narrow definition of the latter. Therefore, in this chapter, we define accountability as the management of diverse expectations generated within and outside the organization (Romzek and Dubnick, 1987), taking into account the different forms of accountability in education—such as political, public, and professional—as well as managerial accountability (Conway and Murphy, 2013; Romzek and Dubnick, 1987; Sinclair, 1995). How and to what extent these different forms play out depends on how they are linked to the use of policy instruments, methods, and tools of governing processes, which differ from country to country. In general, the different forms of accountability offer lenses through which to investigate accountability in practice, which help to understand the mechanisms and consequences of school governing (Skedsmo, 2009). For a school principal in Norway, political accountability means responding to and following up on educational policies and political decisions. This links to public accountability, regarding the fulfilment of a school's mandate and function in society and in the local community. Managerial accountability specifically refers to the principal's leadership position and responsibility to superiors at the municipal level—in other words, hierarchical relationships; it is about monitoring inputs and outputs, and improving educational outcomes. Similarly, legal accountability delimits how a principal is answerable to regulations—in Norway there has been a trend towards regulating more areas of school practice by law (Mølstad and Hansèn, 2013), which in turn strengthens other types of accountability.

Professional accountability refers to the principal's commitment to a community of professionals, requiring adherence to professional standards. Arguably, due to the nature of work in schools, professional accountability has always existed. Professional accountability also concerns how codes of ethics, more recently introduced by professional organizations, have become a familiar part of the rhetoric that informs professional work in schools, although the influence of these codes is uncertain (Mausethagen, 2013b). Finally, and again relating to professional accountability, teachers and principals are also accountable for personal values—being true to one's basic values such as respect for human dignity and an acceptance of the responsibility for affecting the lives of others. This type of accountability is regarded as particularly powerful and binding in education; stress is likely if personal values conflict with other forms of accountability (Mausethagen, 2013b). Thus, different accountabilities exist in parallel and are negotiated locally, which causes challenges when they conflict.

First, using these forms of accountability as points of departure enables us to take a more nuanced look at accountability. Second, it takes account of how principals must balance diverse expectations and priorities. Third, it acknowledges that school governing involves the coordination of key actors' work by different means, such as curriculum guidelines, national test results and so on. Policy implementation and school governing depend on how key actors coordinate initiatives to meet different accountabilities, and this interaction may have both intended and unintended consequences (Skedsmo, 2009).

The Norwegian education context

Norway has a long and deep-rooted tradition of comprehensive schooling, social inclusion, and egalitarianism, and of steering by means of a national curriculum and legislation (Gundem, 1993a). More than 97 percent of Norwegian students are in the public school system, which is expected to serve as a 'social melting pot' and to promote social equality and democracy (Aasen et al., 2013). This 'Nordic model of education' (Telhaug et al., 2006) has historically tied education to the development of the social-democratic welfare state, emphasizing the redistributive role of the state and promoting social inclusion through equality of access and outcomes (Karlsen, 1993; Sejersted, 2005). Teachers and principals have traditionally had substantial autonomy (Gundem, 1993b; Slagstad, 1998). For example, teachers exercise a great amount of discretion in their work, which implies government-backed trust that professionals do their jobs in the best possible ways. A prominent example of professional autonomy is the national curriculum; historically, teachers in Norway have been trusted by the state to teach the curriculum on the basis of their knowledge and values (Mausethagen and Mølstad, 2014; Sivesind and Bachmann, 2008).

Routines for reporting information to national authorities have existed since the strengthening of the education system after World War II. These local reports formed the basis for decisions regarding infrastructure, including buildings, equipment, material and personnel resources (Karlsen, 1993; Telhaug, 1994). They also influenced decisions about compulsory requirements for subjects and courses. Based on the information provided, national authorities (i.e., the Ministry of Education) were responsible for resolving problems and making improvements to education.

The education system in Norway has historically delegated responsibility for primary and lower secondary education to the 428 municipalities, while the 19 counties are in charge of upper secondary education. Decentralization strategies were initiated in the 1980s to encourage and strengthen local initiatives and to introduce a bottom-up approach to school development (Engeland, 2000). It was assumed that local engagement would promote motivation and learning among students, helping to build a sense of belonging to the local community and thus supporting individual identities as well. In this way, schools were important in supporting rural areas and encouraging continuous settlement. There was also political consensus about the importance of decentralization as a means of restructuring and renewing public sector procedures and practices (Engeland, 2000). In policy documents from the early 2000s, municipalities and counties are defined as 'school owners' that are in charge of quality management, local curriculum planning and professional development for teachers. However, the introduction of new assessment and accountability policies raises the question of whether central coordination has been strengthened in such a way that municipalities are left with less autonomy (Møller and Skedsmo, 2013a).

A report from the Organization for Economic Co-operation and Development (OECD, 1988) questioned Norway's lack of documentation on educational quality and suggested that quality assurance systems be developed. During the 1990s, such systems were developed mainly under the umbrella of 'school-based evaluation,' focusing on developing local schools as organizations (Nyhus and Monsen, 2012). At the same time, the policy debate around a national quality assurance system (including national testing) continued during the 1990s, and various committees published numerous white and green papers, at the behest of the Royal Ministry of Education and Research (Skedsmo, 2009). The debate was characterized by negotiations on such issues as governing structures, centralization, and decentralization, and the roles and responsibilities of national and local authorities (Skedsmo, 2009).

Parallel to discussions around how to measure and document educational quality, various strategies were implemented to renew the public sector in general, known as new public management (NPM). The Norwegian version of NPM emphasized decentralization and delegation and was accompanied by the introduction of management by objectives (MBO) during the 1990s (Christensen, 1991). MBO was proposed to solve problems related to strongly divided and inflexible governing structures, unclear division of tasks and responsibilities, and a lack of national coordination and consistency, all of which encourage disclaiming responsibility (Møller and Skedsmo, 2013b). While MBO was seen as 'a central condition for local autonomy' (Skedsmo, 2009), it took almost 15 years until such a system was introduced.

Education reforms of the 1990s also suggested the need for increased attention to student learning and outcomes (Haug, 2003), and the mediocre first Programme for International Student Achievement (PISA) results, published in 2001, and subsequent intermediate PISA results, received a great deal of political and public attention, which highlighted problems in Norwegian education and legitimized subsequent reforms in the 2000s

(Elstad, 2010; Skedsmo, 2009). Together, these developments have shifted attention towards the outcomes of education.

In the early 2000s, two green papers in particular (Government of Norway, 2002, 2003) highlighted the need for more attention to learning processes and the results of individual students. These two documents laid the groundwork for the introduction of the National Quality Assessment System (NQAS), which was presented in White Paper No. 30 (2003–2004). A national test was trialled during the fall of 2004, and the first version of NQAS was introduced in 2005. White Paper No. 30 also introduced key principles for the Knowledge Promotion Reform, introduced in 2006. This national curriculum for basic education is based on competency aims at the end of Grades 2, 4, 7, and 10 and places greater emphasis on developing students' basic skills (i.e., reading, writing, oral skills, digital skills, and numeracy).

Assessment policies and accountability practices in Norway

As described above, there has been a shift in Norway's education policy since the early 2000s. Along with public sector reforms, school governing processes have changed. Previously, the curriculum provided direction but teachers were not bound by external assessment of student achievement. However, the introduction of NQAS meant greater state coordination, monitoring, and control (Skedsmo, 2009, 2011); the teaching profession views this shift towards external control of outcomes as a sign of distrust.

The main argument for launching NQAS in 2005, and in particular for national testing, was the declared need for more access to and use of data to improve school quality and outcomes. NQAS included a toolkit comprising a mix of new and traditional assessment tools—national testing and international comparative achievement studies such as PISA, Trends in International Mathematics and Science Study (TIMSS), and Progress in International Reading Literacy Study (PIRLS) were new, while the School-leaving Examination (exit exam after completing upper secondary school), the Craft Certificate (the qualifying certificate for vocational education), and grades are traditional tools that were kept (Skedsmo, 2009, 2011.). However, now that NQAS also includes grades as a central element, grading is no longer simply a matter of teachers assigning grades to students in individual schools but has become part of the basis for national measurement, comparison and concern (Prøitz, 2013).

During this introductory phase of NQAS, considerable attention was given to national testing. In particular, the publishing of school results and ranking of schools attracted criticism in the media, and the School Student Union of Norway even boycotted the tests. Because evaluation of the national tests revealed quality deficiencies (Lie *et al.*, 2005), the new government instituted a moratorium in 2005. Validity and reliability were improved when the tests were reintroduced in 2007; results are again made publicly available after some years of restricted availability. Nevertheless, while national testing aims to determine whether schools successfully meet national curriculum objectives, teachers are encouraged to use the tests for formative purposes—that is, to guide students and to improve their own teaching practices.

NQAS thus represents a shift towards output-oriented school governing, accompanied by a realignment of traditional input-oriented approaches. In particular, national testing provides a basis for emerging forms of accountability practices in which schools are increasingly perceived as units of measurement. We argue that accountability policies are embedded in current national assessment policies, and that demands for accountability are expressed in terms of expectations about the use of student results. This implies that key actors are held more accountable for educational outcomes, as national test results represent a benchmarking tool for schools and municipalities to compare their results with averages at municipality, regional, and national levels (Skedsmo, 2009). Teacher accountability in Norway is therefore primarily mandated through national testing (Mausethagen, 2013b). However, how accountability practices play out depends on how results are used, which varies greatly between municipalities (Engeland *et al.*, 2008; Skedsmo and Hopfenbeck, submitted).

The ways in which assessment policies are formulated determines the flexibility and discretion teachers, principals, and municipalities are given to make decisions about pedagogical practices in pursuit of curricular aims (Ministry of Education and Research, 2003–2004). This form of decentralization emphasizes school and teacher accountability that is framed within a discourse of 'freedom', 'trust,' and 'responsibility.' In other words, one might say that trust and flexibility are traded for improved learning outcomes; the state remains a strong actor in pursuing systemic change (Karseth and Sivesind, 2010; Skedsmo, 2009). However, there is little knowledge about how these dynamics play out locally and how notions of performance are developed through school governing processes.

In addition, input-oriented means of governing align with outcome control, such as competency aims and state-initiated programs with specific targets (e.g., to improve basic competencies). Thus, guidelines for municipalities, principals, and teachers on how to use national test results to improve educational practices represent a new form of input-oriented governing (Skedsmo, 2009). Moreover, outcome control has been reinforced by new regulations with direct impacts on local practice. For instance, municipalities are required to implement quality management systems to ensure school quality, and students are entitled to two assessment conferences per year with teachers and parents, which link outcome control and student assessment to legal compliance.

Studies of accountability in Norwegian education

In the following review of studies of accountability in Norwegian education, we first examine studies that depict how the policy climate has shifted towards managerial accountability. Second, we look at studies that address how assessment and accountability policies are perceived by municipal administrators, principals, and teachers, and how such policies play out locally. Third, we consider studies that focus specifically on the role of principals in accountability and assessment.

Studies of policy developments over time

One way of looking at the relatively recent policy shifts in Norway is by drawing broad historical lines. Aasen *et al.* (2013) provide an overview of what they describe as 'knowledge regimes' in the Norwegian education system after 1945. Of these, they characterize the current and most influential as the 'market-liberal knowledge regime.' While previous knowledge regimes have mainly promoted input-based governing, the market-liberal knowledge regime emphasizes an outcome-based approach. The authors argue that ideas about human capital and individual merits are important features of this knowledge regime, a development that has been influenced by transnational organisations such as the European Union and the OECD. Aasen *et al.* (2013) hold that equity has been redefined as equivalence in recent policy documents, so that schooling is increasingly understood as an individual and private good, and equity and the notion of a shared culture is de-emphasized. Yet, it is important to note that although this knowledge regime is increasingly influential, it coexists with social-democratic values of promoting social equality and democracy (Aasen *et al.*, 2013). It is therefore reasonable to argue that when both of these knowledge regimes present ideas about education that coexist in practice, it presents certain dilemmas in the field.

Other studies focus on recent policy developments related to accountability in Norwegian educational policy. For example, Møller and Skedsmo (2013b) investigate the ways in which ideas related to NPM have been introduced and interpreted in the Norwegian educational sector. They identify three areas of discursive struggle: the first is linked to ideologies and the national history of schooling, the second to contested discourses of professionalism (Mausethagen and Granlund, 2012), and the third to strategies for modernizing and improving education. Although monitoring educational outcomes became part of the policy agenda in 1988, Møller and Skedsmo (2013b) describe how the discourse that holds teachers more accountable became more prominent after the weak PISA results. And although teachers' individual autonomy was emphasized, they argue that the introduction of NQAS in 2004 marked a shift in how trust in teachers was communicated. In the same period, a discourse of strong leadership also emerged, reconfiguring hierarchical relationships in schools and redefining teachers as followers (Møller and Skedsmo, 2013b). Outcome-oriented approaches to school governing gained ground, reinforced by new input-oriented methods and new laws and regulations about assessment procedures. Taken together, these tighter state coordinating mechanisms are to be followed by municipalities that, as of 2006, are defined as 'school owners.'

In his book, *The Struggle for the Knowledge School*, the Norwegian state secretary from 2001 to 2005 recalls how it was no longer possible to deny that the country's educational system had a significant knowledge and skills problem, which had worsened in recent years (Bergesen, 2006). He outlines how the PISA results motivated the government to introduce new reforms. Policy makers also began to place greater emphasis on the importance of the 'good teacher,' highlighting that it is not resources or structural conditions that have the strongest impact on student learning but the quality of the teacher (Bergesen, 2006). Moreover, administrative competence became a central issue in the reform process, together with an emphasis on assessment and student outcomes.

Introduction of new assessment tools and accountability

Only a few studies address how accountability policies in Norway have been perceived and enacted by principals and teachers, particularly after the introduction of NQAS in 2004 and the Knowledge Promotion Reform of 2006. Skedsmo (2009) examines both the purposes of assessment policies and how principals perceive the use of new and old assessment tools. Through an analysis of policy documents from 1990 to 2005, she investigates the argumentation leading to the establishment of NQAS, finding that information provided by the assessment tools increasingly focused on student performance, the development of local follow-up procedures and the use of specific methods to increase student performance and professional development. Skedsmo (2009) emphasizes that the dominant policy discourse relates to using information about outcomes to improve administrative practice, while concealing the government's agenda for oversight and monitoring educational quality. Moreover, it seems to be taken for granted that municipalities, principals, and teachers need the same information to initiate improvements—and that they know how to improve. Findings from a survey of Norwegian principals show that new assessment tools were perceived as an administrative system, linked to local reporting and control and only loosely coupled with practices that might help students to improve their learning (Skedsmo, 2009). The author suggests the need for greater awareness of the design and function of assessment tools because how these tools are implemented is likely to create new patterns of interaction between national authorities, local authorities, and schools.

Roald (2010) addresses the introduction of the national evaluation system and how principals and local authorities interact with data analysis and development projects. Based on interviews, he notes how difficult it is for schools and municipalities to use assessment and evaluation data for improvement purposes. The national discourse on quality and everyday work in schools presents two different narratives of what education is about and how to enhance its quality. Roald (2010) argues that increased access to data may even be counterproductive if the data are not treated in ways that enhance collective insight and knowledge among teachers and politicians, and he asks whether the evaluation system increases or limits learning within organizations. He thus presents translating information into action within schools and municipalities as an important challenge, as information and systems alone do not create new knowledge and development. Roald emphasizes that productive assessment cultures must be built from below, that quality processes are only developed when principals, teachers, students, and parents are 'co-producers.'

Elstad (2009) presents a qualitative study on how media attention following test results gives rise to complex emotional processes among teachers that in addition to initiating improvement, may provoke hostile reactions and panic measures. He demonstrates how emphasizing results and hierarchical accountability reveals social norms that operate through shame, and how collegial pressure may be triggered by 'naming, shaming and blaming' practices, such as the league tables published by the media. However, Elstad (2009) finds that this public shaming may also generate normative change when incremental steps are taken, and he calls for more empirical work inside schools to explore how professional standards in particular influence local norms and actions.

These studies by Roald (2010) and Elstad (2009) are part of the Achieving School Accountability in Practice (ASAP) project, which commenced with the introduction of NQAS in 2005 and first addressed how to consolidate governing and accountability in Norwegian schools. Both studies emphasize lack of theoretical sense-making of the encounter between accountability and everyday schooling. Elstad *et al.* (2008) state that their project documents how education governing in Norway is increasingly marked by managerial accountability, which is expected to continue. However, they also question further development in light of conflicts of interest between politicians and teachers, emphasizing the need for further research on 'accountability the Norwegian way'—that is, according a relative degree of trust to the profession with few incentives or penalties attached to school performance.

The implementation of the Knowledge Promotion Reform was evaluated by several studies. In one, Møller *et al.* (2013) describe how national authorities have a hierarchical and top-down understanding of implementation practices, even though 'steering from below' and increased professional autonomy were important parts of the policy discourse when the reform was initiated. The study found that five years after the reform's implementation, municipalities, and schools experienced a decrease in autonomy. However, increased knowledge of the Knowledge Promotion Reform did result in changes to schools and teacher practices. For example, increased access to aggregated performance data has proven useful for school leaders and municipalities in prioritizing development work, and the emphasis on assessment and assessment data has been important in increasing understanding of the reform rationale and promoting shared professional language (Aasen *et al.*, 2012). Implementing and anchoring NQAS, however, are described as particularly challenging.

Møller *et al.* (2013) see the teaching profession as being too critical of control regimes, saying that they must also recognize demands for documentation as largely legitimate. The researchers argue that if the profession does not become more involved in the dialogue around these issues, accepting accountability as a part of professionalism, its status may be adversely affected. Karseth and Engelsen (2013) argue that although the reform was intended to increase teacher autonomy, teachers' discretionary powers have been diminished by a regulation that outlines explicit criteria for assessing student competence, thereby conscribing teachers' didactic practices. They also argue that the ways in which competence aims are measured narrow the broader aims of education and creates a more product-oriented curriculum. Rønning (2013) notes other possible implications by way of findings that teachers have become more performative at the expense of deeper conversations with students. Additionally, Nordahl and Hausstätter (2009) find that the number of students receiving special needs education increased after the introduction of the 2006 reform, and Bakken and Elstad (2012) believe that social inequality has increased. More research is needed on these social effects, but overall, student performance has increased since the introduction of the reform (Kjærnsli and Roe, 2010).

Two evaluation projects by the Norwegian Directorate of Education and Training (Allerup *et al.*, 2009; Seland *et al.*, 2013) have investigated national testing. The reports suggest that teachers and principals place greater emphasis on summative than formative aspects of the tests, that teaching practices may become directed towards national tests, and in spite of being generally accepted, the tests create some discomfort for teachers. Seland *et al.* (2013) find that national tests are mostly integrated into schools' practices; but while principals claim to gain useful information from them, teachers do not generally agree and are more concerned with being unable to provide useful formative feedback to students. These studies, do not, however, address tests' summative aspects or why teachers are more sceptical than principals about their usefulness.

In her doctoral dissertation, Mausethagen (2013b) reports that four specific issues increase tension around national testing from a teacher's perspective: professional knowledge, the curriculum, formative aspects of teaching, and loyalty to students. These internal aspects of teachers' work are seen as being challenged by external or managerial accountability. First, from the perspective of individual teachers' emotions, national testing challenges what they perceive as their main teaching tasks, which are reliant on internal explanations, concepts, and models. Second, national testing challenges the profession's collective knowledge base and autonomy. Mausethagen's (2013b) findings imply that when national testing challenges central epistemic aspects of teaching, it is harder for teachers to accept the tests or the control that they represent. In order to create relevance and legitimacy for new (mandated) expectations, professional discourse is reshaped. Although national testing to a limited extent is explicitly resisted, findings suggest that the tests are not as integrated or influential as policy makers wish (Mausethagen, 2013c).

In their study of how local actors interpret and respond to national assessment policies, Skedsmo and Hopfenbeck (submitted) find that national test results shape municipal quality assurance systems. Both superintendents and principals use results to monitor student outcomes over time, and to set and legitimize priorities for school development. The use of tests is accompanied by new or reinvented organizational routines, such as meetings between key actors in local school systems, contracts that include performance targets for principals and teachers and, to some degree, performance-based salaries. These routines imply that chains of accountability relationships are established to clarify roles and responsibilities. However, the focus on test results, the routines initiated, and the links to accountability processes vary widely across municipalities. Regardless of accountability pressures within a municipality, however, all principals want their schools to do well on national tests. Principals are also concerned about how to follow rules for omitting students from the tests. Currently, national tests are compulsory for all students in Grades 5, 8, and 9. However, according to the Guidelines for National Testing (Norwegian Directorate for Education and Training, 2014), students eligible for special education or specific language training, may be excused from testing. In collaboration with parents, principals decide which individuals are excluded from testing, which is often inconsistent and perceived as unfair.

The role of principals

These policy developments have raised new expectations for municipalities, schools and in particular, principals. Here, we focus on recent studies that have examined implications for principals.

In her doctoral dissertation, Skedsmo (2009) finds that principals experience leadership dilemmas in using new assessment tools. Principals report concrete dilemmas in planning, priority setting, and defining good results. National tests define acceptable results for student achievement. On the other hand, key actors often perceive these measures as too narrowly defined. Principals feel that they are primarily accountable for providing good educations for all students, indicating a focus on equity and social inclusion, as guided by professional norms and responsibilities (Skedsmo, 2009).

Through different project phases from 2004 until 2009, the Norwegian component of the International Successful School Principalship Project (ISSPP) has focused on principals' notions of success, leadership approaches, and factors that contribute to sustaining success in schools. Case studies were conducted in 12 schools, and after five years, the researchers returned to three schools to assess possible changes (Møller *et al.*, 2009b). Both municipal-level players and parents recognized all three as taking good care of students with special needs. Despite the new expectations for improving student outcomes on national tests, the researchers found continuity in these schools. Although they also found more explicit talk about improving student outcomes, principals remained focused on meeting students' needs—success was defined as finding the appropriate teaching strategies for diverse students. That is, they monitor students' progress through a variety of assessment practices and quality indicators. So far, school principals in these municipalities have paid less attention to students' academic performance on national tests because there have been few, if any, related incentives or sanctions (Møller *et al.*, 2009a). Thus, how principals are accountable reflects the socially sanctioned dominance of certain ideologies and the subjugation of others. Accordingly, principals frequently describe themselves as being caught in the cross-fire between politicians, parents, and staff members' increased expectations (Møller, 2012).

NQAS and the different requirements for reporting between local levels have influenced new procedures for performance monitoring (Aasen *et al.*, 2012; Hopfenbeck *et al.*, 2013), which has changed school plans and priorities, especially in primary and lower secondary education. There are, however, large variations between schools in terms of how and to what extent performance information is being used. By establishing data practices, e.g. the use of test results, for monitoring students' learning progress, principals play a pivotal role in developing and sustaining such practices (Skedsmo and Hopfenbeck, submitted). However, this requires that principals be able to interpret and apply the results for school development purposes; many find it difficult to prioritize efforts on the basis of such data, and both principals and teachers find it difficult to assess the extent to which data leads to improved student outcomes. Moreover, Skedsmo and Møller (2016) find that the overall school governing system in Norway—and, in particular, the use of tools to measure performance and hands-on management—entails strong commitment to data use, user orientation, and holding key actors accountable for outcomes. Performance expectations are closely related to national test data, and economic incentives connected to management contracts have also been introduced to motivate achievement. The study also points to some dangers inherent in this strong performance orientation; namely, aspects of education that cannot be tested receive less attention, which requires principals to champion these aspects and to justify their priorities to their municipal superiors (Skedsmo and Møller, 2016).

Summary of accountability studies

To date, most studies have been qualitative, comparative case studies of schools and municipalities; relatively few studies have addressed how testing, accountability, and assessment are perceived locally in Norway; most have largely explored the more systemic changes stimulated by the introduction of NQAS in 2004 and education reform in 2006, for which questions primarily relate to how the reform and evaluation systems have been implemented rather than to how teachers and principals perceive accountability policies. Other contributors have presented only preliminary suggestions for possible social effects of the reforms (both positive and negative). While these studies do provide important insights into both systemic and individual reforms, the current review highlights the need for research that delves into how teachers, principals, and municipalities handle the new expectations created by performance management and accountability tools. Investigating accountability from below—that is, taking account of actors' perspectives—provides insights into the dynamics of performance management and managerial accountability, and how assessment policies advance new ideas about professional accountability. In Norway, the apparent decrease of trust in principals and teachers has generated a response from the teaching profession, which has become more proactive in emphasizing their knowledge base and justifying their actions (Mausethagen, 2013b); thus, teachers have concurrently enacted and negotiated managerial and professional accountabilities. It is clear that the dynamics of educational accountability are very complex, so research design must take this complexity into account.

New national and local modes of governing: Possible tensions and dilemmas

We now discuss new modes of governing and emerging accountability policies and practices in the Norwegian context. Three themes in particular are of immediate relevance: tensions between control and development, issues related to trust and distrust, and central versus local school governing.

First, one might reasonably suggest that it is principals and teachers' professional responsibility to ensure that knowledge about student performance initiates learning and development feedback loops for schools and individuals. Indeed, assessment tools such as national testing may have been created for just this purpose. In the first phase, assessment policies in Norway were characterized by trust in the profession in that policy makers seemed to believe that teachers and principals would participate in learning and development processes without extrinsic motivations or sanctions. In this regard, policy makers relied on professional accountability for continuous learning processes based on professional knowledge and responsibility. However, in the last couple of years, several national initiatives have been introduced to steer and control local learning and development processes. One example is the formulated inspection criteria, which schools and municipalities use as check lists. Another example is the national guidelines for developing local criteria for student assessment. Some municipalities have introduced risk management to school governing, in which school leaders are required to identify risk factors that may hinder goal attainment. However, several principals and teachers have engaged in media debates to protest the use of detailed quality indicators and reporting requirements that take time away from teaching and student learning (e.g., Klassekampen, 2014). These objections indicate tensions around local control mechanisms and managerial accountability practices that seem to contradict professional accountability, norms and ethics, which become personal dilemmas for principals and teachers.

Second, one could say that managerial accountability has taken form with a 'Norwegian touch,' in that it still places a certain amount of trust in professionals. However, in the national discourse related to data use and accountability, a certain embedded distrust creates tensions and suggests paradoxes in how these policies are formulated (Skedsmo, 2009). Although the control of outcomes represents a break from tradition, the loyalty of the profession to the state, derived from historically mandated responsibility for the curriculum, could remain—unless teachers' feel that the state and the profession are no longer working together towards the same goals or that managerial accountability practices weaken rather than enhance student motivation and learning. This might also lead to conflicts between managerial accountabilities and professional beliefs and ethics, or between professional and personal accountabilities. Again, such experiences strengthen the control and accountability function of assessment tools while diminishing their developmental aspects. Another factor that could undermine trust is how, despite the lack of incentives and sanctions, managerial accountability creates tensions among colleagues within a school that aims to 'perform well' (Mausethagen, 2013c), which suggests that collegial relations exert a strong influence on teachers and principals' work, a finding that sheds light on the more subtle, informal dynamics of accountability. As such, the introduction of managerial accountability implies that local practices could become 'high-stakes' issues for teachers and principals in the local community.

Third, the ways in which quality assurance systems are designed in many municipalities, where accountability practices are enacted, may lead to tighter municipal control and monitoring of school outcomes. Expectations about using test results to raise student achievement and subsequent test results may lead to a one-sided focus on teach-to-the-test practices, which detract from other important aspects of education. To date, only a few municipalities attach formal incentives or penalties to test results, such as pay for performance or school sanctions. Nevertheless, schools are keen to perform well because of concerns about their municipal reputations. Some municipalities rank schools according to national test results, while others do not. In addition, using management contracts and performance appraisals for principals strengthens the basis for managerial accountability practices (Skedsmo and Møller, forthcoming). Previous research has shown that the ways in which district superintendents and principals negotiate accountability pressures impact how teachers experience and enact managerial accountability (Hallett, 2010; Wills and Sandholtz, 2009), and whether it is experienced as something that mainly controls or supports learning and development. In the Norwegian context, then, there is a need to explore local variations in the design of quality assurance systems and to examine the possible tensions between governing and accountability practices in particular contexts.

Concluding remarks

This chapter has explored questions about educational accountability in the Norwegian context, focusing on recent policy changes and their implications for principalship. Like elsewhere, education policy and practices in Norway are influenced by transnational ideas that are adapted to cultural traditions and specific contexts (Ozga and Jones, 2006; Phillips and Ochs, 2003). An understanding of contextual issues helps to clarify how educational accountability plays out in Norway, where there remains trust in the profession and limited use of incentives. The Norwegian situation illustrates the emergent nature of accountability policies and practices, typically characterized by the existence and interplay of different accountabilities.

To gain more insights into these dynamics, we see the need for more research into the national and local integration of performance data into organizational routines and accompanying accountabilities. Also, existing research has not yet addressed the implications of new modes of governing that create relationships in which local authorities and schools become more dependent on national decisions and priorities (cf. Ozga, 2009; Skedsmo, 2009), as increased central regulation may create new interaction patterns between national authorities, municipalities, and schools.

References

Aasen, P., Møller, J., Rye, E. M., Prøitz, T. S., and Hertzberg, F. (2012). *Kunnskapsløftet som styringsreform – et løft eller et løfte?* Forvaltningsnivåenes og institusjonenes rolle i implementeringen av reformen: Nordisk institutt for studier av innovasjon, forskning og utdanning.

Aasen, P., Prøitz, T. S., and Sandberg, N. (2013). Knowledge regimes and contradictions in education reforms. *Journal of Education Policy*, 28(5), 718–738. doi: http://dx.doi.org/10.1177/0895904813475710

Allerup, P., Velibor, K., Kvåle, G., Langfeldt, G., and Skov, P. (2009). *Evaluering av det nasjonale kvalitetsvurderingssystemet for grunnopplæringen*. Report. Agder Research (Vol. 8). Kristiansand.

Bakken, A. and Elstad, J. I. (2012). *For store forventninger? Kunnskapsløftet og ulikhetene i grunnskolekarakterer*. (Vol. 7). Oslo: NOVA.

Bergesen, H. O. (2006). *Kampen om kunnskapsskolen (The "battle" of the knowledge school)*. Oslo: Universitetsforlaget.

Christensen, T. (1991). Virksomhetsplanlegging – staffasje eller effektivt styringsverktøy? In Lægreid, P. (ed.) *Målstyring og virksomhetsplanlegging i offentlig sektor*. Bergen: Alma Mater Forlag AS, 83–91.

Clarke, J. and Newman, J. (1997). *The Managerial State: Power, politics and ideology in the remaking of social welfare.* London: Sage Publications Ltd.

Conway, P. and Murphy, R. (2013). A rising tide meets a perfect storm: New accountabilities in teaching and teacher education in Ireland. *Irish Educational Studies*, 32(1), 11–36.

Elstad, E. (2009). Schools which are named, shamed and blamed by the media: school accountability in Norway. *Educational Assessment, Evaluation and Accountability*, 21(2), 173–189. doi: 10.1007/s11092-009-9076-0

Elstad, E. (2010). PISA i norsk offentlighet: politisk teknologi for styring og bebreidelsesmanøvrering. In E. Elstad and K. Sivesind (eds) *PISA – Sannheten om skolen?* Oslo: Universitetsforlaget, 100–122.

Elstad, E., Langfeldt, G., and Hopmann, S. (eds) (2008). *Ansvarlighet i skolen. Politiske spørsmål og pedagogiske svar.* Oslo: Cappelen Damm Akademisk.

Engeland, Ø. (2000). Skolen i kommunalt eie – politisk styrt eller profesjonell ledet skoleutvikling? PhD thesis. Faculty of Educational Sciences: University of Oslo.

Engeland, Ø., Langfeldt, G., and Roald, K. (2008). Kommunalt handlingsrom: Hvordan forholder norske kommuner seg til ansvarsstyring i skolen? In G. Langfeldt, E. Elstad and S. Hopmann (eds), *Ansvarlighet i skolen. Politiske spørsmål og pedagogiske svar.* Fagernes: Cappelen Akademisk Forlag, 178–203.

Fuller, B. (2008). Liberal learning in centralising states. In B. Fuller, M. K. Henne and E. Hannum (eds) *Strong States, Weak Schools: The Benefits and Dilemmas of Centralised Accountability* (Vol. 16). Bingley: Emerald Group.

Government of Norway (2002). Green Paper: Proposal for framework for the national system of quality assessment of the Norwegian comprehensive education (*NOU 2002:10, Førsteklasses fra første klasse. Forslag til rammeverk for et nasjonalt kvalitetsvurderingssystem av norsk grunnopplæring*).

Government of Norway (2003). Green Paper: Improving quality in comprehensive education for all students *(NOU 2003:16, I første rekke. Forsterket kvalitet i en grunnopplæring for alle).*

Gundem, B. B. (1993a). *Mot en ny skolevirkelighet? Læreplanen i et sentraliserings- og desentraliseringsperspektiv.* Oslo: Ad Notam Gyldendal.

Gundem, B. B. (1993b). Rise, development and changing conceptions of curriculum administration and curriculum guidelines in Norway: The national-local dilemma. *Journal of Curriculum Studies*, 25–3, 251–266.

Gunter, H. and Fitzgerald, T. (2013). New public management and the modernisation of education systems. *Journal of Educational Administration and History*, 45(3), 213–219.

Hallett, T. (2010). The myth incarnate. Recoupling processes, turmoil, and inhabited institutions in an urban elementary school. *American Sociological Review*, 75(1), 52–74.

Haug, P. (2003). *Evaluering av Reform 97. Sluttrapport frå styret for Program for evaluering av Reform 97.* Oslo. Norges Forskningsråd.

Heilig, J. V. (2011). Understanding the interaction between high-stakes graduation tests and English learners. *Teachers College Record*, 113(12), 2633–2669.

Hopfenbeck, T. N., Tolo, A., Florez, T., and El Masri, Y. (2013). *Balancing Trust and Accountability? The Assessment for Learning Programme in Norway.* Report for the OECD.

Karlsen, G. (1993). *Desentralisert skoleutvikling. En utdanningspolitisk studie av norsk grunnskole med vekt på 70- og 80-tallet.* Oslo: Ad Notam Gyldendal.

Karseth, B. and Engelsen, B. U. (2013). Læreplanen for Kunnskapsløftet: Vekjente tråkk og nye spor. In B. Karseth, J. Møller and P. Aasen (eds) *Reformtakter. Om fornyelse og stabilitet i grunnopplæringen* (pp. 43–60). Oslo: Universitetsforlaget.

Karseth, B. and Sivesind, K. (2010). Conceptualising curriculum knowledge within and beyond the national context. *European Journal of Education*, 45(1), 103–120. doi: 10.1111/j.1465-3435.2009.01418.x

Kjærnsli, M. and Roe, A. (eds) (2010). *På Rett Spor. Norske Elevers Kompetanse i Naturfag, Lesing og Matematikk.* Oslo: Universitetsforlaget.

Klassekampen (2014). Vil ikke ha målehysteri. January, 29. www.klassekampen.no/article/20140129/ARTICLE/140129957

Lie, S., Hopfenbeck, T., Ibsen, E. B., and Turmo, A. (2005). *Nasjonale prøver på ny prøve. Rapport fra en utvalgsundersøkelse for å analysere og vurdere kvaliteten på oppgaver og resultater til nasjonale prøver våren 2005 (Testing national tests).* Oslo: Department of Teacher Education and School Development, University of Oslo.

Mausethagen, S. (2013a). Governance through concepts: The OECD and the construction of 'competence' in Norwegian education policy. *Berkeley Review of Education*, 4(1), 161–181.

Mausethagen, S. (2013b). Reshaping teacher professionalism. An analysis of how teachers construct and negotiate professionalism under increasing accountability. PHD thesis, Oslo and Akershus University College, Oslo.

Mausethagen, S. (2013c). Talking about the test. Boundary work in primary school teachers' interactions around national testing of student performance. *Teaching and Teacher Education*, 36, 132–142.

Mausethagen, S. and Granlund, L. (2012). Contested discourses of teacher professionalism: current tensions between education policy and teachers' union. *Journal of Education Policy*, 27(6), 815–833.

Mausethagen, S. and Mølstad, C. E. (2014). Licence to teach? Læreplananalyse og profesjonsutvikling. In Elstad, E. and Helstad, Kristin (eds) *Profesjonsutvikling i skolen*. Oslo: Universitetsforlaget, 152–169.

Ministry of Education and Research (2003–2004). White Paper No. 30. Kultur for læring (Culture for learning). Oslo: Ministry of Education and Research.

Mintrop, H. (2004). *Schools on Probation: How Accountability Works (And Doesn't Work).* New York: Teachers College Press.

Møller, J. (2012). The construction of a public face as a school principal. *International Journal of Educational Management*, 26(5), 452–460.

Møller, J. and Skedsmo, G. (2013a). Centralization and decentralization as twin reform strategies. In L. Moos (ed.) *Transnational Influences on Values and Practices in Nordic Educational Leadership – Is there a Nordic Model?* Dordrecht: Springer, 61–72.

Møller, J. and Skedsmo, G. (2013b). Modernizing education: NPM reform in the Norwegian education system. *Journal of Educational Administration and History*, 45(4), 336–353.

Møller, J., Vedøy, G., Presthus, A. M., and Skedsmo, G. (2009a). Fostering learning and sustained improvement: The influence of principalship. *European Educational Research Journal*, 8(3), 359–371.

Møller, J., Vedøy, G., Presthus, A. M., and Skedsmo, G. (2009b). Successful principalship in Norway: Sustainable ethos and incremental changes. *Journal of Educational Administration*, 47(6), 731–741.

Møller, J., Prøitz, T. S., Rye, E., and Aasen, P. (2013). Kunnskapsløftet som styringsreform. In B. Karseth, J. Møller and P. Aasen (eds) *Reformtakter. Om fornyelse og stabilitet i grunnopplæringen.* Oslo: Universitetsforlaget, 23–42.

Mølstad, C. E. and Hansén, S.-E. (2013). Curriculum as a governing instrument: A comparative study of Finland and Norway. *Education Inquiry,* 4(4), 735–753.

Nordahl, T. and Hausstätter, R. (2009). *Spesialundervisningens forutsetninger, innsatser og resultater. Situasjonen til elever med særskilte behov for opplæring i grunnskolen under Kunnskapsløftet. Evaluering av Kunnskapsløftet – gjennomgang av spesialundervisning.* Elverum: Høgskolen i Hedmark.

Norwegian Directorate for Education and Training (2014). *National Guidelines for National Testing.* Retrieved from www.udir.no/Upload/Nasjonale_prover/2013/SKOLEEIERVEILEDNING_2014_BM-rev-12-09-2014.pdf.

Nyhus, L. and Monsen, L. (2012). School development as communication processes. *Policy Futures in Education,* 10(4), 461–474.

OECD (Organisation for Economic Co-operation and Development) (1988). *Reviews of National Policies for Education Norway.* Paris: Department of the Examiners, Organisation for Economic Co-operation and Development.

Ozga, J. (2009). Governing education through data in England: From regulation to self-evaluation. *Journal of Education Policy,* 24(2), 149–162.

Ozga, J. and Jones, R. (2006). Travelling and embedded policy: The case of knowledge transfer. *Journal of Education Policy,* 21(1), 1–17.

Phillips, D. and Ochs, K. (2003). Processes of policy borrowing in education: Some explanatory and analytical devices. *Comparative Education,* 39(4), 451–461.

Prøitz, T. S. (2013). Variations in grading practice – subjects matter. *Education Inquiry,* 3, 555–575.

Ranson, S. (2003). Public accountability in the age of neo-liberal governance. *Journal of Education Policy,* 18(5), 459–480.

Roald, K. (2010). Kvalitetsvurdering som organisasjonslæring mellom skole og skoleeigar. PhD thesis, University of Bergen.

Romzek, B. S. and Dubnick, M. J. (1987). Accountability in the public sector: Lessons from the Challenger tragedy. *Public Administration Review,* 47(3), 227–238.

Rønning, W. (2013). Kunnskapsløftet i klasserommet – lærernes praksis, tenkning og utfordringer for videre læringsarbeid. In: Reformtakter. Om fornyelse og stabilitet i grunnopplæringen. Oslo: Universitetsforlaget. In Karseth, B, Møller, J. and Aasen, P. (eds) *Reformtakter. Om fornyelse og stabilitet i grunnopplæringen.* Oslo: Universitetsforlaget, 1–118.

Sahlberg, P. (2007). Education policies for raising student learning: The Finnish approach. *Journal of Education Policy,* 22(2), 173–197.

Sejersted, F. (2005). *Sosialdemokratiets tidsalder. Norge og Sverige i det 20. århundre.* Oslo: Pax.

Seland, I., Vibe, N., and Hovdhaugen, E. (2013). Evaluering av nasjonale prøver som system (Evaluation of the system of national standardised testing). Oslo: NIFU.

Sinclair, A. (1995). The chameleon of accountability: Forms and discourses. *Accounting Organizations and Society,* 20(2/3), 219–237.

Sivesind, K. and Bachmann, K. (2008). Hva forandres med nye standarder? Krav og utfordringer med Kunnskapsløftets læreplaner. In G. Langfeldt, E. Elstad and S. Hopmann (eds) *Ansvarlighet i skolen. Politiske spørsmål og pedagogiske svar.* Fagernes: Cappelen Akademisk Forlag, 62–93.

Slagstad, R. (1998). *De nasjonale strateger (The national strategists).* Oslo, Norway: Pax Forlag.

Skedsmo, G. (2009). School Governing in Transition? Perspectives, Purposes and Perceptions of Evaluation Policy. PhD thesis, University of Oslo.

Skedsmo, G. (2011). Formulation and realisation of evaluation policy: inconcistencies and problematic issues *Journal of Educational Assessment, Evaluation and Accountability, 23*(1), 5–20.

Skedsmo, G. and Hopfenbeck, T. (submitted). Integrating sustainable school improvement and assessment policies: A study of how local educational authorities and schools respond to new national expecations.

Skedsmo, G. and Møller, J. (2016). Governing by new performance expectations in Norwegian schools. In: Gunter, H.M., Grimaldi, E., Hall, D. and Serpieri, R. (eds). *New Public Management and the Reform of Education in Europe.* London: Routledge.

Telhaug, A. O. (1994). *Norsk skoleutvikling etter 1945 (Norwegian school development after 1945).* Oslo: Didakta.

Telhaug, A. O., Mediås, O. A., and Aasen, P. (2006). The Nordic model in education: Education as part of the political system in the last 50 years. *Scandinavian Journal of Educational Research, 51*(3), 245–283.

Wills, J. S. and Sandholtz, J. H. (2009). Constrained professionalism: Dilemmas of teaching in the face of test-based accountability. *Teachers College Record, 111*(4), 1065–1114.

16 Accountability policies across Austria, Germany, France, the Netherlands, and Norway

Jorunn Møller

Within new approaches to governing education in Europe, the pressure for increased educational accountability has become a major theme in the public debate, clearly implying new expectations of public reporting (Gunter and Fitzgerald, 2014).

Conceptualizing educational accountability

"Accountability" means having to answer for one's actions, and particularly for the results of those actions. It is a multi-layered concept that defines the relationship of control between different parties, but it is also connected to trust (Møller, 2009). The discourses of accountability are often a mixture of several forms of accountability (Elmore, 2005; O'Day, 2002; Sinclair, 1995). The many ways of describing accountability differ in the way they respond to the following four key questions: who is accountable? To whom are they accountable? For what are they accountable? And what are the consequences of the accountability regime? Within new modes of governing, "to whom" usually refers to the district and/or state agencies, while "who" is often the local school (O'Day, 2002: 305). Schools are primarily accountable for student performance, which is generally defined as measured achievement on tests in basic academic subjects. Student performance is normally evaluated against externally set standards that define acceptable levels of student achievement, and the evaluation is frequently accompanied by a system of rewards or intervention strategies. It may also include penalties such as a low ranking on league tables. As such, accountability is a social practice pursuing particular purposes, defined by distinctive relationships and evaluative procedures (Ranson, 2003).

While Sinclair (1995) differentiates between political, public, managerial, professional, and personal accountability, O'Day (2002) demarks the line between bureaucratic and professional accountability, and Elmore (2005) between external and internal accountability. Evetts (2009) takes recent reforms and the configuration of professionalism in knowledge-based work as a departure for discussing new approaches to governing and accountability. She distinguishes between organizational professionalism and occupational professionalism. The first incorporates standardized work procedures and hierarchical structures of accountability. It relies on external forms of regulation and accountability measures. In contrast, occupational professionalism includes collegial authority, discretionary judgment, and relational trust between employers and employees, and accountability is guided by codes of professional ethics. Evetts (2009) argues that recent governing reforms in which output measures and standardized practices are distinctive hallmarks seem to favor organizational professionalism. Although organizational and occupational professionalism must be understood as ideal types of professionalism and need not to be seen as mutually exclusive, her framework is helpful for understanding how the context of professional work in schools and school leadership is changing.

One might assume that new expectations of public reporting and external accountability create both challenges and possibilities for school leaders, but exactly how these affect the work of school leaders across countries and across local contexts is an unsettled question, one that depends on national and local organizational work contexts. On the one hand, by tracing historical and cultural patterns of social development across different regions in Europe, it is possible to identify how, in recent years, the governing of education and the position of school leaders have changed radically. Benchmarking and league tables have been developed, schools are held accountable for their students' achievement, and the Programme for International Student Assessment (PISA) findings have triggered the establishment of new accountability systems. Also, there seem to be numerous examples of policy copying, following site visitations, study tours, and electronic networking amongst national agencies and authorities. On the other hand, it is well known that the socio-cultural context influences what is defined as effective school leadership, and the overviews presented in this book show how leadership and accountability are framed by different historical and socio-cultural contexts.

Comparing approaches to leadership and accountability

The five chapters on accountability in Austria, France, Germany, the Netherlands, and Norway lay the foundation for this chapter. All five chapters include an analysis of and reflections upon changes in educational accountability and include some of the implications these changes seem to have for school leadership. As such, the authors encourage a discussion about the role of the nation-state in education policy, the mediating role of local schools, and how school leaders use the opportunities provided to address challenges connected to reforms in education. Each of the five countries has gone through major changes in education during the last 10–20 years, largely inspired by new managerial ideas. The push to reform is closely connected to the modernization of the public sector as a whole, often characterized as new public management (Hood, 1991; Pollitt and Bouckaert,

2004), or, more recently, as "post new public management." (Christensen and Lægreid, 2011) These policies generally aim to reduce public expenditures and bureaucratic structures by fostering competition and the marketization of public services. An important element of this approach is to monitor efficiency and effectiveness by measuring outcomes.

A "national and cultural touch" on new forms of governing

The interplay between educational reform and the constant reworking of the centralization and decentralization binary is present in all five countries. Change has involved shifts in policy, legislation, curriculum, expectations of school principals, and the organization of schools. Triggered by the PISA results, the schools have been reformed under a policy of decentralized centralism. This is particularly evident in Germany, Austria, and Norway. Benchmarking and league tables have been developed, schools are held accountable for the students' results, and new accountability systems have been established.

However, although new forms of governing and accountability regimes have been developed in all five countries, it is possible to trace how national education legacies are influencing and modifying the new policy recipes of decentralization, marketization, and output-oriented systems of quality control. For example, a common trait within national assessment and evaluation is relatively low-stakes measurement. In addition, there is no publication of league tables based on national tests. In particular, it seems as though teachers have historically enjoyed, and still have, a relatively high degree of autonomy and trust.

The legal regulation of education is also prominent in these countries. In Austria, it is characterized by a model of "bureaucratic-professional double regulation," which means a high level of centralist state input on regulations and high levels of teacher self-control within this framework (see Chapter 11). In Germany, several school supervisory authorities have been transformed into authorities of school support and improvement, while at the same time external school inspections are mandated to evaluate schools as self-responsible bodies in terms of educational and organizational matters (see Chapter 13). The Norwegian model implies a combination of output-oriented reforms and input regulation. Although there is variety present across different municipalities, it seems that resistance from the professional world is still effective in contrasting the managerial attack to professional self-regulation. Still, new evaluation technologies have been developed and hierarchical relationships in schools have been reconfigured, positioning the principal with more power compared to teachers (see Chapter 15).

In the French chapter, it is questioned whether the new managerial state is relevant to France today. It is highlighted how the reform agenda in France brings together the French passion for equality, professional interests, European influences, and ideological wars. Another feature of the French education system is its centralized and bureaucratic dimension. Rules play a very important role, and equality is a major concern, whether it is in traditional bureaucratic forms or in new approaches to redistribution, such as giving more to those who have less. This is the legacy of Napoleon, who created the modern administration for which laws and regulations are today the backbone of decision-making, but it is also the result of school standardization policies rooted in the creation of professional bodies and a national curriculum for all schools. This bureaucratic and centralized organization is challenged today by the promotion of some features of the new public management. It is too early to say what part of the accountability, external or internal, will be implemented in the French education system (see Chapter 12).

The Netherlands represents a different history. The chapter highlights how top-down, standards-based reforms do not fit well within the Dutch educational system, which has been strongly decentralized for many decades. Few intermediate hierarchical administrative structures between government and schools play a prominent role. Instead, small and, what the authors describe as, unprofessional boards, responsible for the hiring and firing of principals and teachers play a vital role. However, even though there are weak mechanisms to promote a systematic approach of accountability in and between levels, the national inspectorate seems to influence the local interpretation of what is at stake because of regular school visits and public reports. On the one hand, the inspectorate encourages self-evaluation at the school level; on the other hand, central elements of how schools are achieving national standards are also assessed, and school boards are held accountable by the inspectorate for meeting national standards. Thus, the inspection practice is ambivalent in this context (see Chapter 14).

Challenges and possibilities for school leadership

The chapters do not seem to contest the policy rhetoric about a governing model that calls for accountability, surveillance, measurement, and standards in a critical way, though some questions are raised regarding strengthened centralized administrations and the related consequences for principals. For example, the Austrian chapter shows how the recent modernization of the Austrian school governance system seems to leave stakeholders somewhat ambivalent. Principals are responsible for quality improvement and human resource development, but at the same time they have little freedom of decision when it comes to personnel selection and termination (see Chapter 11).

France's Ministry of Education has encouraged audits, and indicators of accountability have been introduced to schools through national programs of performance, though schools retain a large degree of autonomy. The data collected by the National Inspectorate are mainly used to measure inequality gaps between students according to their social background, and it does not have a great impact on schools' cultures. The support of the inspectorate remains unsteady, even if its audits are actually appreciated. Most principals limit their role to providing data on achievement, but without challenging teachers' judgment on students (see Chapter 12).

The German chapter also highlights how school principals, above all, are in charge of administrative tasks; this is due to long-lasting bureaucratic traditions in Germany. Although all states have gone through a shift towards a more output-oriented system of quality control, so far, new public management reforms have not yet challenged the traditional bureaucratic governing model to any appreciable extent regarding the role of a principal. The principals have restricted authority over staff employment and dismissal and very limited control over financial resources and curricula.

The Norwegian chapter takes as its departure that the country was during the 1990s, by and large, reluctant to implement accountability policies, but a change was motivated by the publication of the first PISA report. A national quality assessment system (NQAS), which implies new modes of school governing, was introduced. The demands for accountability were expressed in terms of expectations about the use of student results on different levels within the school system. The Norwegian chapter highlights how the discourse related to data use and accountability creates tensions within the school. "Performing well" may become a goal in itself, despite the low-stakes context, and from the teachers' perspective, new modes of external control can be seen as a sign of distrust. The national discourse also includes strong leadership and entrepreneurs as vehicles for the modernization project in public education, and the logic of "contractualism" has been institutionalized in some municipalities, implying closer surveillance of school principals from above (see Chapter 15). Although there is a variation across the many municipalities in Norway, and it is in the local arena that accountability practices are played out, and explicit expectations and measures of performance for principals may create both pressures and strains. For some, this may also serve as motivation to initiate and follow up with school improvement plans (Skedsmo and Møller, forthcoming).

The Dutch chapter emphasizes that the data-driven work in classrooms and schools creates new opportunities for school leadership because of large leeway in interpreting new modes of accountability policy. First and foremost, it has created new opportunities for the leadership of small school boards. In the chapter, the work of one specific school board is used as case to exemplify new opportunities for school leadership. The authors argue that, because the Inspectorate is now holding local school boards accountable for meeting national standards, the school boards interfere much more into the practices of teaching compared to 20 years ago. Hence, the balance between the political and professional power over education is more blurred, and it is unclear who, at the local level, obtains more autonomy. However, as demonstrated by the case, depending on how the members of the school board use their power position, there are opportunities for teachers to develop professionally within new forms of governing. In the case reported in the chapter, the school board collaborated closely with researchers from a university to implement the use of performance data to enhance educational quality. The authors argue that it is vital to engage principals in the work of developing assessment instruments and procedures to ensure school improvement when a new accountability regime is introduced (see Chapter 14).

Concluding remarks

The five chapters offer an account of the commonalities and differences of diverse policy trajectories through which, on the one hand, new approaches to governing and accountability have inspired educational reforms and, on the other hand, managerial elements have been mediated through the country-specific histories. The cross-country synthesis shows how different legacies are influencing managerial policy recipes. Marketization strategies are mainly identified in the Netherlands, while France is still a unitary, centralized state with a legalistic tradition strongly rooted in public administration. In Austria and Germany, the model of "bureaucratic-professional double regulation" seems to mediate the entering of new public management, creating "stop-go dynamics" of change; hence, old public management features remain, such as hierarchy as the leading mode of regulation. At the same time, new tools for holding schools and principals accountable are introduced, and at the national level an "evaluation machinery" has been built to measure the systems' effectiveness. In Norway, one of the main tensions is between discourses rooted in socially democratic ideologies linked to notions of equity, participation, and comprehensive education and discourses of strong leadership, competition, and privatization to improve quality in education. As such, tensions and paradoxes are produced due to multiple and conflicting rationales in the current education policy in these countries.

Although managerial accountability has more the status of an "anticipated future" in general, it is possible to identify how the use of new evaluation technologies to monitor student outcomes can be read as a shifting field from occupational professionalism towards organizational professionalism. The accounts of change describe a shift from the notions of collegiality, discretion, and trust to increasing levels of bureaucracy, standardization, assessment, and performance review. As Evetts (2011) has argued, the exercise of professionalism is now increasingly organizationally defined and includes the logics of the organization, and, to some extent, the market. Organizational professionalism has been expanded, but resistance from the teaching professions is still effective. A long history of relational trust in teachers seems to trump the need for monitoring in local schools. This particularly seems to be the case in France. Local traditions and national educational legacies ensure that new approaches to governing due to global forces are played out differently in national contexts, a phenomenon which Beck (2000) has termed "glocalization."

Across the five European countries discussed herein, various strategies for school governance can be identified, but also within each country, there is a variety across districts and municipalities, as underlined in the Norwegian chapter. If the external accountability environment in which the schools operate is rather weak, it may explain some lack of uniformity, but it may also be the case that solutions to the question of accountability are more based on values of teachers and principals as enacted in their daily practice. In addition, how much each of the countries has adopted the new global ideas of education as human capital and individualistic quest seems to be influenced by their legacies about schools as a force for public good.

The studies reported in these chapters have primarily viewed the issue of accountability from the perspective of external policies that intend to influence schools, rather than from the perspectives of schools. Although the chapter from the Netherlands exemplifies how a partnership between a school board and researchers manages to balance the control and school improvement aspects by using the leeway for local interpretation of policy, the focus in all chapters has mainly been on discussing the policies designed to make schools accountable to external authorities. As a consequence, based on these chapters, we know less about what conditions within schools determine to whom, for what, and how teachers are accountable. It is, however, possible to highlight some challenges that principals across countries encounter.

First, the chapters have shown how standards have become almost like a mantra for school reformers. Alongside this development, we can see the emerging need to make both principals and teachers accountable. Therefore, it is likely that the risks associated with school leadership will escalate and that the need for calculated strategies of risk assessment and management will increase significantly.

Second, in the current climate of accountability, it is likely that a great deal may be at stake for the principal in his or her interaction with superiors and public relations. Contexts will vary, but what principals across countries will have in common is the reality that a school principal is continuously "on stage." He or she is engaged in a public performance before colleagues, parents, students, and citizens, and is performing within a role that is, in many ways, prescribed by the dominant culture (Møller, 2012).

Third, job advertisements for principals often seek outstanding, innovative, and creative leaders with vision, but at the same time they also want a principal who will ensure that the school will implement the national and local policies, contribute to raising standards, and develop the school according to the requirements outlined by the ministry and the local authorities. As such, these advertisements signal paradoxes; they simultaneously call for exceptional leaders and loyal bureaucrats (Thomson, 2009).

Depending on what is at stake at the national and local levels, and the professional and personal capacity of the school leaders, these challenges will be handled or processed differently. The International Successful School

Principalship Project (ISSPP) has, during the last six years, constructed many accounts regarding this issue (Day and Gurr, 2014; Day and Leithwood, 2007). Principals leading successful schools look upon themselves as guardians of certain values that are now at risk, and they work hard to mediate government policy and external changes, so that they can be integrated with the school's values. In the Norwegian chapter, such a conflict between managerial accountability and professional beliefs and ethics is emphasized as a possible dilemma, which may undermine relational trust in the future. On the one hand, there is a need to find a balance between professional and political power over education. On the other hand, there is a need to sustain trust in the school in order to improve teaching and learning (Møller, 2009). At present, a lot of faith is placed in assessment tools, and test results tend to legitimize new accountability initiatives both at the national and local levels. While the public has a right to know how well our schools are educating future citizens, those who shape accountability systems for schooling should also be held accountable for doing it in a responsible way.

References

Beck, U. (2000). *What is Globalization?* Cambridge, UK: Polity Press.
Christensen, T. and Lægreid, P. (2011). Beyond NPM? Some development features. In T. Christensen and P. Lægreid (eds) *The Ashgate Research Companion to New Public Management* (pp. 391–403). Farnham, England: Ashgate Publishing Ltd.
Day, C. and Gurr, D. (eds) (2014). *Leading Schools Successfully. Stories from the field.* London: Routledge.
Day, C. and Leithwood, K. (eds) (2007). *Successful Principal Leadership in Times of Change: An International Perspective.* Dordrecht: Springer.
Elmore, R. F. (2005). Accountable leadership. *The Educational Forum*, 69(2), 134–142.
Evetts, J. (2009). New professionalism and new public management: changes, continuities and consequences. *Comparative Sociology*, 8(2), 247–266.
Evetts, J. (2011). A new professionalism? Challenges and opportunities. *Current Sociology*, 59(4), 406–422.
Gunter, H. and Fitzgerald, T. (2013). New Public Management and the modernization of education systems; editorial. *Journal of Educational Administration and History*, 45(3), 213–219.
Hood, C. (1991). A public management for all seasons? *Public Administration*, 69(1), 3–19.
Møller, J. (2009). School leadership in an age of accountability: tensions between managerial and professional accountability. *Journal of Educational Change*, 10(2), 37–46.
Møller, J. (2012). The construction of a public face as a school principal. *International Journal of Educational Management*, 26(5), 452–460.
O' Day, J. (2002). Complexity, accountability, and school improvement. *Harvard Educational Review*, 72(3), 293–330.
Pollitt, C. and Bouckaert, G. (2004). *Public Management Reform. A Comparative Analysis* (2nd edn). New York: Oxford University Press.

Ranson, S. (2003). Public accountability in the age of neo-liberal governance. *Journal of Educational Policy, 18*(5), 459–480.
Sinclair, A. (1995). The chameleon of accountability: forms and discourses. *Accounting, Organizations and Society, 20*(2/3), 219–237.
Skedsmo, G. and Møller, J. (2016). Governing by new performance expectations in Norwegian schools. In H. Gunter, D. Hall, R. Serpieri and E. Grimaldi (eds) *New Public Management and the Reform of Education: European Lessons for Policy and Practice*. London: Routledge.
Thomson, P. (2009). *School Leadership. Heads on the Block*. London: Routledge.

17 Educational accountability around the globe
Challenges and possibilities for school leadership

Pierre Tulowitzki

As is pointed out in the beginning of the US chapter, one thing to bear in mind is that schools have always been accountable. A possible "age of accountability" therefore doesn't mean that school leaders are facing something completely new. However, the form and the extent of accountability have changed in many countries as well the chains of accountability (cf. Elmore, 2005; Kuchapski, 1998).

As this book shows, despite many cultural differences, a general shift towards accountability appears to be taking place. Looking at all the countries featured in this book as a whole, it is fair to say that there is a dynamic in many accountability systems. What is the case today might change rapidly. While some advantages of systems with increased accountability are shown throughout this book—making a system more transparent, revealing elements that are not up to a certain standard and thus highlighting opportunities for improvement—the emphasis of accountability systems doesn't always seem to be ideally suited for improving learning and teaching. While this book highlights instances where accountability policies can be used for the latter (see for example the Dutch chapter), too often it seems the case that it is mostly used for the former (see for example the chapter from India).

As accountability has become a more prominent feature of twenty-first century education systems, the question arises how this impacts educational leadership and what possibilities might arise from this development. Elmore (2005) argues that school leaders form their conceptions of accountability regardless of accountability policies. According to him, they do so based on individual beliefs, collective norms, and formal mechanisms. This can be viewed as two planes of accountability: internal and external. Based on what can be seen in this book from various countries around the world, this dualism exists quite often. In many places there seem to be formal, policy-driven and/or codified levers in place that influence principals' actions, i.e. external accountability. At the same time we see instances in which external accountability does not seem to reach principals as they follow their own accountability systems, i.e. internal accountability.

A recommendation to draw from this is for school leaders to be aware of these two planes of accountability and how to link them up. In addition, many academics have been advocating for a shift towards schools as learning organizations (cf. Fullan, 1995; Giles and Hargreaves, 2006). This equates transformation into an organization "where people continually expand their capacity to create the results they truly desire, where new and expansive patterns of thinking are nurtured, where collective aspiration is set free, and where people are continually learning to see the whole together" (Senge, 1990: 8). As this definition implies, learning organizations are dynamic organizations. This entails that any accountability system would have to be adaptable to shifting priorities and organizational structures. A claim to draw from this would be that systems of external accountability need to be de-emphasized or at least made flexible as learning organizations need to have the space to establish a self-contained accountability system, (at least partly) determining their own frame of accountability.

In coping with the logistics of accountability, i.e. gathering and formatting the necessary data, technology can serve as a facilitator. Imaginable would be a 'digital school' where all grades and all administrative data (attendance, budgetary data etc.) are treated digitally. This in combination with a standardized yet adaptable accountability framework could make for a form of accountability that does not overburden a school's resources. On a small scale, this vision has actually been implemented in several places, for example individual projects schools in Scotland (John, 2008) and Sweden (Pedersen, 2004) or more recently in a pilot program in France involving 72 secondary schools (Ministère de l'Éducation nationale, de l'Enseignement supérieur et de la Recherche, 2014). The aim of this program is to bring information and communication technology (ICT) not only into the classrooms, but also into all aspects of school life including school management. However, globally speaking, the current ICT infrastructure in many schools is not yet adequate for something like this to be implemented. The openness of leaders and staff to switch to such a system is also difficult to gauge, as is the competence level of school leaders and staff with regard to digital matters. Literature and research on this topic is practically non-existent, which can be seen as an indication that an all-digital school is, at the moment, not a realistic option.

While it is tempting to define yet another adjective leadership and elaborate on principles of 'accountable leadership' (Elmore, 2005), this would also put a huge emphasis on matters of accountability. It stands to argue that school leadership should be focused on creating the best conditions for learning for students; something that entails the learning of adults and organizational learning as a means to improve student learning. 'Accountable leadership' therefore would seem like a step in the wrong direction.

A challenge with systems of (external) accountability in many countries is that actions either do not have consequences or that the systems are heavily sanction-oriented. In other words, many systems have warning mechanisms in place when schools fail to meet accountability demands. Some systems have sanctions for when this happens. However, there is often no bonus or reward if demands are met or even exceeded. If the school spends more than the allotted budget, there is a warning or a sanction or the excess spending is revoked. Yet, if the school spends less than the budget it often does not get to keep the money saved or another form of reward. This seems like a missed opportunity to encourage schools to make economic decisions that enable them to spend excess resources in a way that promotes student learning. In addition, it is also a missed opportunity for school leaders to get a certain degree of (financial) maneuverability.

The preceding chapters provide much information on how accountability is framed and how it is implemented. The structures and challenges of accountability policies and practices are widely reported. However, beneficial effects are mentioned less frequently. When looking at the empirical evidence gathered around the world, its merits with regards to school improvement or creating better learning environments for students are hard to judge. While some studies see a positive impact on student achievement (Hanushek and Raymond, 2005), others find negative or no effects on student achievement (Lee and Wong, 2004) and adverse effects on teacher retention rates (Clotfelter *et al.*, 2004). In addition, just like increased testing led to teaching to the test in many classrooms (with effects worthy of critical debate, cf. O'Day, 2004), increased testing and reporting on a school level might well lead to 'working to the (accountability) test'. In other words, school principals concentrate their efforts on making sure their schools receive favorable results when being assessed instead of actually concentrating on developing their school. There are some indications that this is happening (Møller, 2009). The notion of principals 'working to the (accountability) test' stands in contrast to principals truly reflecting on their schools, developing a vision for student learning, overall improved educational quality overall, and then trying to rally everyone to work towards achieving this vision.

In the current context, several possibilities for school leadership present themselves.

Take back the narrative. Define your school's needs. Have a standard frame of accountability that you customize. This requires a shared endeavor among stakeholders, but must be championed by way of school leadership. In systems where schools are encouraged to be autonomous (like the Netherlands for example), a strong case can be made for this autonomy to extend to matters of accountability. It can be beneficial to schools as well as to the superior authorities to allow the schools to, in part, define what gets taken into account and how it is measured. This can help to ensure that all the data a school considers to be vital to assess its state are measured. School and staff might be more willing to do their part as they might feel a certain sense of ownership for an accountability framework that is custom tailored to their school (see the Hong Kong case). As we know, context matters. So if accountability is to continue and if it is to become an instrument to improve teaching and learning, it should not only cover a school's performance, but also the school context. A school that is operating in very challenging circumstances should be held accountable in a way that is mindful of said circumstances. It falls on the school leaders to make their unique school context known to the hierarchical entities they are or their school is accountable to and to be the driving force to make accountability frameworks fit their school (instead of vice versa).

Get fluent in data. A comprehensive accountability framework often includes lots of indicators. It is important that all parties are able to make sense of every aspect of an accountability system. This includes understanding the purpose behind the collected data (why are these things measured?) but also being able to read and interpret quantitative data (what does this number mean?). A school where the school leader and the staff are 'fluent in data' is a school that can use data to foster school improvement. Never has more data been generated, yet there is a lack of knowledge and tools to make efficient use of the data at hand.

A third opportunity is for school leaders to use what we know to *improve accountability systems*: internal and external. Characteristics of successful schools have been researched and debated for quite a while (cf. Döbert, 2004; Rutter, 1979; Teddlie and Stringfield, 1993). Relatedly, there's a sizeable body of knowledge on characteristics of successful school leadership (Johnson *et al.*, 2008; Leithwood *et al.*, 2008; Mulford and Silins, 2011) and the mighty role context plays in all of this (Belchetz and Leithwood, 2007). Finally, accountability systems for education have also been the subject of analysis (cf. Fuhrman and Elmore, 2004).

As this book demonstrates, many accountability frameworks have evolved to take into account more than student achievement scores. Yet, the question remains whether more sophisticated frameworks are adequate to assess the performance of a school or educational system and to help school leaders and other agents make informed decisions. More research into the impact of accountability systems on schools as well as on productive leadership practices in accountable policy contexts (cf. Leithwood, 2001) is needed. This is also a great opportunity for a more profound exchange between researchers, practitioners, and policy makers. Such a dialogue could well constitute the best chance for creating viable accountability systems that provide ample possibilities for school leadership.

References

Belchetz, D. and Leithwood, K. (2007). Successful leadership: Does context matter and if so, how? In C. Day and K. Leithwood (eds) *Successful Principal Leadership in Times of Change: An International Perspective*, 5, 117–138. Dordrecht: Springer.

Clotfelter, C. T., Ladd, H. F., Vigdor, J. L., and Diaz, R. A. (2004). Do school accountability systems make it more difficult for low-performing schools to attract and retain high-quality teachers? *Journal of Policy Analysis and Management*, 23(2), 251–271. http://doi.org/10.1002/pam.20003.

Döbert, H. (2004). *Features of Successful School Systems. A comparison of schooling in six countries*. Münster: Waxmann.

Elmore, R. F. (2005). Accountable leadership. *The Educational Forum*, 69(2), 134–142. http://doi.org/10.1080/00131720508984677.

Fuhrman, S. and Elmore, R. F. (2004). *Redesigning Accountability Systems for Education* (Vol. 38). New York: Teachers College Press.

Fullan, M. (1995). The school as a learning organization: Distant dreams. *Theory Into Practice*, 34(4), 230–235. http://doi.org/10.1080/00405849509543685.

Giles, C. and Hargreaves, A. (2006). The sustainability of innovative schools as learning organizations and professional learning communities during standardized reform. *Educational Administration Quarterly*, 42(1), 124–156. http://doi.org/10.1177/0013161X05278189.

Hanushek, E. A. and Raymond, M. E. (2005). Does school accountability lead to improved student performance? *Journal of Policy Analysis and Management*, 24(2), 297–327. http://doi.org/10.1002/pam.20091.

John, M. (2008). Is the paperless school in sight? August, 1. www.theguardian.com/education/2008/jan/08/link.link2.

Johnson, L., Møller, J., Jacobson, S. L., and Wong, K. C. (2008). Cross-national comparisons in the International Successful School Principalship Project (ISSPP): The USA, Norway and China. *Scandinavian Journal of Educational Research*, 52(4), 407–422. http://doi.org/10.1080/00313830802184582.

Kuchapski, R. (1998). Accountability and the social good: Utilizing Manzer's liberal framework in Canada. *Education and Urban Society*, 30(4), 531–545.

Lee, J. and Wong, K. K. (2004). The impact of accountability on racial and socioeconomic equity: Considering both school resources and achievement outcomes. *American Educational Research Journal*, 41(4), 797–832. http://doi.org/10.3102/00028312041004797.

Leithwood, K. (2001). School leadership in the context of accountability policies. *International Journal of Leadership in Education*, 4(3), 217–235.

Leithwood, K., Harris, A., and Hopkins, D. (2008). Seven strong claims about successful school leadership. *School Leadership & Management: Formerly School Organisation*, 28(1), 27. http://doi.org/10.1080/13632430701800060.

Ministère de l'Éducation nationale, de l'Enseignement supérieur et de la Recherche. (2014). *Collèges connectés: soixante-douze établissements pilotes pour développer les usages pédagogiques du numérique*. November, 21. www.education.gouv.fr/cid72373/colleges-connectes.html.

Møller, J. (2009). School leadership in an age of accountability: Tensions between managerial and professional accountability. *Journal of Educational Change*, 10(1), 37–46. http://doi.org/10.1007/s10833-008-9078-6.

Mulford, B. and Silins, H. (2011). Revised models and conceptualisation of successful school principalship for improved student outcomes. *International Journal of Educational Management*, 25(1), 61–82.

O'Day, J. A. (2004). Complexity, accountability, and school improvement. In S. Fuhrman and R. F. Elmore (eds) *Redesigning Accountability Systems for Education* (S. 15–46). New York: Teachers College Press.

Pedersen, J. (2004). Project work in the paperless school: A case study in a Swedish upper secondary class. *Education and Information Technologies*, 9(4), 333–343. http://doi.org/10.1023/B:EAIT.0000045291.99489.bd.

Rutter, M. (1979). *Fifteen Thousand Hours: Secondary Schools and their Effects on*

Children. Cambridge, MA: Harvard University Press.
Senge, P. M. (1990). *The Fifth Discipline.* New York: Doubleday Business.
Teddlie, C. and Stringfield, S. (1993). *Schools Make a Difference: Lessons Learned from a 10-Year Study of School Effects.* New York: Teachers College Press.

Index

Aasen *et al.* 211
Abbott government (Australia) 7
absenteeism: pupils 110; teachers 122, 134
academic ability 66
Academic Intervention Services (AIS) 46
academic merit, private schools 64
academic performance: in China 87
accountability 6
accountability mechanisms 73–4, 74–5
accountability models 56
accountability stressors 45
accountable leadership 234
accounting 14
accreditation 117–18
Accreditation Standards for Quality School Governance 117–18
Achieving School Accountability in Practice (ASAP) project 213
active management by exception 3
adequate yearly progress (AYP) 36, 38
advertisements, job 230
aided schools 98
Altrichter, H. and Heinrich, M. 142, 172
American Recovery and Reinvestment Act (2009) 42
Anderson, J.A. 79
Angst, Awareness, Action (Desai) 114
annual charters 20
annual planning process 20
annual professional performance review (APPR) 42
Annual Status of Education Report (ASER) 116
Aotearoa New Zealand 18–19; accountability and assessment of school leaders 27–9; assessment practices 23–6; effective schools 30; national assessment and accountability policies 20–2; new possibilities for school leadership 29–31; OECD *Improving School Leadership Country Report* 30; school accountability policy 19–20; school level self-review 22; underachievement of marginalised groups 29
appraisals 22, 29, 146
assessment: in Australia 7–8, 8–10; in Austria 143, 145–6, 147–51; descriptive 23; in France 155; in Germany 169–71; in India 115–16; in New Zealand 20–1, 23–6, 27–9; in Norway 209–10, 212–15; online tools 24; in primary schools 23; school leaders 8–10, 27–9; of students in Austria 145–6; teachers 146; *see also* formative assessment; student assessment
Assessment Program for Effective and Social Outcomes (APASO) 97, 131
audits 159
Australia: accountability and assessment of school leaders 8–10; GERM (global educational reform movement) 6; new possibilities for school leadership 10–15; practice of testing, accountability and assessment 7–8; school accountability policies 6–7
Australian Primary Principals Association (APPA) 10, 11
Austria: bureaucratic-professional double regulation 226, 229; external assessments 148–9; external school inspections 149–51; governance of school systems 142, 143, 151, 152; governance strategies 147–8;

performance standards 143, 148–9, 151; phases of school modernization 142–3, 151; pressure on school leaders 151–2; primus inter pares 144; quality management 143–4; role of school leaders 144–5, 147–51; school profiles 142; student assessment 143, 145–6; teacher and school assessment 146; team inspection 143
Austrian Court of Audit 146
Austrian Ministry of Education 143
Austrian School Education Act (2015) 144, 151
authoritative leadership style 48
autonomy 226; in Australia 15; in Austria 142, 143, 144; in Chile 61; in China 87; in France 156, 160, 163; in Germany 165, 167, 180; in Hong Kong 98; in the Netherlands 184, 186, 189, 191, 235; in New Zealand 28, 29; in Norway 207, 211, 213, 214; in the USA 47, 49

Bahadur, A. 115–16
Bakken, A. and Elstad, J.I. 214
balanced accountability 51
Bangladesh 110
Bass, B.M. 2–3
bastard leadership 9–10
Batra, S. 121
Beck, U. 229
Beer, M. and Nohria, N. 92, 106
bell curve mentality 38
benchmarking 225, 226
Best Academy and Harvest Academy 36
'Big Six' of reading 12
Bloomberg, Michael 43, 45
boards of trustees 19, 21, 22
Böhm-Kasper, O. 173
booklet of skills 159
bottom-up change 92
British Empire 111
Bruns et al. 115, 123–4
budgets 235
Building on Success 31
bullying 9
bureaucratic accountability 54

Central Board of Secondary Education (CBSE) 118
centralization 46, 48, 49
centralized decentralization 131
chain responsibility 203

change: bottom-up 92; climate for 102; as a constant 75; educational leadership 101–5; evaluating progress of 105; Kaizen approach 104; leadership style 102–3; top-down 92; see also organizational change
charter schools, Minnesota 37, 39, 40, 41, 42
Chaudhury et al. 123
child protection 9
Children First reform 47, 48
Chile: capitalist revolution 57; competitive public education system 57–9, 67; disadvantaged schools 69; double accountability 59–67, 67–8; enrolment strategies 62, 63–4, 68; management practice 68–9; mediating national policies 69; role of school leaders 59–62; school leaders' response to double accountability 62–7; SIMCE (Sistema de Medición de la Calidad de la Educación) strategies 62, 65–7, 68; student numbers growth 57; System of Quality Assurance 67–8
China: challenges for school leaders 87–8; designation policies 82–3; educational accountability 80–1; educational reforms 80–1; external evaluation 84–5; impact of evaluation systems 85–7; internal evaluation 84; methodology of case study 82–3; pressures on teachers 133; promotion for teachers 81, 82, 84–5, 86–7; teacher evaluation 80–1, 82–3
'Christmas Tree' problem 133
Chu, H. 80–1
churn, policy 75
classical organization theory 102
climate change 102
'Closing the Gap' initiatives 10
cocktail approach 102
codes of professional ethics 206, 225
co-finance law 58
colonialism: legacy of education in India 111
Commissioner's Regulations 42
Common Core State Standards initiatives 75
community accountability 123–4
competition 6
comprehension 12
comprehensive school reform 189
co-mutuality of accountability 37

conceptual framework 12–15
Constitution of India (1976) 115
constructed environments 34
consultancy, external 104–5
consumer choice 6
contextually literate 13
contingent reward 2–3
continuing professional development (CPD) 104
continuous improvement 104
continuous self-improvement 95
contractual accountability 54
contractualism 228
Cranston *et al.* 8, 9
critical incident technique for fidelity 44–5; critical incidents 45, 46
Cullen, J.B. and Reback, R. 66
cultural leadership 102
culture building 103–4
curriculum and assessment, implementation strategy 46
Curriculum Stocktake 23
cyclical processes 93

Darling-Hammond, L. 38, 54
data fluency 236
data literacy 12, 13–14
data usage 161–2; in Norway 216
de Blasio, Bill 43
decentralization 22, 46, 48, 49, 210; in China 80; in Germany 167; in the Netherlands 189–91, 202; in Norway 207–8
decentralized centralism 226
decision-making, participation in 103
Decree on Student Assessment 145
delegative leadership style 48
Dempster, N. 14
Desai, J.P. 114
descriptive assessment 23
designation policies 82–3
Despatch (Wood) 111, 116
developing countries: quality of education 110
developing (D), QR score 43
diads 196
diagnosis, in French schools 160–1
differentiation 84–5
digital school 234
Directorate of Evaluation, Forecast and Performance (DEPP) 155, 158
disadvantaged schools 69
discourses: of professionalism 211; strong leadership 211

distributed leadership 13, 102, 187
district support 37
double accountability 55, 59–67, 67–8, 68
drugs 9
Duignan, P. 14

Earl, L. 14
Easley, J. and Tulowitzki, P. 49
e-asTTle (NZ) 24
economic filter, private schools 64
Eder, F. 145
Education Act (NZ) (2008) 19
educational accountability 1–4; conceptualizing 224–5
educational infrastructure 74–5
educational leadership 101–5, 202; and accountability 188–9; defined 187–8; in the Netherlands 184–5, 191, 193, 201; in school board policy 193
Educational Leadership Network (ELN) 1, 2, 4
Educational Leadership Practice Survey 30–1
educational management 156
educational quality: poor 110–11; stagnation of 110; universalization of 110
Educational Quality Guarantor System 60
Educational Review Office (ERO) (2007) 74
Education and Manpower Bureau (EMB) 99; circular 97
Education and National Development (India) 112
Education Bureau (EDB) 93, 95, 100; Quality Assurance and School-based Support Division 100
Education Commission Report No. 7 (ECR7) 93
Education Department (ED) 99
Education for All Development Index (EDI) 113
Education for All Movement 110, 113
Education Law §3012-c 42
education plans 28
Education Review Office (ERO) (NZ) 20, 22, 26; effective schools 30; evidence and assessment 25; issues of school leaders 27; recommendations 29–30; on self-regulating students 26
education revolution 7
education sector: investment in 110;

quality of education 110
effective schools 30
Elementary and Secondary Education Act 42
Elmore, R.F. 34, 45, 49, 50, 51, 54, 224, 233
Elstad, E. 213
Elstad *et al.* 213
Empowerment Zone schools 47
English language learners (ELLs) 37
enrolment: distinguishing from competition 64; gaining loyalty from families 64; informing families of good academic results 64; in private schools 61; promoting differentiated characteristics of families 64; in public schools 61; rates in South Asian countries 110; starting pupils at earlier age 64; strategies for improving 62, 63–4, 68
entrepreneurialism 44
equitable learning opportunities 39
equity 211
equivalence 211
evaluation 105
evaluation systems 79; impact of 85–7
Evetts, J. 224–5, 229
evidence: in New Zealand schools 25
evidence-based organizational change 93, 95
examinations: in China 43, 87; in India 116; promotion and graduation exams (PGEs) 43; public 116; *see also* tests/testing
experience 36
expert panels 86, 135
extended schools 199–200
external accountability 55
external consultancy 104–5
external evaluators 82
external expert panels 86, 135
external quality assurance 93, 94
external school review (ESR) 93, 95, 96, 97, 98, 100, 106, 132, 135

Figlio, D. and Getzler, L. 66
Flanagan, J.C. 44
fluency 12
formative assessment 25, 25–6
France: accountancy and finance 159–60; assessment 155; bodies of accountability and inspection 159–60; booklet of skills 159; case study findings 160–3; case study methods 160; centralization and bureaucracy 227; culture of accountability 156; data usage 161–2; diagnosis 160–1; educational management 156; evaluation 158–9; inspection bodies 155–6; minimum competence standards 157; pedagogical freedom of teachers 157; reform agenda 226; role of school leaders 156–7; school accountability 158–9; top-down bureaucracy 156; understanding of accountability 155
free/reduced lunch 36–7, 38, 39
Friedman, Milton 57

Galab *et al.* 123
Gandhi, Mahatma 112
Gaokao 87
General Education Law (LGE) 58
General Inspectorate of Education 159
Georgi, A. 36
Germany: accountability 177–8; accountability through quality assurance/control 165–7; assessment tests 169–71; bureaucratic governing model 165, 166; classification of quality control 171–2; decentralization 167; educational leadership 187–9; inspections 168–9; Länder school system 165, 167; legal regulation of education 226; looking ahead 180; mediocre performance of students 166–7; oversight system 167, 168, 171; preferences and strains in school leadership practices 173–9; quality assurance 174–5, 179, 179–80; quality development 174, 175, 179, 180; quality management 180; school-based management 172; school leadership 172–3; School Leadership Study 173–4; school supervisory authorities 167–8; self-evaluations 169; systems of quality assurance and control 167–71
GERM (global educational reform movement) 6
Gillard government (Australia) 7
Global Initiatives report 111
globalization: education system 92
glocalization 229
governance: in Austrian schools 142, 143, 147–8, 151, 152; new forms of 226–7; in Norwegian schools 217–19

Index   243

government accountability 73–4
grammar schools 173
green papers (Norway) 209
Grover, S. and Singh, N.H. 121, 122
Guidelines for National Testing 215
guru 111
Gurukula system 111
Gymnasium 144, 146

Hanushek, D.A. and Wößmann, L. 114
Harbin 83
hard evidence 85, 133
Harvey, David 132
health: Australian school leaders 8
healthy eating 9
hierarchical relationships 206, 211, 226
high accountability 136–8
high achievers 38
Hill, P.T. and Bonan, J.J. 2
Hong Kong: educational leadership in managing change 101–5; implementation of the SDA Framework 99–101; internal accountability mechanisms 135, 136; loosely coupled education system 98; pressure on teachers 133–4; quality assurance movement 93–4, 100; school policies 93; SDA Framework 95–101, 131, 135; two forms of accountability 132
Hoyle, E. and Wallace, M. 137
Hoy, W. and Miskel, C. 185
Huber, S.G. 173
human capital 110

idle capacity 61
Imai, Masaaki 104
Impact of School Inspection on Teaching and Learning (ISI-TL) 149
implementation/compliance 34, 45–6
improvement models 125
Improving School Leadership Country Report (NZ) 30
incentives: SIMCE scores 67
independent public schools 7
India 110; accountability and responsibility in education 114; colonial legacy 111; community accountability 123–4; context and purpose of school education 111–13; facets of school accountability 115; improvement models 125; leadership and school accountability 121–2; learners' assessment and school accountability 115–16; private sector schools 115; public examinations 116; school accreditation 117–18; school inspection and supervision 116–17; school performance evaluation 117–21; school quality improvement 118–21; student performance 124; teacher accountability 122–3
induction programmes 31
information and communication technology (ICT) 234
innovation 104
Inquiry Teams 47
inspections: in Austria 149–51; in France 159–60; in Germany 168–9; in the Netherlands 190
inspections (Ofsted) 138
inspection system (China) 80
Inspectorate of Education 186, 191
inspectors, school 146
Institute for Quality Development (IQB) 170
instructional accountability 50
instructional fidelity 41
instructional leadership 137–8
instructional oversight, implementation strategies 46
instructional practices 37
internal accountability 54
internal quality assurance 93, 94
internal self-evaluation 132, 135
International Congress School Effectiveness and Improvement (ICSEI) 1, 2
International Successful School Principalship Project (ISSPP) 215, 230–1
intervention programmes, implementation strategies 46

Jacob, B.A. 67
job advertisements 230
job satisfaction 176, 177, 178

Ka Hikitia 31
Kaizen approach 104
Karnataka School Quality Assessment and Accreditation Council (KSQAAC) 118
Karseth, B. and Engelsen, B.U. 214
Kendriya Vidyalayas schools 118
key performance measures (KPMs) 97, 131

Kingdon, G. and Muzammil, M. 122
Kipnis, A. 132
Kiwi Leadership 31
Klein, Joe 43
KMK (Standing Conference of Ministers of Education and Cultural Affairs) 165–6, 167; Institute for Quality Development (IQB) 170
Knowledge Promotion Reform 209, 213–14
knowledge regimes 211
Kogan, M. 171–2
Koretz *et al.* 67
Krishnaratne *et al.* 110–11
Kuchapski, R. 34

Lasley, T.J. 114
leader-follower transactional conditions 2–3
leadership: connections with learning 11, 14–15
leadership styles 102–3
league tables 225, 226; in Australia 7–8; in Chile 59, 61; in China 87; in New Zealand 21; in Norway 209–10, 213; *see also* rankings
learning: connections with leadership 11, 14–15; quality measurements of 61
learning assessments 115–16
learning organizations 234
Lee *et al.* 132, 138
Lee, J.C. and Dimmock, C. 132, 137
Lee, J.C. and Zhu, Y.-P. 132
legal accountability 54, 206
Leistungsbeurteilungsverordnung 145
Leithwood *et al.* 187
Leithwood, K. 54
letter of assignment 160
literacy: professional learning 12
literacy performance 11–12
loosely coupled system 98
Lower-Saxony 168–9
lunch, free/reduced 36–7, 38, 39

Macaulay, Thomas Babington 111
macro level 131; German model 165, 166
Mahmoud, Eric 36
management by objectives (MBO) 208
managerial accountability 206, 218, 229
managerialism, performance-based 206
Maori (indigenous) student achievement 21, 22, 31

marginalized groups 29
market accountability 54, 55, 56
marketization 80, 110, 226, 229
market plus state accountability 56
Marzano, Robert 40
Masters, Geoff 15
Mausethagen, S. 214–15
Melbourne Declaration on Educational Goals for Young Australians (MCEETYA) (2008) 7
meso level: German model 165, 166
micro level 131; German model 165, 166
Millennium Development Goals 110
minimum competence standards 157
minimum levels of learning (MLL) standards 112
Ministerial Council on Education, Employment, Training and Youth Affairs (MCEETYA) 7
Ministry of Education (Austria) 146, 152
Ministry of Education (France) 155, 158, 163, 227
Ministry of Education (MOE) (China) 80
Ministry of Education (NZ) 19, 20, 22; consultation and partnership 31; policy paper on assessment for learning 25; position on assessment 20–1; professional development programmes 23
Ministry of National Education (Chile) 57, 58, 68
Minnesota (case study): accountability factors 37–9; average student scores 35; case methods 36; demographics 35; findings 36–7; performance-based accountability 36, 37; racial gap in educational achievement 35–6; school leaders' response to performance accountability challenges 40–2
Minnesota Comprehensive Assessments (MCAs) 36, 37, 39
Minnesota Multiple Measurement Ratings (MMRs) 38
Minute on Indian Education (Macaulay) 111
missions 101
Møller *et al.* 213, 214
Møller, J. and Skedsmo, G. 211
moral accountability 49–50, 54
moral purpose 14

Index   245

Muijs, D. and Harris, A. 138
multi-accountability 54
Muñoz, Gonzalo 62
MySchool website 7–8, 9

Napoleon 227
National Accreditation Board for Education and Training (NABET) 117, 118
National Achievements Survey (NAS) 116
National Administration Guidelines (NZ) 19
national aspiring principal programmes 31
National Assessment of Education Progress (NAEP) 35
National Assessment Program – Literacy and Numeracy (NAPLAN) 7, 12
National Center for Educational Statistics (USA) 35
National Certificate of Educational Achievement (NCEA) 21, 22, 30
National Commission on Teachers 122
National Curriculum Frameworks (NCFs) 113, 114, 115, 116
National Curriculum (NZ) 19
National Education Guidelines (NZ) 19
National Inspectorate (France) 227–8
National Institute of Statistics and Economic Studies (INSEE) 158
National Knowledge Commission 117
National Mission for Secondary Education 113
National Monitoring Study of Student Achievement (NMSSA) 21
National Policies on Education (NPE) 112, 115
National Policy on Education (1986) 134
National Programme on School Standards and Evaluation (NPSSE) 121
National Quality Assessment System (NQAS) 209–10, 211, 212, 216, 228
National Quality Framework (NQR) 143–4, 146, 151
National Regulations on Educational Inspection 80
national standardized tests *see* standardized tests
national standards (Netherlands) 190
National Standards (NZ) 20, 22, 24, 30; implementation of 24–5
National System of Performance Evaluation (SNED) 61
National University of Educational Planning and Administration (NUEPA) 116–17, 121
Navyoug Schools 118
neoliberalism: Australian school policy 6–7; educational governance 131–2
Netherlands, the: accountability 185–7; autonomy 184, 186, 189, 191, 235; case study 196–201; conceptual framework 185–9; control perspective of accountability 184; data analysis for research purposes 198; data collection for research purposes 197; decentralization 189–91, 202, 227; decentralized characteristics 184; educational leadership 184–5, 191, 193, 201, 202; educational standards 190; improvement perspective of accountability 184; inspections 190; local centralization 191–2; peer review method 193–6; research methods of case study 196–8; results of case study 198–201; school development trajectory 193; *see also* school board(s)
new public management (NPM) 208, 211, 225–6, 227, 228, 229
New Visions for Public Schools 47
New York City (case study): accountability stressors 45; annual progress report 43; case methods 44–5; Department of Education 43, 47; educational reform 43–4; entrepreneurialism among school leaders 44; leadership styles 47–8; performance-based accountability 45–8; performance evaluation mechanisms 42–3; racial minority students 45; reform agenda 47; simultaneous centralization and decentralization 46, 48
New York City Department of Education (NYCDOE) 43; reform agenda 47
New York City Leadership Academy 47
New York State: reform of public education 42
New York State Board of Regents 43
New Zealand *see* Aotearoa New Zealand

New Zealand Council for Educational Research 23; survey 27–8
New Zealand Qualifications Authority 22
No Child Left Behind Act (NCLB) 36, 37, 38, 39, 42, 75
no excuses mindset 39
non-low income students 39
Nordahl, T. and Hausstätter, R. 214
Nordic model of education 207
Norway: assessment policies and accountability practices 209–10; autonomy 207, 211, 213, 214; decentralization 207–8, 210; education context 207–9; education reforms 208–9; legal regulation of education 226; monitoring and improvement 205; national tests 209–10, 210, 214–15, 218; new assessment tools and accountability 212–15; new national and local motor governing 217–19; perspectives on accountability 205–7; PISA results 208, 212; policy developments over time 211–12; quality assurance 208, 218–19; role of school leaders 215–16; school owners 208, 212; studies of accountability and education 210–17
Norwegian Directorate of Education and Training 214
Nusche, D.: on national standardized tests 20
NZ Curriculum 24, 26

occupational professionalism 225
O'Day, J. 224
OECD (Organisation for Economic Cooperation and Development) 18; differentiating accountability types 54; quality assurance systems in Norway 208
Office of School Support 47
Office of the Auditor General (NZ) 22
Ofsted (Office for Standards in Education) 138
online assessment tools 24
oral language experience 12
organizational change 92; evidence-based 93, 95; facilitating 101–5
organizational culture 103–4
organizational integrity 76
organizational legitimacy 76

organizational professionalism 224–5, 229
organizational self 76
organizational theories 105
outcome-based approaches 211
outcome control 209, 210, 218
outcomes 206, 207, 208, 209, 211, 218; national tests 216
overall teacher judgements (OTJs) 24
oversight regulations 167, 168, 171

Pacific Education Plan 31
Pakistan 110
Pandey et al. 124
panels, expert 86
parent-teacher associations (PTAs) 123
participatory leadership style 47–8
passive management by exception 3
pedagogy 14, 190
peer review (Netherlands): case study 196–201; data collection for research purposes 197; guideline for collecting and analysing data 195–6; guideline for executing the review 196
peer reviews 193–6
Penguins' Revolution 58
people, conceptual framework 13
performance accountability 40–2
performance-based accountability 31, 36, 37, 45–8
performance-based managerialism 206
performance indicators (PIs) 94, 97
performance management systems 19
performance measurement 6
performance standards 148, 151
Persistently Low Achieving (PLA) schools 44
personal accountability 49–50
personal formation and transformation 14
personal injuries 9
personal qualities 206–7
personal resilience 14
phenomenology 36
phonics 12
phonological awareness 12
Picot Report 19
Pinochet, General 57, 58
place, conceptual framework 13
planning-implementation-evaluation (PIE) cycle 95, 100, 135
pluralistic institutional environments 75–6

policy churn 75
political accountability 206
post new public management 226
power, sharing of 103
Pratham 116
Preferential School Subvention Law (SEP) 58, 59, 60, 68
primary schools: assessment of students 23; in Chile 69; in New Zealand 21, 22, 23, 24
principal(s) *see* school leader(s)
Principals as Literary Leaders (PALL) project 10–12
private education: in Chile 57
private schools: filters for selection 64
problem students 66
professional accountability 54, 77–8, 206, 217
professional autonomy *see* autonomy
professional development 19, 188, 189; programmes 23, 25
professionalism 101, 224–5, 229
professional standards 19
proficient (P), QR score 43
profiles, school 142
Programme for International Student Assessment (PISA) 18, 58, 67, 115, 143, 145, 165, 226
Progress in International Reading Literacy Study (PIRLS) 133, 209
promotion and graduation exams (PGEs) 43
promotion, teachers 81, 82, 84–5, 86–7
public accountability 206
Public Affairs Centre 113
public education: in Chile 57
Public Report on Basic Education (PROBE) 116
public schools: promoting differentiated characteristics of families 64; stakeholders 39
public schools, independent 7
public school system: in Norway 207
public sector: modernization of 225–6
public shaming 213
pupil absenteeism 110

Qi, T. 80
quality assurance 93–4; evolving model 100; in Germany 165–7, 167–71, 174–5, 179, 179–80; in the Netherlands 191; in Norway 208, 218–19
Quality Assurance Division (QAD) 93

Quality Assurance Inspectorate (QAI) 93
quality cards 189
quality control: classification 171–2; in Germany 166, 167
Quality Council of India (QCI) 117
quality development 174, 175, 179, 180
quality management 143–4, 180
Quality Review (QR) 43

Race to the Top (RTTT) funds 42
racism: in the USA 38
Radnor *et al.* 2
rankings, school: in Australia 7–8; in Chile 59, 61; in China 87; *see also* league tables
Rastriya Madhyamik Shiksha Abhiyan (RMSA) 113, 131
reading 'Big Six' 12
reciprocal accountability 50–1
Regent's Exam 43
reporting information (Norway) 207
Report of the National Commission on Teachers 134
Research, Analysis and Insights into National Standards (RAINS) project 28
resilience, personal 14
response 34
responsibility 114
restricted schools 198–9, 200
result-oriented teaching 186–7, 189, 191, 198, 201; peer review method 193–6; restricted and extended modes 198–200
review, external 132
Revision of the Austrian School Education Act (2011) 152
rewards 2–3
Right of Children to Free and Compulsory Education Act (2009) 122, 123
Riley, P.: on school leaders' health 8
risk management 217–18, 230
Roald, K. 212–13
Robertson and Hill 74, 77
Robinson, M.A. 47–8
Rønning, W. 214
Royal Ministry of Education and Research 208
RTI (Response to Interventions) team 40
Rudd government (Australia) 7

Saint Paul 37
salaries, teachers 20
sanctions 235
Sargant Report 111
Sarva Shiksha Abhiyan (SSA) 113, 123, 131
Scaffold Apprenticeship Model of School Improvement through Leadership Development (SAM) 47
school absenteeism 110
school autonomy 142
school-based management 172
school board(s) 186, 190–1, 191, 202, 228–9; educational leadership 193; peer review method 193–6; perception of 200–1; vision and policy 192–3
School Development and Accountability (SDA) Framework *see* SDA Framework 94
school districts 19
school improvement 136–8
school inspections 116–17, 149–51; in France 159–60
school inspectors 146
school leader(s): accountability and assessment 8–10, 27–9; accountability cultures 3; appraisal practices 29; balanced accountability 51; challenges faced by 76, 87–8; CPD 104; data fluency 236; data usage 161–2; diagnosis in French schools 160–1; entrepreneurialism 44; facilitating organizational change 102–5; health of 8; importance of 27; improving accountability systems 236; institutionalizing a self-renewal framework 95–6; instructional accountability 50; mediating national policies 69; new possibilities 2; personal and moral accountability 49–50; pressure 151–2; protocol for interviewing 97; reciprocal accountability 50–1; response to double accountability 62–7, 68; response to performance accountability challenges 40–2; responsibilities of 8–9; result-oriented teaching 191; role in Austrian schools 144–5, 147–51; role in Chilean schools 59–62; role in French schools 156–7; role in Norwegian schools 215–16; school improvement 136–8; 'on stage' 230; suburban 37, 38; sustainable improvements 49; transformation of role 121

school leadership: appointments 173; challenges and possibilities 227–9, 233–6; in Chile 69; effect of accountability on 2; expanded role 3; focus on 77–8; future of 1; in Germany 172–3; in India 121–2; new possibilities 3, 10–15, 29–31; preferences and strains 173–9; training 121–2; *see also* leadership
School Leadership and Educational Quality 62
School Leadership Study 173–4
School-leaving Examination (Norway) 209
school management committees (SMCs) 123
School of Public Affairs 47
school owners (Norway) 208, 212
school principal(s) *see* school leader(s)
School Quality Assessment and Accreditation (SQAA) 118
school quality improvement 118–21
School Quality Improvement Models (SQIM) 118
school rankings *see* rankings
school reports 28
schools: effective 30
school self-evaluation (SSE) 93, 95, 96, 98, 100, 105–6, 135
School Student Union of Norway 209
school supervisory authorities 167–8
school systems: change processes 67; multi-accountability types 54–5
school-wide vision 103
Schulprofile 142
SDA Framework (School Development and Accountability) 93, 94, 95–101, 100, 131, 135; complex processes of SSE and ESR 98; excessive reforms 98; facilitators at the school organizational level 100–1; facilitators at the system level 99–100; focused attention 101; high staff morale 101, 106; hindrances 96–7, 106; hindrances at school level 98–9; hindrances at system level 98; impact of 97; leading and managing change 95–6; loosely coupled system 98; overambitious plan 98;

professionalism 101, 106; research into the effectiveness of 96; shared values and missions 101; shrinkage of the school system 98; team spirit 101, 106; tools for self-evaluation 100; transformational leadership 100–1, 106
secondary schools: in New Zealand 21, 25
segregation 67
Seland *et al.* 214
self, conceptual framework 14
self-evaluation: in Germany 169; institutionalised 135; internal 132
self-evaluation form (SEF) 138
self-evaluation frameworks 94; tools for 100
self-improvement 95
self-management 6; in New Zealand 19, 22, 23, 29
self-regulation, students 26
self-review, schools 22
Senge, P.M. 234
sexual misconduct 9
shared values 101, 103–4
sharing power 103
Shipps, D. and White, M. 35, 43
short route of accountability 123, 136
silver BBs (ball bearings) approach 40, 41
silver bullet approach 40, 41
SIMCE (Sistema de Medición de la Calidad de la Educación) 59, 61; enhancing/maximizing teaching skills 66; excluding problem students 66; incentives 67; organizing pupils according to academic ability 66; priority to assess the subjects 66; specific teaching methods 66; strategies for improving scores 62, 65–7, 68; training pupils with practice assessments 66–7
Sinclair, A. 224
Sistema de Medición de la Calidad de la Educación (SIMCE) 59, 61
Skedsmo, G. 212, 215
social accountability 124
social inclusion 207
social justice 38
socio-emotional assistance (SA) team 40
sostenedor 57, 61, 68
South Asia: enrolment rates 110
special needs education 214, 216

special service coordinators 187–8, 193, 200, 201
sport safety 9
Sri Lanka 110
staff conferences 173
staff morale 101
stakeholders 39; accountability to 75–6
standardized tests: in Austria 148; in Chile 58–9, 68; in Germany 170; in New Zealand 20–1; *see also* SIMCE (Sistema de Medición de la Calidad de la Educación)
standards: high 37; performance 148–9; and school reform 230; teachers, in China 80–1
Standing Conference of Ministers of Education and Cultural Affairs (KMK) *see* KMK (Standing Conference of Ministers of Education and Cultural Affairs)
state accountability 56
State Report Card 43
statistics 162
Statute of Professionals in Education 58
steering committees 193
Struggle for the Knowledge School, The 212
student assessment: in Austria 143, 145–6; in primary schools 23
student evaluation: in New Zealand 20–1
student learning: quality measurements of 61
student outcomes 208, 210, 212, 215, 216
student progress 20
students: organized according to academic ability 66; training for SIMCE assessments 67
suburban schools, Minnesota 37, 38, 39, 42
Success for All 31
summative activities 25
supervision 167–8
surveillance 136
surveys: Educational Leadership Practice Survey 30–1
SWOT (strengths, weaknesses, opportunities and threats) analysis 95
system, conceptual framework 13–14
System of Quality Assurance 67–8

teacher absenteeism 123, 134

250 *Index*

The Teacher Central 192
teacher evaluation 79; in China 80–1, 82–3
Teacher Evaluation and Designation policy 82
teacher retention rates 235
teachers: accountability in India 122–3; active learners 187; assessment 146; CPD 104; criticisms of 134–5; effectiveness 85; enhancing/maximizing skills 66; evaluation of 79; external evaluation in China 84–5; incentives for 61; internal evaluation in China 84; national testing in Norway 214–15; passive participants 187; pedagogical freedom 157; pressures on 133–4; professional learning 30; team spirit, morale and professionalism 101, 106; working conditions, improved 58; *see also* autonomy; promotion, teachers
teaching methods 66
team spirit 101
technology 234
temples of learning 111
tests/testing 170; assessment 169–71; in Austria 148; in Chile 58–9, 68; in France 158–9; in Germany 169–71; in New Zealand 20–1; in Norway 209–10, 210, 214–15, 218; *see also* examinations; SIMCE (Sistema de Medición de la Calidad de la Educación)
Theory E 92, 106
Theory O 92, 106
Thrupp, M. and White, M.: on implementation of National Standards 24–5
TIMSS (Trends in International Mathematics and Science Study) 21, 143, 145, 209
top-down change 92
training 121–2
transformational leadership 102
transparent accountability procedures 79
Trends in International Mathematics and Science Study (TIMSS) 21, 143, 145, 209
trust 207, 211, 217, 218, 224, 229, 231

Tucker, S. 114
Tu Rangatira 31

underdeveloped (UG), QR score 43
UNESCO 110; *Global Initiatives* report 111
Unified District Information System for Education 112
uninformed consumers 64
United States of America (USA): case study methods 35; context of school accountability in Minnesota 35–42; from policy and practice to possibilities 49–51; New York 42–8; performance-based accountability 31; racism 38
U.S. Census Bureau 35

values: personal 206–7; shared 101, 103–4
values ideological filter, private schools 64
village education committees (VECs) 123
vision, school-wide 103
Viteritti, J.P. 43
vocabulary 12

Wahlstrom *et al.* 48
walkthroughs 46
Wang, Ting 130
Wang, Y.: on teacher surveillance 136
Watson, L. 8
Watterston, J. and Caldwell, B.: on pressure on school leaders 9
Weinstein *et al.* 60
Weinstein, José 62
well developed (WD), QR score 43
World Bank 135–6
World Development Report (2004) 111
Wylie, C. 19, 20; on accountability 28; on appraisals 29; on education plans and school reports 28; on implementation of National Standards 24

Xia, X. 82

Yukl, G. 138